Society in Ancient India

Reconstructing Indian History & Culture

(ISSN 0971-3824)

1. Society in Ancient India; by Sures Chandra Banerji
2. Political Thought in Ancient India; by G.P. Singh
3. Early Indian Historical Tradition and Archaeology; by G.P. Singh
4. Vasantotsava: The Spring Festivals of India; by Leona M. Anderson
5. Ecological Readings in the Veda; by M. Vannucci
6. Vṛndāvana in Vaiṣṇava Literature; by Maura Corcoran
7. Social History of the Tamils (1707-1947); by P. Subramanian
8. Ancient Indian Coinage; by Rekha Jain
9. Buddhism and Socio-Economic Life of Eastern India; by Bimal Chandra Mohapatra
10. Chandragupta Maurya; by P.L. Bhargava
11. Mṛtyu: Concept of Death in Indian Traditions; by Gian Giuseppe Filippi
12. Yama: The Glorious Lord of the Other World; by Kusum P. Merh
13. Sacred Complex of Ujjain; by D.K. Samanta
14. Vedic View of the Earth; by S.R.N. Murthy
15. Society in the Atharvaveda; by B.S. Kharade
16. Orissan History, Culture and Archaeology; by S. Pradhan
17. Education in Ancient India; by Mitali Chatterjee
18. Surā: The Liquor and the Vedic Sacrifice; by M.B. Kolhatkar
19. Human Ecology in the Vedas; by Marta Vannucci
20. Governance in Ancient India; by Anupa Chandra Pandey
21. The Cultural Glory of Ancient India: A Literary Overview; by Sures Chandra Banerji
22. Kauṭilya's Arthaśāstra in the Light of Modern Science & Technology; by Sunil Sen Sarma
23. History of Jainism : With Special Reference to Mathurā; by V.K. Sharma
24. Cultural Tourism in India: Museums, Monuments & Arts – Theory and Practice; by S.P. Gupta; Krishna Lal; Mahua Bhattacharya
25. Ancient Indian Historiography : Sources and Interpretations; by G.P. Singh
26. Republics, Kingdoms, Towns and Cities in Ancient India; by G.P. Singh
27. Facets of Ancient Indian History and Culture : New Perception; by G.P. Singh
28. Kamakhya : A Socio-cultural Study; by Nihar Ranjan Mishra
29. History and Culture of Tamil Nadu as Gleaned from the Sanskrit Inscriptions Vol. 1 (up to *c.* 1310); by Chithra Madhavan
30. Lifestyle of the Vedic People; by Pranati Ghosal
31. History and Culture of Tamil Nadu as Gleaned from the Sanskrit Inscriptions Vol. 2 (up to *c.* 1310 - *c.* 1885); by Chithra Madhavan
32. Matrimonial Alliances and Ancient Indian Polity (*c.*600 to *c.*650); by Preeti Prabhat
33. Artisans and Craftsmen of Northern India; by Kuldeep Singh Thind
34. The Evolution of Historiographical Tradition in Ancient and Medieval India; by G.P. Singh
35. Warfare in Ancient India: In Historical outline; by Soma Basu
36. Sanskrit Education and Literature in Ancient India; by Chithra Madhavan
37. Rājadharma in Mahābhārata; by Priyanka Pandey
38. Interstate Relations in Northern India Circa 800–1200 ; by Shiva G. Bajpai

Reconstructing Indian History & Culture, no. 1

Society in Ancient India

Evolution since the Vedic Times based on Sanskrit, Pali, Prakrit and Other Classical Sources

by
Sures Chandra Banerji

DK PRINTWORLD
Publishers of Indian Traditions

Cataloging in Publication Data — DK
[Courtesy: D.K. Agencies (P) Ltd. <docinfo@dkagencies.com>]

Banerji, Sures Chandra, 1917-2000, **author.**

Society in ancient India : evolution since the Vedic times based on Sanskrit, Pali, Prakrit and other classical sources / by Sures Chandra Banerji.

pages cm. — (Reconstructing Indian history & culture ; no. 1)

Includes passages in Sanskrit.
"First published in India in 1993" — Title page verso.
Includes bibliographical references and index.
ISBN 9788124600795 (HB)

1. India — Social life and customs — To 1200. 2. India — Social conditions — To 1200. I. Title. II. Series: Reconstructing Indian history & culture ; no. 1.

LCC DS425.B36 2026 | DDC 954 23

ISBN 978-81-246-0079-5
First Published in India in 1993
Second impression in 1997
Third impression in 2007
Fourth impression in 2026

Printed and published by:
D.K. Printworld (P) Ltd.
Regd. Office : "Vedaśrī", F-395, Sudarshan Park
ESI Hospital Metro Station, New Delhi - 110015
Phones : (011) 4172 2626, 98713 94815
e-mail : indology@dkprintworld.com
Web : www.dkprintworld.com

PREFACE

OF late, there has been a growing interest among the intelligentsia about the past of India. Social workers, legislators and administrators are keenly feeling the need of re-orientation in the social conditions and outlook. Thanks to quick transport, the world is shrinking. People of different countries are coming closer together not only in the fields of technology and science but also in the cultural plane. Radhakrishnan said that India had been waiting for a new *Smṛti*. Many of our time-worn customs and practices are fast losing relevance to modern conditions.

The present society is a child of the past. Any reform, radical or partial, requires a knowledge of the history of the social conditions. Whatever is old is not sacrosanct however much the obscurantist may plead for it. Likewise, whatever is modern cannot be accepted as infallible. Before we undertake reform, we must have a knowledge of the origin and evolution of the sociological ideas. In some cases, a social practice originated in a most casual way, but passed through various vicissitudes resulting in many changes. A consideration of the historical perspective will reveal the true nature of the original customs. Thus, we shall be in a position to assess the value and importance of it before we think of changing it or giving it up.

Moreover, the evolution of the Indian society from the earliest times is a curiosity to the historians, scholars and general readers.

The present work was undertaken to apprise the reader of the conditions which prevailed in India through ages. The pictures of the society in different epochs have been drawn by different scholars. For example, we have books on the society of the Maurya and Gupta periods. Again, the society reflected in some literary works has been described. For instance, the *Vedic* society and the society in the epics have been studied. But, we do not know of any book in which we can have an integrated picture of the complex society in its evolution from the *Vedic* times through centuries. Thus, for example, if one feels curious to know how the institution of marriage originated and developed, one has to go through a number of books dealing with the matter in different periods. It is expected that the present work will remove this want to a considerable extent.

Folk-life of ancient India has not received the adequate attention of scholars. An attempt has been made here to set forth the salient features of the life of the common people as reflected in works in Sanskrit, Pāli and Prākrit.

For our purpose, we have relied mainly on the following classes of literary works: *Vedic Saṃhitās, Brāhmaṇas, Ūpaniṣads, Kalpasūtras, Vyākarana*, Epics, *Purāṇas, Arthaśāstra, Smṛtiśāstra, Tantra* and Classical Sanskrit literature.

Besides works in Sanskrit, we have also consulted the Buddhist Pāli works, particularly the *Jātakas*, and the Jaina works in Prākrit and Apabhraṃśa.

The present work has no pretension to completeness. It is, however, hoped that an overall picture of the society has been delineated in a general way bringing out the highlights from a direct study of the literary records.

The author's labour will be rewarded if this work succeeds in giving the reader a coherent picture of the society in its evolution from the earliest times.

Sincere thanks are due to the Publisher, who has evinced love for indology, for readily agreeing to undertake the publication of the work.

CALCUTTA **S.C. Banerji**

CONTENTS

ABBREVIATIONS

ABJ	*Andhabhūta-jātaka*
AJ	*Asampadāna-j.*
ALJ	*Asilakṣaṇa-j.*
APJ	*Apaṇṇaka-j.*
ASJ	*Asaṃkhya-j.*
ASMJ	*Aśātamantra-j.*
AV	*Atharvaveda.*
AYBJ	*Ayācita-bhakta-j.*
BaJ	*Baka-j.*
Bhk	*Bhavisayatta-Kahā* (Dalal & Gune)
BJ	*Bhīmasena-j.*
BMJ	*Bandhana-mokṣa-j.*
BVJ	*Bherīvāda-j.*
CSJ	*Cullaśreṣṭhi-j.*
DDJ	*Devadharma-j.*
DMJ	*Durmedha-j.*
DN	*Dīgha Nikāya*
DP	*Dhammapada*
DPA	*Dhammapada Aṭṭhakathā*
DS	*Dharmasūtra*
GJ	*Godhā-j.*

GS	*Gāthāśaptaśatī* of Hāla *(Gs.* following *Āśva., Pār.* etc.; stands for *Gṛhyasūtra)*
GV	*Gauḍavaho,* ed. N.G.S. Ahmedabad, 1975
H	*Harṣacarita,* ed. Kane where the page of the text is intended, it is indicated by p. At other places, the references are to the pages of the notes.
IJ	*Illīsa-j.*
JC	*Jasahara-cariu*
K	*Kirātārjunīya*
Ka	*Kādambarī*
Kad	*do,* (Kale, 1928).
Kaj	*Kāka-j.*
KaMJ	*Kaṇḍina -mṛga-j.*
KaTJ	*Kaṭāha-j.*
KJ	*Kharādiyā-j.*
KKC	*Karakaṇḍa-cariu*
KLJ	*Kulāyaka-j.*
KM	*Karpūramāñjarī*
KMJ	*Kuraṅga-mṛga-j.*
KPJ	*Kapota-j.*
KrJ	*Kṛṣṇa-j.*
KUJ	*Kuddāla-j.*
KUM	*Kuṭṭanīmata*
KVJ	*Kūṭavāṇija-j.*
LIJ	*Lipta-j.*
LJ	*Laṅguṣṭha-j.*
LOJ	*Lośaka-j.*

M	*Mṛcchakaṭika*
MAJ	*Mahilāmukha-j.*
Mbh	*Mahābhārata*
MCJ	*Mitacinti-j.*
MIJ	*Mitravindaka-j.*
MJ	*Matsya-j.*
MLJ	*Mṛdulakṣaṇa j.*
MS	*Manu-smṛti*
MUJ	*Munika-j.*
MVJ	*Mahāśīla-j.*
N	*Naiṣadha-carita*
NJ	*Nanda-j.*
NKC	*Nāyakumāra-cariu,* (ed. H. Jain), 1933
NMJ	*Nyagrodha-j.*
NPJ	*Nalapāna-j.*
PaJ	*Parṇika-j.*
PGJ	*Pañcaguru-j.*
PJ	*Phala-j.*
PPJ	*Pūrṇapātri-j.*
PRJ	*Puṣparakta-j.*
Ram	*Rāmāyaṇa*
RV	*Ṛgveda*
S	*Śiśupālavadha*
SaJ	*Saṃyama-j.*
SalJ	*Sālitta-j.*
SanJ	*Sanjīva-j.*
SBE	*Sacred Books of the East Series*
SIMJ	*Śīla mīmāṃsā-j.*
SJ	*Sṛgāla-j.*

SKJ	*Satyaṃkila-j.*
SMJ	*Sammodamāna-j.*
SNJ	*Śīlavannāga-j.*
SS	*Srautasūtra*
SV	*Sumaṅgalavilāsinī*
Svapna	*Svapnavāsavadatta, Kala,* 19
SVJ	*Serivāṇija-j.*
TAJ	*Taru-j.*
TANJ	*Taṇḍulanālī-j.*
TDJ	*Trayodharma-j.*
TJ	*Tittira-j.*
TPJ	*Tailapātra-j.*
UBJ	*Ubhatobhraṣṭa-j.*
UJ	*Udañcana-j.*
VaiJ	*Vairi-j.*
VBJ	*Visvāsabhojana-j.*
VJ	*Vartaka-j.*
VMJ	*Vātamṛga-j.*
VVJ	*Visavanta-j.*
YS	*Yājñavalkya-smṛti.*

1

INTRODUCTION

Sanskrit Literature

A General Survey

BEFORE taking up an account of the Indian society, reflected in Sanskrit literature, we shall give a rapid survey of this literature.

The *Ṛgveda* is regarded as the earliest written record of the Indo-Europeans. We find in it a civilisation of a considerably high degree. It has been aptly said that *Vedic* civilisation has dawn but no twilight. The same remark is applicable to the *Vedic Saṃhītā*. In it we have a literature of considerable refinement. There must have been a long period of development culminating in the *Veda*. But we do not as yet have any specimen of the preceding period. The age of the *Ṛgveda* is still uncertain. Most modern scholars would place it about 1500 B.C.

The other *Vedic Saṃhitās* are the *Yajus* (*YV*), *Sāma* (*SV*) and *Atharvan* (*AV*).

While the *RV* contains *Mantras* mainly about the various aspects of nature, conceived as deities, the *YV* contains matters for ritual application. The *SV* is a collection of hymns to be sung in sacrifices. The *AV* contains matters reflecting popular beliefs and practices. In it we have matters designed to prolong life, heal diseases, ward off evils, counteract the venom of snakes, cause mischief to enemies etc. It is a *Veda* of magic of two kinds, viz. white and black. Many amulets are mentioned; these are believed to ensure various kinds of welfare.

The *Vedic Saṃhitās* are followed by *Brāhmaṇas*. These are prose works dealing exhaustively with the procedure of *Vedic* rites and rituals. Their contents may be divided as *Vidhi* (injunctions), *Arthavāda* (explanation) and *Upaniṣad* (secret doctrines). The

Upaniṣadic portion belongs mainly to *Āraṇyakas* or forest-texts. These represent the thoughts of the sages resorting to the solitude of forests. The *Upaniṣads* deal with sublime thoughts about the philosophy of life, its goal, the nature of *Brahman*, the Supreme Being and the ways to His realisation.

Then came the *Sūtra* period in which the earlier knowledge was systematised and presented in mnemonic aphoristic style. The entire body of *Vedic Sūtras* is designated as *Kalpasūtra*. It comprises the following :

Śrauta –	dealing with *Vedic* rites and rituals.
Gṛhya –	containing rules and regulations about domestic rites like *Upanayana, Vivāha* etc.
Dharma –	dealing with rules regarding the personal and social life of the people, law etc.
Śulva –	containing directions about the measurement of sacrificial altars.

The *Kalpasūtra* is a *Vedāṅga* or *Vedic* accessory. It is necessary for conducting life according to *Vedic* injunctions. While it is ritualistic, there are exegetical *Vedāṅgas* too. These comprise

Śikṣā –	rules about phonetics.
Vyākaraṇa –	grammar.
Nirukta –	etymological rules.
Chandaḥ –	metrics.
Jyotiṣa –	astronomy.

The *Veda* and the *Upaniṣads* contained germs of philosophy. As time rolled on, philosophical ideas took a clear shape, and were developed through centuries. An attempt at systematisation of the philosophical ideas resulted in the formulation of *Sūtras* about the different systems of thought. The systems were mainly six, viz. *Nyāya, Vaiśeṣika, Mīmāṇsā, Vedānta, Sāṃkhya, Yoga*. In course of time, elaborate commentaries were written to elucidate the ideas contained in the cryptic *Sūtras*. For example, the commentary of Śaṅkara on *Vedānta-Sūtras* is very well known.

After the *Vedic* period came the epics, viz. the *Rāmāyaṇa* (*Ram*) and the *Mahābhārata* (*Mbh*). We have no means of determining when the epics originated. It appears that epic stories were sung by two classes of people, viz. *Sūtas* or bards living in royal courts, and *Kuśīlavas* or travelling singers. After a long period of oral transmission these came to be written and redacted through centuries. The *Mbh*, in its present form, perhaps dates back to the 4th century A.D. and the present *Ram* to a century or two earlier.

Another important class of Sanskrit literature is the *Purāṇas.* The precise date of origin of this type is unknown. The early *Purāṇas*, however, appear to have been composed or compiled in the period between the fifth century B.C. and sixth century A.D. They deal with all sorts of subjects ranging from creation to genealogies of kings. In short, these can be called epitomes of Indian civilisation and culture.

A considerable role is played by *Tantras* in the social life of India. They give freedom to all, irrespective of caste, creed and sex, regarding religious rites and observances. They teach ways to liberation (*mukti*) through enjoyment *(bhukti)*. The ascetic practices of the Brāhmaṇical religion are not favoured. The conventional *Smṛti* rules are disregarded. For instance, even a low-class man, who has attained a high level of *Tantric Sādhana*, is to be saluted by a *Brāhmaṇa*. One's mother is supposed to be one's best spiritual guide. For *Kumāri-pūjā,* even a low-class girl of the requisite qualification can be selected by a *Brāhmaṇa. Tāntric* ideas already appeared in the *Atharvaveda*. Some regard *Tantra* also as *Śruti* which is generally used to refer to the *Veda. Tāntric* ideas and practices may have been co-eval with the *Veda*, but no *Tāntric* work earlier than the fifth or sixth century A.D. is available.

Classical Sanskrit literature, with which we are concerned in the present work, is supposed to have come into being in the post-Pāṇini period. Pāṇini (c.4th cent. B.C.) regulated the Sanskrit language with strict rules. Thus, the unfettered earlier language began to move through the grooves of grammatical rules.

In course of time, a vast literature comprising prose, poetical and dramatic works, came into being. Already in the *YV* we find prose portions. The *Brāhmaṇas* are prose works. The *Mahābhāṣya* of Patañjali (c.2nd cent. B.C.) contains prose of a considerably developed style. The *Avadānas*, containing stories of the Buddha in his previous births, are in prose. Of the later prose writers, the most noteworthy are Daṇḍin, author of the *Daśakumāra-carita*, Subandhu, author of the *Vāsavadattā*, and Bāṇabhaṭṭa who composed the *Kādambarī* and the *Harṣacarita.*

Poetical compositions date back to the *Vedic* period. But, at present we do not have any poetical work before Aśvaghoṣa (c. 1st or 2nd cent. A.D.). His *Buddhacarita* and *Saundarnanda* are well-known poetical works. By far the greatest classical poet is Kālidāsa. He composed the *Kāvyas* called *Raghuvaṃsa, Kumāra-sambhava* and the *Meghadūta*. Of the *Kumāra-sambhava* cantos *ix* to the end are believed, on certain grounds, to have been spurious. Kālidāsa's authorship of the *Ṛtu-saṃhāra* is also doubted by some scholars. Besides the above, several other poetical works are ascribed, not on convincing grounds, to the master-poet. (Vide S.C. Banerjee, *Kālidāsa Apocrypha*, Banaras, 1988).

Of the poets, following Kālidāsa, the following are the most famous: Bhāravi, author of the *Kirātārjunīya,* Bhaṭṭi, author of the *Bhaṭṭikāvya*, Kumāradāsa, author of the *Jānakī-haraṇa,* Māgha, author of the *Śiśupālavadha*, and Śrīharṣa, author of the *Naiṣadha-carita.*

In the domain of drama also, we do not have the work of any author preceding Aśvaghoṣa. His *Śāriputra-prakaraṇa* is the earliest extant drama. As in the realm of poetry, so in that of drama, Kālidāsa stands pre-eminent. His *Abhijñana-śakuntala* is by far the best work, and is universally acclaimed. Besides, there are the *Mālavikāgnimitra* and the *Vikramorvaśīya.*

Among the other dramatists, famous are Bhāsa (13 dramas including the *Svapnnavāsavadatta)*, Śūdraka (*Mrechakaṭika*), Viśākhadatta (*Mudrārākṣasa)* and Bhavabhūti (*Uttara-rāmacarita, Mahāvīracarita* and *Mālatīmādhava*).

Middle Indo-Aryan Literature

Before examining the social conditions, reflected in this literature, we should have an idea of the literature of the period. We shall, therefore, give here a rapid survey of this literature with special reference to the works on the basis of which an account will be given here.

The Indian languages, belonging to the Aryan group, are believed to have passed through three broad stages of evolution. These are Ancient Indo-Aryan, comprising *Vedic*, Epic and classical Sanskrit, Middle Indo-Aryan, including Pāli, Prākrit and Apabhraṃśa, and New Indo-Aryan like Hindī, Bengali, Nepālī Oriyā etc. The languages, thus evolved, are spread over northern India particularly in its eastern and western wings excepting a small pocket in the extreme North-west. The languages of the major part of South India are of Dravidian origin, and thus belong to an entirely different family.

The literature, written in Middle Indo-Aryan languages, is Middle Indo-Aryan literature. When and how the Middle Indo-Aryan language started cannot be said with certainty. There has been considerable divergence of opinion regarding the derivative meaning of the word Pāli. According to some, it comes from *Paṃkti* denoting the lines of the canonical literature written in Pāli. Others think that it is derived from *Pallī* denoting a village. Thus, according to them, it was originally the language of the rural people. The fact seems to be that, side by side with Sanskrit, the language of the elite, there was a spoken language which was a corruption of Sanskrit and, in some cases, Pāli. This theory accords well with the Buddha's instructions to disseminate his teachings in the own language (*sakāya niruttiyā*) of the people; by people he obviously meant the common people. In this connection, it may be pointed out that, in Sanskrit dramas, the female and low characters generally speak in Prākrit. Pāli is regarded as the oldest form of Prākrit. That Prākrit was widely in vogue as a spoken language of the masses seems to be proved also by the existence of several dialects of it, e.g. Māhārāṣṭrī, Śaurasenī, Māgadhī etc. According to some, *Prākṛta* is derived from *Prākṛti* or nature. So, the language that spontaneously developed among the people came to be called Prākrit.

We do not know if *Vedic* language was ever a spoken tongue. There are, however, evidences tending to prove that Sanskrit, as standardised by Pāṇini (c. 4th cent. B.C.), was a spoken language in however limited a circle. The absence of dialects in Sanskrit tends to show that it did not gain very wide currency among the people as a spoken language.

Orthodox grammarians, perhaps more out of a spirit of glorifying Sanskrit, the *deva-bhāṣā* as they called it, than of respect for history, declared Sanskrit to have been the basic language out of which Prākrit developed (*Prakṛtiḥ, saṃskṛtam, tatra bhavaṃ tata āgatam vā Prākṛtam*)[1]. The etymological meaning of *Saṃskṛta* (refined), however, tends to point to an opposite process—from the crude Prākrit to the refined Sanskrit. But, in reality, the refinement of Sanskrit seems to point to its improvement on the *Vedic* language.

Prākrit is believed to have passed through three stages of development, viz. Old, Middle and Late. The last stage is represented by Apabhraṃśa, the immediate predecessor[2] of the New Indo-Aryan languages, e.g. Hindī, Behārī, Nepālī etc. Daṇḍin, in his *Kāvyādarśa* (i. 36, 37) holds that Apabhraṃśa denotes the language of the *Ābhīras* (cowherds) and the like.

There were various dialects of Apabhraṃśa, viz. *Vrācaṭa, Nāgara, Upanāgara* etc. According to some scholars, these dialects can be divided into three regional groups, viz. *Pūrvī, Paścimī* and *Dakṣiṇī*.

As regards the vocabulary of Prākrit, it may be observed that it contains several classes of words, viz. *Tatsama* (pure Sanskrit), *Tadbhava* (derived from Sanskrit) and *Deśī* (local or regional).

Pāli literature is broadly divided into two classes, Canonical and Non-canonical. Canonical Pāli literature comprises the *Tipiṭaka* (three baskets), called *Vinaya, Sutta* and *Abhidhamma.*

The *Vinaya-piṭaka* consists of the *Pātimokkha, Khandhaka* and *Parivāra*. The *Pātimokkha* contains lists of lapses of the monks and the corresponding rules for atonement. The *Sutta-vibhaṅga* (exposition of *Suttas*) is divided into two parts, *Pārājika* and *Pācittiya.* Comprising two parts, called *Mahāvagga* and *Cullavagga*, the latter deals, inter alia, with distinctions between degrees of various crimes like theft, murder etc. The former deals with offences for which punishment for monks was expulsion from the *Saṃgha* (order). The *Khandhakas*, also containing two parts, *Mahāvagga* and *Cullavagga,* deals with various rules regarding the order. Information about some diseases and their medicines as well as legal matter is available in it. The *Cullavagga* contains edifying anecdotes concerning the life of the Buddha and the history of the order. The *Parivāra* contains various matters relating to Ceylon.

The *Sutta-piṭaka* is divided into five *Nikāyas* (collections), viz, *Dīgha, Majjhima, Saṃyutta, Aṅguttara* and *Khuddaka.* The last one comprises the *Dhammapada* containing verses on moral and ethical principles; it is considered to be a gem of Pāli literature. The same *Nikāya* has the *Jātaka* containing stories about the

Bodhi-sattvas or the previous existences of the Buddha. Each *Jātaka* story, in its present form, consists of the following parts:

(1) *Paccuppanna-vatthu*	It states the occasion on which the Buddha narrated the story.
(2) *Atīta-vatthu*	The story of a past existence.
(3) *Gāthās*	Verses.
(4) *Veyyākaraṇa*	Brief exposition.
(5) *Samodhāna*	Generally containing the identification of the distinguished personages, mentioned in the first part, with those mentioned in the second.

The *Abhidhamma* comprises seven sections :

(i) *Dhammasaṃgaṇi*	–	dealing with psychological ethics.
(ii) *Vibhaṅga*	–	generally dealing with the different categories and formulae treated of in the *Dhammasaṃgaṇi.*
(iii) *Dhātu-kathā*	–	a discourse on the elements, e.g. 5 *Khandhas,* 12 *Āyatanas* etc., the Eightfold path.
(iv) *Puggala-Paññatti*	–	it discusses six designations and grouping of human types successively by one to ten.
(v) *Kathā-vatthu*	–	contains heretical questions on the Buddha and Buddhism and answers in defence and glorification of these two.
(vi) *Yamaka*	–	deals with psychological, ethical and eschatological matters.
(vii) *Paṭṭhāna-pakaraṇa*	–	The non-canonical Pāli works may be divided under the following heads :

1. Those preceding the commentaries
2. Famous commentaries
3. Historical works
4. Compendiums
5. Poetical compositions
6. Grammar
7. Rhetoric and Prosody
8. Lexicography

Of the works of the first class, the following are original :

Nettipakaraṇa – on textual and exegetical methodology.
Peṭakopadeśa – instructions regarding the *Tipiṭaka.*
Milindapañho – questions relating to Buddhism, asked by Greek king Menandros and answers by Thera Nāgasena.

The other works of this class are expository and the result of collective efforts of those who are known as *Aṭṭha-kathācāryas* (masters of commentaries). Of such works, a very well-known one is the *Jātakaṭṭhakathā.*

The works of the second class were written by Buddhadatta, Buddhoghosa and Dhammapāla. Their commentaries on the *Piṭakas* are valuable not only for the exposition of the text but also from the social, religious and historical points of view. Besides the famous trio above, there were also other less known commentators.

The historical works are

Dīpavaṃsa – chronicle of the island of Ceylon.
Mahāvaṃsa – an enlarged and refined version of the above.
Cūlavaṃsa – a sort of supplement to the *Mahāvaṃsa.*
Buddhaghosuppattī – biographical account of Buddhoghosa, named above.
Saddhamma-Saṃgaha – history of Buddhism from the time of Buddhist councils in India down to 14th century A.D.

Sandeśa-kathā	–	discussion on the *Abhidhammatthasaṃgaha* of Anuruddha and *Abhidhammatthavibhāvanī* of Sumaṅgalasāmī etc. contains information about some kingdoms, e.g. Suvaṇṇabhūmi, Cīna etc. and about the relation between Burma and Ceylon.
Mahābodhi-vaṃsa	–	history of the Bodhi-tree.
Hatthavana-gallavihāra	–	*Vaṃsa*-account of king Siri Saṃghabodhi and the mansions and memorials built by him for performing religious rites.
Dāṭhāvaṃsa	–	contains valuable information about the tooth-relic and the history of Ceylon.
Chakesa-dhātu-vaṃsa	–	describes topes built on the hair-relic by different persons.
Gandha-vaṃsa	–	accounts of many Pāli works and their authors as well as of anonymous works.
Sāsana-vaṃsa	–	history of Buddhism in India (up to third Buddhist Council), Ceylon and Burma.

The works of the fourth class include abridgements and manuals of different parts of the canonical literature.

The noteworthy poetical works are :

Anāgata-Vaṃsa	–	prophecies purported to have been made by the Buddha himself.
Jina-carita	–	biography of the Buddha.
Telakaṭāha-gāthā	–	of the Sanskrit *Śataka* type, it is in the form of ethical instructions and noble thoughts.
Rajjamadhu	–	of the *Śataka* type, it deals with the Buddha's graceful appearaance and knowledge. It contains praise of the *Saṃgha* and

		Nirvāṇa.
Rasavāhinī	–	stories relating to India and Ceylon. It contains information about social conditions, particularly of common people.
Saddhammopāyana	–	principal topics relating to Buddhism.
Pañcagati-dīpana	–	deals with the condition of a person in the other world according to good and bad deeds done in this.

The grammatical works, which are of no use for our present purpose, may be divided into three classes, viz. *Kaccàyana*-school, *Moggallāna*-school and the *Saddanīti* group.

The works of the other two classes may be passed over as these throw little light on folk-life.

Like Pāli literature, Prākrit literature also can be broadly divided into two classes, viz. Religious and Secular. The religious works are called *Siddhāntas* or *Āgama*. Of the two principal sects of the Jainas, viz. *Digambara* and *Śvetāmbara*, the works of the latter are better known to the scholarly world.

The works of the *Siddhānta* class comprise the following types of compositions :

1. *Dvādaśāṅga*
2. *Dvādaśa Uvaṅga* (*Upāṅga*)
3. *Daśa Paiṇṇa* (= *Prakīrṇa*)
4. *Ṣaṭ Cheyasutta* (= *Chedasūtra*)
5. Four *Mūlasūtras*
6. Others comprising *Nandi* or *Nandisutta* (= *Nandisūtra*)
7. *Anuogadāra* (= *Anuyogadvāra*).

The main topics, discussed in the above works, are the analysis of the main tenets of Jainism, the way of a Jaina ascetic's life, the conduct of ordinary Jains, their activities, re-birth etc. To relieve monotony spicy stories and legends have been occasionally introduced. In the narrative portions, there are some creations as well as borrowings from the *Rāmāyaṇa* and the *Mahābhārta*.

Not much is known about the religious literature of the early

Digambars. Some works of the other sect, e.g. *Dvādaśāṅga,* have been recognised in this sect too. The religious works of the later *Digambaras* can be classified as follows :

1. *Prathamānuyoga* – containing *Purāṇic* stories.
2. *Karaṇānuyoga* – dealing with cosmogony and cosmology.
3. *Dravyānuyoga* – philosophical works.
4. *Caraṇānuyoga* – dealing with religious rites.

These are collectively called *Caturveda.*

Among the secular works should be mentioned *Paṭṭāvalīs* and *Therāvalīs* containing information about the teachers and prominent personages of the different Jaina sects.

According to tradition, one Guṇāḍhya composed the *Bṛhatkathā* in Paiśacī Prākrit[3]. It is untraceable today and therefore considered lost. The title suggests that it was a huge work containing narratives.

On the oldest works the earliest commentaries are called *Nijjutti* (= *Niryukti*).

The secular works can be broadly divided into the following classes :

A. Poetical Works
B. Prose and *Campū* (mixed prose and verse)
C. Drama
D. Philosophy and the Rules of Conduct of the Jainas.
E. Grammar and Lexicon.

Poetical Works

The principal works are :

Setubandha, variously called *Rāvaṇavaho (Rāvaṇa-vadha), Dahamuhavaho (Daśamukha-vadha).*

Paümacariya (*Padmacarita*) - *Rāmāyaṇa* story with modifications to suit the Jaina doctrine.

Gauḍavaho (*Gauḍavadha*) - biographical account of Yaśovarman, king of Kanauj, and patron of the poet.

Mahāvīracariya

Kumārapāla-cariya
Supāsanāha-cariya
Sumatinātha-cariya
Taraṅgalolā
Taraṅgavatī
Surasundarī-caria
Kaṃsavaho

Prākrit lyrics are of two kinds, religious and secular. Of the religious lyrics, which are of a considerable number, but which are of no use for our present purpose, the most renowned is the *Uvasaggahara-stotra.* The *Sattasaī* (*Saptaśatī)* of Hāla Sātavahana is a collection of excellent lyrical verses throwing lurid light on folk-life.

Of the metrical didactic works, the well-known are the *Uvaesa-mālā (Upadeśamālā), Kathākośa, Kumārapāla-pratibodha,* etc.

Among the anthologies, the *Vajjālagga* and the *Prākṛta-Sūkta-ratna-mālā* deserve special mention.

A very interesting work is the *Vidagdha-mukha-maṇḍana,* supposed to have been composed in the period between 630 and 950 A.D. It deals with enigmatology and *Citra-kāvya.* The languages, used in it, are pure Sanskrit, pure Prākrit, mixture of these two and Avahaṭṭha.

Prose and Campū

Works in prose are rare. Most of the works are in prose interspersed with verse. Well-known among these works is the *Samarāicca-kahā.*

Of the works of the *Kathānaka* (short stories) class, mention may be made of the following :

Kathākośa, Kathā-ratnākara, Kālakācārya-kathānaka Kathā-mahodadhi.

Drama

The *Karpūra-mañjarī* is the most renowned, and the others are insignificant.

Philosophy and Rules of Conduct of the Jainas

A large number of such works appears to have been composed. Kundakunda alone is credited with the authorship of 83 works of which only seven are available at present. His best known work is the *Pañcātthikāyasāra* (= *Pañcāstikāya-sāra)* or *Pavayanasāra-pañcatthiya-saṃgaha* (= *Pravacanasāra-pañcastikāya-saṃgraha).* The *Chhappāhuḍa* (Skt.*-prābhṛta)* is also attributed to him.

To Devendrasūri are attributed six works, e.g. *Karmavipāka, Ṣaḍaśītikā etc.*

There are several other works too, e.g. *Pavayana-sāra, Samaya-sāra,* etc.

Grammar and Lexicon

These works do not fall within the purview of our study.

Coming to Apabhraṃśa literature, we find that some verses of the *Vikramorvaśīya* of Kālidāsa (c.5th cent. A.D.) are in this language. If these were not later interpolations, these serve as the earliest extant specimen of this language.

Apabhraṃśa verses occur in the following Sanskrit works :

Kuvalayamālā of Uddyotana (end of 8th cent. A.D.)

Prabandha-cintāmaṇi (1304 A.D.)

Śuka-saptati (12th cent. A.D. or later)

Vetāla-pañcaviṃśati (according to some, 13th or 14th cent. A.D.)

Śārṅgadhara-paddhati (an anthology of 14th cent A.D.)

Kathāratnākara (1600 A.D.).

The Apabhraṃśa works can be broadly divided into two classes, Jaina and non-Jaina.

From the literary point of view these works can be divided into the following classes :

A. Jaina *Prabandha.*

B. Spiritual or mystic works of Jainas.

C. Jaina didactic poetry.

D. Bauddha *Dohā.*

E. Lyric.

F. Miscellaneous.

Jaina Prabandha

The works of this class are religious, and may be classified as *Purāṇa,* Biography and Narrative literature.

The *Purāṇas* are in imitation of the Brāhmaṇical *Purāṇas*. The main works are *Paümacariu, Harivaṃśa, Mahāpurāṇa, Pāṇḍva-*

purāṇa, Padmapurāṇa.

The principal biographical and narrative works are : *Jasahara-cariu, Nemināha-cariu, Bhavisayatta-kahā, Naya-kumāra-cariu, Karakaṇda-cariu, Sudaṃsana-cariu, Kathākośa,* etc.

Spiritual and Mystic Works

Paramātma-prakāśa, Dohā-pāhuda etc.

These are of no use for our present purpose.

Jaina Didactic Poetry

Upadesa-rasāyana-rasa, Caccarī etc.

Bauddha Dohā

These verses deal with spiritualism and the means of attaining salvation, their authors being designated as *Siddhācāryas.*

Lyric

Besides the lyrical verses in the *Vikramorvaśīya,* the *Kumārapāla-carita* etc. there is a lyrical poem called *Sandeśa-rāsaka* by Abdur Rahman.

Miscellaneous

Of the works of this type, the following have some relevance to our study :

> *Ḍākārṇava* (mixed Sanskrit and Prākrit. Portions are in Śaurasenī Apabhraṃśa, according to some)
> — a Buddhist *Tāntric* work.
> *Prākṛta-paiṅgala* (c. 14th cent.)
> — a work on metrics, containing many illustrative Apabhraṃśa verses[4].

INDIAN SOCIETY—ITS ANTIQUITY AND CHARACTERISTICS

Indus Valley Civilisation

Indian civilisation is one of the earliest civilisations of the world. If Egypt was a gift of the Nile, India was a gift of the Indus. The relics of the Indus Valley civilisation of Mohenjodaro and Harappa[5], perhaps dating back to the pre-*Vedic* period, bear witness to a highly developed condition. The urban civilisation of this valley reveals brick-built houses, public baths, swimming pools, scientific system of drainage, well-constructed roads, terracotta work of various kinds, figures of human beings and deities, seals etc. Some seals and stone images testify to the artistic skill of the people.

Of the ornaments, used in that age, we know the following : necklace, ring, bangle, head-ornament, waist chain, earring, anklets etc. Besides gold and silver, copper, bronze, ivory were used in jewellery.

Some earthen vessels were painted.

Among the implements for daily life were the axe, chisel, knife, sickle, hook (for catching fish), razor etc. For domestic work needles, spinning machines etc. were in use.

Knife, mace, bow, arrow etc. were defensive weapons.

The relics contain toy carts, chains, dice etc.

Wheat, barley, and dates appear to have been widely used as food.

In dress both cotton and wool were used.

Agriculture played the most prominent role in economic life. Bull, sheep, buffalo, elephant, camel etc. were the principal domestic animals. The dog was also there.

Among craftsmen we find the following : potter, weaver, carpenter, mason, blacksmith, goldsmith, jeweller, ivory worker, stone-cutter etc. Metal-work was developed; we have evidence of molten metal poured into moulds, mixing alloy etc.

There is evidence of foreign trade. The main items of import were tin, copper and precious stones.

From the figures of mother-goddesses it seems that the Female Energy (*Śakti*) was considered to be the root of creation. A male figure, surrounded by animals, as represented on seals, seem to be the precursor of the later Śiva. He has three faces and two horns on two sides of the head-ornaments. Some think it to be the forerunner of the trident of Śiva. Some stone chips seem to have been worshipped as *Śivaliṅgas* (Phallus). It is supposed that trees, stones and animals etc. were worshipped. Serpent-worship was, perhaps, in vogue.

The present relics appear to date back approximately to a period round about 3000 B.C. (between c. 2300-1750 B.C. according to some). Some scholars, however, think that the ravages, caused by the flood-waters of the Indus, destroyed the civilisation several times. If so, the original civilisation was much older. The script on the seals, when deciphered, may throw light on the antiquity of this civilisation.

The Dravidians[6] are supposed by some to have been the architects of this civilisation.

Vedic Civilisation

It is generally believed that the Indus Valley civilisation was followed by the *Vedic* civilisation[7]. Some scholars think that the *Vedic* people were barbarous, and that they devastated the earlier civilisation and built up their own. Others are of the opinion that the *Vedic* people were highly civilised, and that they absorbed the earlier inhabitants into the Aryan fold and drove away the rebels. Scholars are usually of the opinion that the Aryans migrated from Central Asia through Persia and settled in the fertile land watered by the Indus. Gradually they spread towards the east. They encountered stiff resistance from the Dravidians of the south where they penetrated with difficulty.

The migration theory with regard to the Aryan influx is more widely accepted than the invasion theory.

The *Ṛgveda,* the earliest written record of the Aryans, appears to have been orally transmitted through centuries till at last it was compiled. The date of the present *Ṛgveda Saṃhita* is a subject of controversy. Most modern scholars believe that it took the present shape approximately round about 1500 B.C.

The Aryans, in their expansion in the different regions of India, met with tough opposition by the earlier non-Aryan settlers. Those who submitted to them were admitted into the Aryan fold. They appear to have been employed as *dāsas* (servants or slaves). Some identify the *dāsas* with *Śūdras*.

That the Aryans spread far in the east is proved by the mention of the tiger, dwelling in the Gangetic valley, in the *Atharvaveda* which is believed to be later than the *Ṛgveda*.

The *Vedic* family was patriarchal. The Government was monarchical. The tribal Chiefs used to govern the respective tribes. In the upper strata of the society people used to perform sacrifices.

In a late hymn of the *Ṛgveda* (x. 90), there is the only reference to the four castes. The *Brāhmaṇa, Kṣatriya, Vaiśya* and *Śūdra* are stated to have sprung from the mouth, arms, thighs and feet respectively of the Great Primeval Being. The gulf of difference between the upper castes on the one hand and the *Śudras* on the other is clear from the *Atharvaveda*.

A class of men was called *Vrātya*. They had no respect for the *Veda* and the *Vedic* rites. In course of time, they seem to have been very powerful; so much so that, in the *Atharvaveda*, they have been deified. The priest came to be looked upon with great respect by the people in this *Veda*.

Material prosperity and happiness were desired by the people. Male and female servants, good houses, good children etc. were some of the things the *Vedic* Aryan aspired to have. Money was sweeter than honey even in that remote age. It is stated (*RV* X.27.12) that money makes even an uncouth person look handsome.

The *AV* depicts an atmosphere wholly different from that found in the *RV*. While the *Ṛgvedic* seer indulges in flights of imagination, and soars on the wings of fancy, the seer of the *AV* moves on the sordid soil of the earth. The *AV* reveals real popular beliefs and practices as yet uninfluenced by the sacredotal class. The following divisions of its contents show how the people thought and worked :

Bhaiṣajya –	Songs and incantations supposed to cure diseases.
Āyuṣya –	Prayers for long life and sound health.
Pauṣṭika –	Blessings to ensure happiness and success in undertakings.
Ābhicārika –	Curses directed against demons and enemies and exorcism.

Besides the above, the *AV* contains incantations for expiation, unity among family members, magic songs in connection with love, marriage etc.

The *AV* is a precursor of the *Āyurveda* and *Tantra*.

This *Veda* contains information about talismans and magical practices designed to achieve various purposes including victory in war and destruction of enemies. There are magic formulae for counteracting the effects of snake venom.

Buddhism and Jainism

Buddhism arose in the 6th century B.C. as a protest against sacredotal practices. It denied *Vedic* authority and dispensed with idle speculations on the existence of God. It laid greater stress on self-discipline and meditation, and advocated monkhood and mendicancy. Instead of blind adherence to conventional ideas and practices, it preached a rational approach, and did away with the external formalities of religious life. Non-violence and love were the sheet-anchor of this religion. It raised its voice against caste-distinction.

Jainism arose about the same time. It carried the creed of non-violence much further, and considered the life of even an insect to be sacred. It preached the creed of rigorous ascetic practices to a limit that weaned away many people. It had much in common with Buddhism. Like the former it deified *Vedic* authority.

Atheism

Side by side with the orthodox religion, there were also atheistic ideas in the society. The *Lokāyata* or the materialistic school, which traces its origin to Cārvāka, did not recognise *Vedic* authority. The Brāhmaṇical rites and practices were declared to be nonsensical, and designed by crafty *Brāhmaṇas* to achieve selfish ends. It advocated hedonism, and did away with the other world. It did not recognise anything which is beyond perception.

The *Sāṃkhya* philosophy declared that the existence of God cannot be proved.

PhilosophicalSchools

The six orthodox systems of philosophy exercised profound influence on the society. The most powerful impact was created by *Vedānta* which declared all creatures to be like sparks from the One Eternal Fire, i.e. *Brahman*. This went a long way in fostering a sense of unity among the people and compassion towards other creatures. The Yoga philosophy taught people how to concentrate the mind and that mind control was at the root of peace and progress. It advocated various Yogic practices some of which are relevant even today.

Upaniṣads

The *Upaniṣads* did not do away with sacrifices and other religious rites. But, they did not look upon the same as the sole means of salvation. The *Iśā Upaniṣad* clearly says that, while sacrifices enable one to cross the ocean of death, knowledge of the Supreme Being (*Brahman*) ensures the elimination of rebirths. In a way, the *Upaniṣads* prepared the ground for Buddhism.

Epic Society

The epics, *Rāmāyaṇa* and *Mahābhārata*, had not always their present forms. The stories originated much earlier than their existing forms. Perhaps several centuries elapsed between their origin and later compilation. The epic stories used to be sung by *Sūtas* (bards) in royal courts and *Kuśīlavas* or travelling singers. Even after the epic stories were written there were additions, alterations and interpolations. Each of the epics exists in different recensions.

Scholars like Winternitz believe that the *Mahābhārata* took the present shape about the fourth century A.D. and that the *Rāmāyaṇa* assumed the final form a century or two earlier.

The *Rāmāyaṇa* mentions two cultures besides the Aryan. Of these, one was that of the monkeys (*Vānara*), friendly towards the Aryans and the other that of the demons (*Rākṣasa*), hostile to them. Both of them belonged to South India. Some think that the so-called *Vānaras* were not actually monkeys, but human beings with the monkey as their totem. Their peculiar appearance and grotesque gestures and postures were perhaps responsible for their designation as *Vānara*. The dark-skinned, fierce-looking and ferocious *Rākṣasas* did not owe allegiance to the Aryans; rather they tried to cause harm to them. The *Rākṣasas* had abundant material prosperity and considerable martial skill. But, they were sensual, wild and eaters of human flesh.

The *Rāmāyaṇa* mentions low-class people and tribes like Niṣādas, Śabaras etc. A tribe was called Gṛdhra. They either used the vulture as their symbol or used to move from one place to another like birds.

This epic mentions also *Yakṣas* and *Nāgas*. The *Yakṣas* were very powerful and handsome; originally they were perhaps closely related to the *Rākṣasas,* and later driven away to the northern region. The *Nāgas* used snakes as their symbols. It seems that they established a kingdom including Ceylon and Malabar. The *Nāga* women were renowned for their beauty. Rāvaṇa is said to have abducted many such women.

There is mention also of *Asuras* hostile to *Rākṣasas*. The *Asuras* are stated to have indulged in various sinful acts.

A class of women, called *Apsaras* (nymph) is met with in the *Ram*. Due to their exquisite beauty, they were regarded as semi-divine. They are said to have disturbed the penance of sages.

Though generally conforming to the orthodox Brāhmaṇical religion, the epic contains atheistic ideas.

The main characteristics of the *Mbh* society are as follows : Though the traditional *Varṇāśramadharma* appears to have been generally followed in the epic, yet it testifies to the popularity of Vaiṣṇavism and Śāktism. None of these two faiths shows conventional adherence to the *Vedas*. The *Pañcarātra* sect of the *Vaiṣṇavas* and the *Pāśupatas* among the *Śaivas* claimed a large number of adherents. The Buddhists and the Cārvākas used to propagate anti-*Vedic* doctrines openly.

This epic betrays a number of departures from the traditional Brāhmaṇical religion. The ideal of one husband of a woman has been violated in Draupadī's having five husbands. There are instances of people of a lower class attaining an exalted position like *Brāhmanas* by dint of merit. Kṛṣṇa himself was a non-*Brāhmaṇa*. Vidura, though of a comparatively lower class, became an object of reverence by his character and conduct. It seems that the low-born person was not necessarily debarred from responsible work and deprived of respect.

Purāṇic Society

The *Purāṇas* contain valuable material for the sociological study of ancient India. No definite date can be suggested for the *Purāṇas*. In some cases, different chapters of a single *Purāṇa* appear to have been composed or compiled in different periods. By and large the early *Purāṇas* came into being approximately between the second century A.D. and the sixth.

One of the objects of the *Purāṇas* was to give freedom to women and *Śūdras* in certain religious rites and practices. They were denied the right to *Vedic* rites, and had been groaning under the grinding weight of repression and feeling an urge for emancipation in this field. The result was that a large number of them embraced Buddhism which allowed the same privileges to all irrespective of caste and sex. This caused an erosion of the

Brāhmaṇical society, and the sacredotal class, which depended on the people for their maintenance, felt the need for works like the *Purāṇas*.

During some centuries preceding and following the birth of Christ, three heterodox faiths exerted wide and deep influence on the populace. These were Buddhism, Jainism and Ājivakism. The semi-*Vedic* worship of the Trinity, viz. Brahmā, Viṣṇu and Maheśvara, and the non-*Vedic* Śaktism were powerful forces to reckon with.

The *Vaiṣṇavas* were broadly divided into two sects, viz. *Pañcarātra* and *Bhāgavata*. Bhāgavatism was very popular among the non-Brāhmaṇical and foreign tribes of whom mention may be made of the following : *Kirāta, Hūṇa, Pulinda, Pukkasa, Ābhīra, Suhma, Yavana* and *Khasa (Bhāgavata Purāṇa,* ii. 4.18). The rights and privileges in religious matters, denied to women and *Śūdras* in the traditional Brāhmaṇical *Śāstras*, have been given to them by the *Vaiṣṇavas*; women and *Śūdras* were allowed directly to worship Viṣṇu.

The *Pāśupatas* resorted to some reprehensible practices, e.g. to remain naked or to put on a loin cloth, living in a cemetery, erotic gestures and postures, defiance of *Varṇāśrama-dharma*. They drew the foreigners into their fold, and gave the right of direct worship to women and *Śūdras*. The *Kāpālikas*, wearing matted locks and garlands of human bones, used to carry blood-smeared human skulls in their hands and using sacred threads made of hair, roamed the streets

The *Purāṇas* tell us that the political sway of the Nandas, Mauryas, Andhras etc. dealt a severe blow to the traditional Brāhmaṇical religion. *Śūdra* kings are known to have themselves performed *Aśvamedha* sacrifice. They extended very liberal patronage to Buddhists and Jains.

The Buddhists advocated mendicancy and the Jains severe asceticism. The privileges in religious performances, given by them to women and *Śūdras*, considerably undermined the Brāhmaṇical society. There were other reasons also for the weakening of this society. One was the invasions by foreigners from the north-west and the other the spread of Tantricism among the masses.

Onslaughts on the Brāhmaṇical religion and society continued till the first quarter of the fourth century A.D. when the Guptas came to power. The Gupta kings revived the Brāhmaṇical religion battered by hostile forces for a long time.

Tāntric religion spread through Vaiṣṇavism and Śaivism. The Buddhists also had many *Tantras*. *Tāntric* influence is noticeable roughly from the fifth century onward. In course of time, *Tantras* influenced *Purāṇas* and *Smṛti*.

The embracing of Buddhism and the adoption of *Tāntric* practices led to the decadence of the traditional Brāhmaṇical religion and society. It was at this juncture that the *Brāhmaṇas* tried, in various ways, to restore their lost glory through the *Purāṇas*. Among the revivalist tactics was the introduction of a network of *Vratas* designed to secure various kinds of material welfare. Gift to *Brāhmaṇas* in *Vratas* was declared to be conducive to happiness. Gift to one having a large family to maintain was considered to be particularly beneficial. Among the articles of gift were such daily necessities as oil, salt, umbrella, sandals etc. Special merit was ensured if the performer of a *Vrata* could carry the articles of gift at his own cost to the house of the donee. *Vittaśāṭhya* (deceitful economy) has been condemned. This means that one should spend in gift as much as one's purse permits. Though prostitutes and *Śudras* were looked down upon, and relegated to a very low social position, yet in matters of gift even a *Brāhmaṇa*, versed in the *Veda*, was allowed to receive gifts from them. All this indicates that, in the society of those times, the economic condition of the *Brāhmaṇas* became critical, and they hit upon various devices to earn money through the medium of religion.

Dharmaśāstra and Arthaśāstra

Works on *Dharmaśāstra* are full of sociological material. It is, however, difficult to say how far the rules and regulations were observed in real life. Besides rules about *Varṇāśrama*, the *Smṛti* works mention the various vocations of the people and contain a mine of information on crimes and punishment.

The *Arthaśāstra*, though a treatise on politics and statecraft, contains sidelights on social conditions.

Society Reflected in Classical Sanskrit Literature

Various prose, poetical and dramatic works reveal a society in which what actually happened and not what was ideal according to *Smṛti* and other *Śāstras*. For example, the *Mṛcchakaṭika* and the *Caturbhāṇī* depict how rogues and rakes worked often overtly and sometimes in the guise of pious people. The *Mṛcchakaṭika* and the following are some of the noteworthy works which utilise theft as an effective and popular motif : *Daśakumāracarita, Pañcatantra, Cārudatta* (of Bhāsa), *Kathāsaritsāgara, Puruṣa-parīkṣā* (of Vidyāpati), *Vetāla-pañcaviṃśati, Śukasaptati* and *Kathārṇava* (of Śivadāsa).

Magical practices have been described in some works, e.g. *Daśakumāracarita, Kathāsaritsāgra* etc.

The wiles and tricks of prostitutes and demimondes have been delineated in some works, e.g. the *Caturbhāṇī, Kuṭṭanīmata*, etc. Vasantasenā of the *Mṛcchakaṭika* is an accomplished and virtuous courtesan, and has none of the frivolities and frolics of her profession.

Abduction of women, illicit sexual relation, drinking, gambling – these are some of the frailties and vices referred to in various works.

Music, dance, horse-race and some of the entertainments are mentioned in different works.

Various arts and crafts are referred to in several works. Other means of livelihood are also mentioned.

Elements of Indian Population

An analysis of the elements of Indian population reveals that it comprises the following principal types :

Aryans or Indo-Aryans

Upper class Hindus who are tall, fair-complexioned, sharp-nosed, speaking Sanskritic languages.

Dravidians

Mostly inhabiting South Peninsular India, differing, to some extent, in physical features, from the Indo-Aryans and speaking Tamil, Telugu, Malayalam and Kanarese languages which are non-Sanskritic and some of which have a few loan-words from Sanskrit.

Primitive Tribes

Like Kols, Bhils and Muṇḍās residing in hills and jungles, short, dark, snub-nosed, speaking languages were absolutely different from those of the above two types.

People with Mongolian Features

Beardless, yellow-complexioned, snubnosed, having flat faces and prominent cheekbones, mostly dwelling in the slopes of the Himalayas and the mountains of Assam.

In various works, we have references to the following principal tribes : Kirāta, Śabara, Barbara, Pulinda.

The term *Bhūta* appears to have been used to indicate some tribal people who presumably inhabited the regions near the Vindhyas. Their language was called Paiśācī Prākrit in which the now lost *Bṛhatkathā* is said to have been composed.[8]

The term *Mleccha* is often met with in different works. Generally it is taken to denote the people beyond the purview of the four castes and stages of life. Some would derive the word *Mleccha* from *Vāc* (speech) thus hinting that the *Mlecchas* used an alien tongue. As a matter of fact, however, what distinguishes them from the Aryans is not an alien language, but an alien culture. Buddhist sources use *Milakkha*[9] (equivalent of *Mleccha*) to refer to the non-Aryan people, the Andhra, Tamil etc.[10]

REFERENCES

1. Hemacandra. *Prakṛtiḥ saṃskṛtaṃ tatra bhavatvat prākṛtam (Prākṛta-candrikā)*. The *Prākṛta-sañjīvanī* is of the same opinion. Daṇḍin also appears to share the same view in his *Kāvyādarśa* (i. 33).
2. The New India Aryan languages are said to have developed out of *Avahaṭṭha*, the last stage in the evolution of Apabhraṃśa.
3. cf. *bhūta-bhāsāmayīṃ prāhur adbhutāṇthām bṛhatkathām*
4. Supposed by some to be of Bengal origin. The verses, dealing with the exploits of Kṛṣṇa, breathe the typically devotional atmosphere of Bengal. At one place, there is the word *Rāī* which is widely used in Bengal for Rādhā. (At least one verse, viz. *oggara bhattā* etc.).
5. Archaeologists claim to have unearthed evidence about the existence of several independent cultures of which the Sothi Culture of the Sarasvati valley and the chalcolithic rural city of Baluchistan and Sind are supposed to have been pre-Harappan. Vide A Ghosh, *The Indus Civilisation* etc. in V.N. Misra and N.S. Mate (ed.) *Indian Pre-history*, 1964. A.D. Pusalker tries to identify the Sothi culture with the *Ṛgvedic* civilisation, See *The Quarterly Review of Historical Studies*, VII, No. 4, 1967-68.
6. Some Finnish scholars claim that the Harappa script is Proto-Dravidian. Vide A Parpola et al, *Decipherment of the Proto-Dravidian Inscriptions of*

the Indus Valley Civilisation, Copenhagen, ordinary script, 1969; *Further Progress in the Decipherment of the Proto-Dravidian·Indus Script,* 1969.

7. The researches of Tilak and Jacobi point to a period of *Vedic* age, several millennia earlier than the Indus Valley Civilisation, See Tilak, *The Orion....* Jacobi in *Indian Antiquary,* June , 1894. *Vedic* parallels with Gāthie Avestan, Kauite and Pritanni inscriptions appear to indicate the origin of the *Ṛgveda* to the middle of the second millennium B.C. Some would identify the Harappan culture with the later *Vedic* Civilisation on the ground that both reflect agro-urban society.
8. c.f. *bhūta-bhāṣāmayṃ prāhur adbhutārthāṃ bṛhatkathām. Kāvyādarśa* of Daṇḍin, I. 38.
9. Eg. *Vinaya Piṭaka,* III. 28
10. Vide Buddhaghoṣa's Commentary.

2

POPULAR BELIEFS AND PRACTICES

The Vedic Age

EVER since the dawn of civilisation, human beings have been holding some naive beliefs and performing certain rites. However much civilisation may progress, whatever heights may be reached in the realm of knowledge, these beliefs and practices linger on. Indeed, ideas in human mind die hard. The earliest written record of the Indians, the *Ṛgveda,* reveal many such ideas and observances. The sense of awe and wonder, inspired by the mighty and beautiful aspects of nature, led them to think of powerful forces behind them. Disease and distress, affecting their worldly life, led them to suppose the existence of malevolent forces or spirits causing the evils. Similarly health and happiness made them infer the existence of benevolent forces controlling the same. Thus, in the factory of human mind came to be manufactured a number of gods, ghosts, imps, spirits, elves, nymphs, etc. The Aryans, among whom the *Ṛgveda* originated, mixed with the aboriginal non-Aryans of the land. Often at feud with them, the Aryans subjugated them, and appear to have used many of them as their slaves. No wonder, therefore, that the Aryans imbibed many non-Aryan ideas and adopted some of their practices. The *Atharvaveda* is a veritable mine of information about the beliefs of the people not sophisticated by the influence of the sacredotalism or Brahmanical class. The general impression is that the *AV* was later than the *RV.* But, the more primitive nature of the beliefs and practices have led some scholars to believe that the former may have been compiled later than the latter; but, the *AV*, perhaps, reflects the ideas of a remoter age. We shall briefly deal with the main popular beliefs and practices found in Sanskrit literature right from the *Vedic* Age.

The *Vedic* people appear to have believed in the existence of the spirits of forests, trees and plants. Spirits of a dangerous nature were supposed to haunt the forests. *RV* X. 97, 146 throw some light on the ideas of the people about forests.

Some prayers (e.g. *RV* X. 87. 12) reveal the belief that the worshipper of gods could see demons and sorcerers.

The agricultural implements were regarded as gods.

Traces of totemism are found in *Ṛgvedic* names of some persons. For instance, Kaśyapa (name of a sage) is supposed to have been derived from *Kacchapa* (tortoise). Some tribes are called *Matsya* (fish), *Aja* (goat), *Śigru* (horse radish). Sects of priests are called *Gotama* (ox), *Vatsa* (calf), *Sunaka* (dog), *Kauśika* (owl), *Māṇḍūkya* (frog). Tracing descent from plants and animals has been a practice among the aborigines of many lands.

Bad dreams were looked upon with great fear; so much so that an entire hymn is addressed to *Duḥsvapna* (bad dream), itself conceived as a deity who is implored to save the worshipper from unpleasant dreams. Such dreams were supposed to frustrate desire, and affect not only people but also cattle. The making of a garland or neck-band in a dream was regarded as ominous. A reference may be made to *RV* VIII. 47.15 in connection with dreams.

The *RV* betrays belief in ghosts, goblins, spirits and demigods. Certain demons were supposed to cause harm in the guise of some beasts and birds, e.g. dog, owl, hawk etc. *RV* III. 30.17 seems to indicate that some demons assumed the form even of roots (*Mūradeva, Sahamūla*). The various kinds of mischief, believed to be caused by them, included the killing of people and cattle, causing ailments, loss of milk to cows, etc. Demons were believed also to obstruct the flow of rivers, rainfall and to cause darkness, drought, etc. and to induce people to use harsh words. Some demons were fancied to possess hideous forms, e.g. three heads, six eyes, three feet and red complexion. *RV* I. 35.10; VII. 104.15 f.f.; X. 14.9 etc. may be referred to in this connection.

RV X. 14.9 reflects the belief that a funeral place is haunted by ghosts and evil spirits. An interesting superstitious practice was to draw a circle round the people on the funeral spot. The circle demarcated the living from the dead, and was believed to avert premature death (*RV* X. 18.4). Two malevolent *Ṛgvedic* demi-goddesses are Kṛtyā and Nirṛti. Kṛtyā was believed to attack people whom they turned blue or red and cause estrangement between husband and wife. Nirṛti was supposed to cause various mischiefs including death. Pigeons were believed to be agents of Nirṛti, causing harm to humans and cattle. For Kṛtyā and Nirṛti, reference can be made to *RV* X. 85. 28 f.f. and I. 38. 6; X. 114.2 f.f., 165. 1.

Yātudhāna seems to have been the appellation of some evil spirits or demons causing harm including the theft of cow's milk. The word *Yātumāvat* probably denotes one practising deceptive and mischievous magic or witchcraft.

Sasarparī (*RV* III. 53.15, 16), also called *Pakṣyā* and perhaps identical with *Pakṣiṇheti* (*RV* X. 165.2, 3), was supposed to be an evil spirit capable of bestowing great power.

The *Vedic* people appear to have been aware of different kinds of poison and their adverse effect on the human body. A curious belief was that some poisons could be cast into the sun.

Madhuvidyā (literally, science of sweetness), which appears to have been a mystical doctrine, was supposed to transform poison into nectar. The recitation of the names of ninety-nine rivers was supposed to counter-act the effects of poison. Twenty-one female peacocks and *Saptasvasārah*[1] (lit. seven sisters) were also believed to destroy the effects of poison. Prayers to particular deities were also supposed to be efficacious. Mongooses were supposed to be capable of removing the effect of poison. References to the following passages may be made in this connection : *RV* I.191.9. 10, 13,14, 15, 16; VII. 50, 1, ,2, 3.

The curious idea of transferring human diseases to other creatures and objects occurs in *RV* I.50.12. For exmaple, the disease called *harimāṇa* is stated to be transferable to the parrots and turmeric. Certain rivers were believed to heal the malady called *Śipada* (*RV* VII. 50.4). The *Vedic* people believed that one of the causes of ailments was the entry of demons into the body (X. 162). The healing effect of incantations is mentioned in *RV* 161, 163.

Certain passages reflect the popular faith that divine grace could effect rejuvenation. Reference may be made to *RV* I. 110; 116. 10; IV. 33.3; V. 74.5; X. 39.4, 7 etc.

Yakṣas and *Druhas* (*RV* II. 23.16, 35.6 etc.) denoted evil spirits taking delight in killing people and possessing untruthful persons. *Kṣvimkās* (X. 87.7) were a class of malefic spirits or birds shouting and eating raw flesh.

Rakṣasvin (*RV* I. 12.5; VII. 94.12; VIII. 22.18 etc.) appears to denote sorcerers controlling evil spirits and possessing the power of causing mischief.

RV X. 49.5, X. 145, X. 159.1 reveal the belief that one could bring another under control. Certain creepers were a means to winning over the husband and co-wife. Some methods of the husband winning over his wife were also believed in.

Paṇis (*RV* II. 24.6) and *Dāsas* (VII. 99.4) were believed to be capable of producing illusion (*Māyā*).

Ṛgvedic people believed in miracles caused through divine favour. For example, a blind man can see, a lame person can walk (II. 15.7; IV. 19.9). Lost eyesight can be restored through the grace of the Aśvins (I. 47.5, VIII. 5.25 etc.). Apalā, deserted by husband due to a skin-disease, is said to have been cured by divine grace. By Aśvins, Ghoṣā is stated to have been cured of leprosy (*RV* I. 117). The fire, into which Atri was cast, is said to have been made cool by the same gods (*RV* I. 112.7). *RV* I. 117.13, IV. 33.3 etc. refer to rejuvenation effected by gods. A barren cow is said to have given milk, and the wife of a eunuch got a son. Wine is said to have flowed from a horse's hoof (*RV* I. 116.7, 117.6). We hear also of a river made fordable by divine help (*RV* VII. 18).

In the ideas of the *Vedic* people about gods and their activities, we find some folk elements. Anthropomorphic and theriomorphic traits, attributed to gods, betray folkish attitude. While some gods are supposed to have human forms, others are conceived as possesed of the appearances of certain beasts and birds. The gods are believed to take food like human beings. Their mental attitudes also are sometimes like those of men and women; gods are not free even from some of the common human frailties. For example, the sun is fancied as following *Uṣas* (Dawn) even as a man (lustfully) follows a woman. Elsewhere she is stated to have the sun as her lover. *Pūṣan* is conceived as a paramour of *Uṣas*. *Uṣas* is fancied as revealing her body as a female dancer. Yamī is described as trying to seduce her brother, Yama, to incestuous sexual enjoyment. The conception of *Rudra* is typically folkish. *Rudra* (roarer) represents storm and plague, the things that are dreaded by the cattle-owner. His sons are the Maruts, the Hurricanes.

It is wrong to assume that all the people were religiously minded. The *Vrātyas* furnish an example of non-conformism. They appear to have been averse, even hostile, to *Vedic* religion and resorted to practices adverse to the orthodox Aryans.

Of the omens and portents, stated in the *RV*, the following are noteworthy. The bird *Kapiñjala* (variously explained as Francoline, partridge, heath-cock or sparrow) was believed to foretell future events. Its cry to the right of the house was regarded as auspicious and to foil the attempts of thieves and other wicked people as also to ensure the birth of sons and grandsons (II. 42.3). Pigeons, supposed to be messengers of Nirṛti, were believed to harm men and cattle (X. 165. 1-3). They were sought to be appeased by worship. The screech of an owl, regarded as the agent of Yama (god of Death), was considered to be ominous (X. 165. 4). There were pacificatory rites in honour of Yama so that the owl might not cause any mischief.

The *Atharvaveda* reflects popular beliefs and practices in a far larger measure than any other *Vedic Saṃhitā*. A larger number of spirits and demons are supposed to haunt human habitations causing harm to cows, horses and heroes and to devour the embryo in the womb. Some are believed to attack people in dream after assuming the forms of their brothers or fathers. Others pierce women in their hips. Demons of a particular class are described as having grotesque figures, red faces, horns on heads and hands, the front parts of the feet turned backward and heels turned forward. One spirit has a thousand eyes. *Moradevas*, belonging to another class, were neckless. *Kimīdins* are a dangerous sort of spirits causing illness and destroying cows' milk. References may be made to *AV* I. 7, I. 16.1, II. 25, III. 9, VIII. 4.24, 6.12 etc.

Of sorcery, witchcraft and magic we hear a lot in the *AV.* There were also means of counteracting the effects of the same. Many passages, e.g. I. 2.27, 12.27, 25.2; II. 11.3, 19-26; VI. 13.1-2 etc., throw lurid light on both white and black magic. Fire and water appear to have been widely used in magical rites.

Gandharvas, living in the sky, with *Apsaras* as their wives, are supposed to be fond of music, dance and association with women. Moving in the forms of dogs, monkeys, and youths with lively hairs, they are believed to cause mental restlessness, addiction to gambling and to devour sacrifical offerings. In this connection, a reference may be made to *AV* II, 2.3 f.f., 4.5; IV 37.1-2, 11 etc.

Some demons are believed to attack a bride or try to enjoy her (*AV* IV. 37.11). If wood and straw, hung up for sacrifice, are found to be moving, the presence of a demon can be inferred.

Curses, pronounced by the enemy, a female relative or an angry *Brāhmaṇa* are looked upon with horror. There are means to counteract their effects. We may refer to *AV* I. 23.22, 147.3, 4; II. 12.10, 23.7; III. 53.21-24 etc.

Amulets of a large variety play an important role in the life of the people of this age. These are used for various purposes, viz. counteracting the effects of a curse, healing diseases, nullifying *abhicāra* or practices designed to cause mischief, even ruin, to others. The names of some of the amulets are *Vīrudh, Sadampuṣpā, Trivṛt, Tilaka, Jaṅgīḍa, Śatavāra*, etc. For amulets, the following passages, *inter alia,* may be adverted to : *AV*; IV. 20; V. 28; VIII. 5.8, 9; XIX. 34.1, 36.6 etc.

The odium, attached to bad dreams in *AV*, is far more intensive than in the *RV*. These are supposed to be the offspring of such female deities as *Abhūti, Nirbhūti*, etc. and to forebode imminent danger, even death. The practices for averting bad dreams are found in the *Kauśikasūtra*, 48th *Kāṇda.* 9-13. The same work gives a list of charms against bad dreams. The charms are *AV* IV. 17.5; VI. 45.1; VII. 100.1; IX. 2.2,3; X. 3.6; XVI. 5 etc.

The atmosphere of the *AV* is so much surcharged, in fact saturated, with magic, that even politics and medical science are not free from it. Certain rites are prescribed for ensuring loyalty among subjects, the acquisition of a vast kingdom, sovereignty, etc. Some amulets, viz. one made from the *Palāśa* tree, one named *abhivartamaṇi* and one made of gold are prescribed for the security and prosperity of kings. Several rites and amulets are found to prevent and cure some diseases.

For the safety of agricultural operations and a rich harvest certain magical rites were performed. Some rites were supposed to ensure the safe delivery of babies.

Some magical practices are prescribed for man and woman to win the love of each other. There are processes for arousing passion in a woman and for increasing virility. *Subhagaṃkaraṇa* is a rite meant for making one full of youthful charm.

Symbolical and mimetic magic is a characteristic feature of *Atharvavedic* magic. The *Kauśika-sūtra* contains such practices. For instance, one has to break into two a piece of grass flung at the enemy. The breaking of the blade of grass symbolises the breaking of the armed foes into two (*KL* VI. 10). The burning of a chameleon, which is killed, symbolises the burning of a dead man (*K* XL VII. 39 ff., 54 ff.); this ensures the killing of an enemy. In a festival, relating to ploughing (*K* X16 ff.), the wife asks the husband if the ploughing has been done. To this the reply of the husband is always 'Yes'. Before undertaking a business tour, a merchant places balls of dung on the limbs of a friendly priest, and asks him—how is the day? The latter replies—it is good and lucky (*K* I. 15).

There are incantations and magical rites to prevent snake-bites as also to counteract the effects of the venom. For example, *AV* V. 13 is a charm against snake-poison. In this connection, the use of some words of non-Aryan origin, e.g. *Taimāta, Apodaka* (*AV* V. 6), *Āligī, Viligī* (stanza 7), *Urugulā, Asikni* (st. 8) etc. testify to the ideas of common people and the words used by them.

In the *Kauśika-sūtra*, we find some processes of divination or forecast of future events. For example, in a ceremony for the bride securing a husband, he will be known to come from the side from which the crowd appears (*K* XXXIV. 24). A girl for marriage is asked to pour a handful of consecrated water. If she pours it to the east, it is a good sign about her suitability (*K* 37. 11-12). A pitcher of water, covered with a piece of new cloth, is kept upon a bed. The remnants of an offering, made with the recitation of *AV* II. 1, are placed over it. Two girls, below the age of puberty and with their faces covered with cloth, are asked to remove the pitcher. A lost object is to be known to exist in the direction to which they take the pitcher (*K* 37. 4-5).

A few naive beliefs of a miscellaneous nature may be noted. From *AV* V. 31.8; XI. 8 we learn that the burial of various articles at cross-roads was believed to cause the destruction of enemies. It was extremely ominous if such evil birds as a pigeon or a crow, with flesh in beak, fell upon a person or struck him with something which dropped from its beak (*K* 51.7 ff; 46. 4.6 ff.). *AV* V. 27.29 and VII. 64 were used in pacificatory rites to avert the evil effects in such a case. A bridal procession, passing near a huge tree, was supposed to be beset with dangers caused by evil spirits. *AV* XIV. 2-9 was recited to avert such an evil. From *AV* XIV. 2.22, 23 we learn that a newly married girl, on reaching her father-in-law's house, used to take a *Brahmin* boy on her lap; this was supposed to ensure the brith of a male child to her. From the *K* we know that the custom of trial by ordeal was in vogue; it was resorted to for ascertaining the truth of a charge against a person in the absence of documentary evidence, witness, etc.

The priests of the *AV* were believed to possess supernatural power. They were regarded as controlling adverse forces, by magical means. Even his speech could heal a dangerous malady like insanity. *AV* II. 14.6; IV. 36; V.30-1-2; VI. 101.1-4, VII. 70. 4-5 may be referred to in this connection.

It was believed that premature death might be prevented by certain rites and incantations. The grain and sesame, offered in honour of the dead, were believed to become respectively a cow and its calf in heaven to give milk to the departed one. The dead person was supposed to go to the sun with his eyes, to the wind with his soul, to heaven and earth or water and plants with his other senses. It was believed that the king sat near Yama in the other world to realise the unpaid revenue from the departed ones. III. 29.1 contains a prayer for exemption of revenue after death.

A superstitious belief was that the appearance of teeth in the upper jaw of a child earlier than in the lower one spelt danger to the lives of parents. *K* prescribes rites (46. 43-46) with the recitation of *AV* VI. 140 to avert the danger.

K reveals the belief in evil stars, especially the one called *Mūla.*

From the *AV* (18.2.34) we learn that there were different modes of disposing of the dead body, *viz.* cremation, burial, throwing into water, exposing in an open place.

The *Ṛgvedic* conception of Rudra has undergone considerable modification in the *AV* with a more popular bias. With a thousand eyes, equipped with bow, arrow and mace and accompanied by a fierce-looking roaring dog, he is extremely powerful. He is believed to be able to cause destruction of the world, and to make people suffer from diseases and effects of poison. He can cure diseases and heal the wounds caused by weapons.

The *AV* betrays a secular and popular influence on society in comparison with the *RV*. The *Vrātyas*, the non-conformists holding atheistic view and adopting practices hostile to the

Aryans, were looked down upon in the *Ṛgvedic* times. But, in *AV* they were admitted into the Aryan fold. They were even deified (*AV* XV. 1-8).

Age of Brāhmaṇas

Certain curious practices are referred to in the *Brāhmaṇas*. From the *Śatapatha Brāhmaṇa* (I. 9.2.12) we learn that a wife did not take meals in presence of her husband. Though the husband used to take food in presence of the wife serving it, yet one desiring a vigorous son was debarred from this practice (*Śatapatha*, 10.5.2.9).

Some beliefs and practices, relating to the disposal of the dead body, are noteworthy. Just before death a person's body was placed on the ground, purified with cowdung and spread over with grass. After expiry the body was washed and anointed; the hair and beard of the departed were closely trimmed and the nails pared. Afterwards the body was garlanded, and covered with a new garment. The female members of the house used to surround the body, wail loudly and beat their chests and thighs. In the cremation ground, incantations were recited to prevent the evil spirits from harming the spirit of the departed or obstructing its union with the Fathers (*pitṛs*). The burning over, the mourners dispersed. They passed under a yoke made of the branches of a sacred tree and, entering the house, touched sanctifying articles such as water, fire, cowdung, mustard and barley.

An interesting practice is that the dead body used to be weighed in a balance in order to ascertain the merit or sin of the departed soul (*Śatapatha*, II. 2.7.33). If his merit outweighed his sin, the soul was believed to enter the heavenly region and become immortal like the gods. Otherwise, the soul was considered to enter hell. This practice is found in Zoroastrianism too.

In connection with the selection of a piece of land for raising a mound in memory of the deceased, some crude beliefs are noticed. If the ground is inclined to the north, the children of the dead person will be prosperous. If it be inclined to the south, his issues will soon follow him (*Śatapatha*, 13. 8.1).

After the burning of the body, the ashes were preserved in an earthen pot.

Kalpasūtras

Some *Gṛhyasūtras*, e.g. *Gobhila* (II. 1.3-8), *Āśvalāyana* (I.5. 4-6), *Kāṭhaka* (14, 4-9), lay down an interesting method of testing the worth of a bride to be chosen for marriage. Clods of earth are to be collected from the following places and kept before her: a sacrificial altar, a pool of water, a cow-pen, a furrow, a road-crossing, a gambling place, a cemetery, a barren spot. She is asked to choose any one of them. If she chose any one of the first four, she was regarded as fit for marriage. If she chose any of the last four, she was to be rejected. Some provide for a ninth clod made of a mixture of the above eight. The girl choosing it is fit for marriage.

According to *Bharadvāja Gṛhyasūtra* (I. 11) there should be four lumps with the earth collected from a sacrificial altar, a field, cow-dung, earth from a cemetery. A girl, choosing any one excepting the fourth, is acceptable. According to *Āpastamba Gṛhyasūtra* (I. 3. 14-17), the following articles are to be placed in covered pots before the girl : different kinds of seeds mixed up, loose earth from an altar, earth-clod from a field, cow-dung, a lump of earth from a cemetery. If she chooses any one excepting the fifth, she is acceptable.

It seems that the above practice of testing a girl was gradually dying out as it was crude. Bharadvāja and Āpastamba declare that one should marry a girl pleasing to one's heart and eyes. This view was, perhaps, the precursor of the later injunction of *smṛti-śāstra* to the following effect—*Voḍhur-manaścakṣuṣo-rānandakarīm udvahet.*

According to some authorities, girls of the following descriptions should be avoided for marriage : having the name of a star, river or trees; girls having such names as have the letters *r* and *l* in the penultimate position (*Āpastamba Gṛhya*, 13.10-13).

According to the *Kāṭhaka Gṛhya* (23. 1-4), while the bridegroom starts for the bride's house, a sister of his catches hold of a hem of his upper garment from behind with a weapon in hand and escorts him up to a tank. *Sāṅkhāyana* (I, 12.1-2) provides that he should be escorted to the bride's house by delighted young women who are not widows. According to *Baudhāyana* (I. 1.24-25) the bride, ceremonially given away, should, with an arrow in hand, behold the bridegroom.

An interesting practice in the marriage ceremony is that the bridegroom places *darbha* grass of a circular shape on the bride's hand. On this circle is fitted the hole of the right yoke of a chariot. On this hole is placed a piece of gold and the girl is washed through the hole. Then she is girdled with a cord (*Yoktra)*. A cart or chariot is placed near the nuptial fire. The bridegroom is tied to the right yoke and the bride to the left. Then they are unyoked. The tying to the yoke perhaps symbolised that they would shoulder the responsibilities of life in a united manner. The customs of washing the bride and girdling her appear to be hinted at in *Atharvaveda* XIV. I. 40-41 and XIV. I. 42.

In the *Pāṇigrahaṇa* rite, it is provided by some *Gṛhyasūtras* that one, desiring the birth of sons only, should seize only the thumb of the bride. One, desiring daughters only, should catch hold of her fingers only. For the birth of both sons and daughters, he should seize her hand on the hairy side alongwith her thumb and fingers. (e.g. *Āśvalāyana*, I. 7. 3-5; *Āpastamba*, II. 4. 11-15).

In the *aśmārohaṇa* rite, the bridegroom made the bride get upon a stone. It was believed that, by this rite, she would be firm like a stone, overcoming the wicked and trampling on those having evil designs. It was also supposed to ensure firm and steadfast conjugal love.

The rites, following the first arrival of the wife at the husband's house, included the placing of a boy in her lap; it was believed to ensure the birth of male children to her. Another practice was showing of the *dhruvatārā* (polestar) to the bride; this was supposed to make her stable (*dhruva*) in the husband's family.

Among the rites to be observed in the cremation ground, according to some *Gṛhyasūtras* (e.g. *Āśvalāyana*), we find that the wife of a deceased male was to lie beside the corpse; she was then made to rise. The practice appears to have been a demonstration of the wife's fidelity to the husband even after his death. Another curious custom was to sacrifice a cow, cut off its limbs and put them on the corresponding limbs of the dead; this was supposed to make the departed one escape the two fierce hounds believed to guard the gates to the abode of Yama (Vide *Kauśika-sūtra* 81. 20-29 and *Āśvalāyana-G.S.,* IV. 3.19-21). Before entering their houses, the persons who attended the funeral ceremony were to chew leaves of *Nimba* tree, sip water, touch water, fire, cowdung, seeds of white mustard, oil and to tread on a stone; these were believed to purify them.

According to *Gṛhyasūtras* (e.g. *Gobhila*, III. 3. 29-34; *Āpastamba* VIII. 23.8-10 etc.), the following events are supposed to portend bad luck and calamities for the householder : the post of a house putting forth shoots, beehive in a house, one pigeon flying into the house, footprints on the hearth, skirt of his garment blown by the wind upon him, a bird voiding dung on his body, a drop of water falling on him under a cloudless sky, a tornado overtaking him, a cow suckling another cow, a bad dream, breaking down of a spar of the roof or the middle post of the house, bursting of the water-barrel, touch of piled up fire altar or a sacrificial post, hearing a humming sound in the ears, quivering of the eyes, sun-rise or sun-set while he is asleep without any sickness, sight of a solitary jackal or a solitary she-wolf, appearance of an ant-hill in the house. Expiatory rites are prescribed for counteracting the evil effects of the above.

Certain superstitious practices are prescribed in *Gṛhyasūtras* to achieve particular objects. Thus, for example, *Āpastamba* (VIII. 23.6) ordains that, in order to ensure the steadfastness of a companion, pupil or servant, one should pour one's own wine into the horn of a living animal, and sprinkle it thrice round him to the accompaniment of a *mantra* when the person concerned is asleep. Certain formulas are prescribed for appeasing the anger of others (e.g. *Āpastamba*, VIII. 23.2). Certain magical rites are prescribed for one who wishes to guard one's wife against a paramour, achieve prosperity in trade and victory in debates (e.g. *Āpastamba*, VIII. 22.19; *Bharadvāja*, II. 28.61, 4 etc.).

Gaining the favour of a person, enjoyment of riches, increase of horses, elephants and cattle, prevention of involuntary death, misfortune, acquisition of a huge quantity of gold, happiness, long life, maintenance of the means of livelihood, acquisition of villages, glory, status of a ruler – these are some of the objects for which magical rites are prescribed in the *Gobhila-G.S.*, IV. 5-6; 8.9-25;9.

In facing some risk or while visiting a place which might be dangerous, one is required by *Gṛhyasūtras* to recite certain *mantras*. Thus, for example, *Āpastamba* (VIII. 22.14-19) prescribes *mantras* for one about to mount an elephant, a horse, a chariot, a camel or an ass and while boarding a ship. Yawning and sneezing were also supposed to be unusual events calling for the recitation of *mantras*. While coming to a road-crossing, a dung-heap, a big tree, a place infested by snakes, a cemetery, a cow-pen or some other dangerous place one was to recite some *mantras* (vide *Hiraṇyakeśi*, I. 18.8-13; *Pāraskara*, III. 15.13-20).

The veneration of snakes appears to have been a common popular practice. In this connection, it may be added that, even now-a-days, many people, particularly in the rural areas, attribute supernatural powers to serpents, and regard them as divine. At the *Śravaṇā* ceremony, there was the practice of presenting, besides other articles of adornment, a comb, collyrium, flowers and an unguent to snakes (*Pāraskara Gṛhya*, II. 14.17, *Sāṅkhāyana Gṛhya,* IV. 15.8; *Āpastamba*, VII. 18.11). *Baudhāyana-Gṛhyasūtra*, III. 10.4, provides that the flour of rice, barley or *Śyāmāka*, cooked with ghee or sugarcane juice and some other things, should be offered to snakes.

The *Kauśika-sūtra* is a mine of magical rites for achieving various objects such as victory for king, protection of cattle and crops, safety and security for merchants in their journey and enterprise, increase of intellect, protection of building from fire, changing the course of a river, ensuring rainfall, cure of diseases, acquisition of children, prevention of abortion and sterility, ensuring marriage, controlling a run-away wife, winning over a rival woman or a husband attached to other women, suppressing paramours etc. There are rites for restoring sexual vigour to a man. There are practices relating to witchcraft as well as those for counteracting them. Elsewhere this work deals with omens and portents and practices designed to remove their evil effects.

The *Dharmasūtras* contain many superstitious ideas relating to study, food, sins and expiation and miscellaneous matters[3]. We note a few interesting ones here. Eating with a woman has been prohibited (*Baudhāyana*, I. 2.5, *Vasiṣṭha*, XII. 31). It is stated that such a practice results in the birth of weaklings. The remnants of the food of the preceptor were believed to cure a pupil of his disease (*Baudhāyana*, II. 1.25). According to *Gautama* (IX. 17-18) talk with a *Mleccha*, other unholy or impious persons taints a person with impurity. *Samudra-saṃyāna* or a sea-voyage to another island was regarded as a sinful practice causing degradation (*Baudhāyana*, II. 2.2).

Vedic study was considered harmful on certain occasions, e.g. when the wind blew carrying dust, when the sound of some musical instruments was heard, when dogs, jackals and asses cried, when the rainbow was seen, rainfall out of season after one had taken a meal on the occasion of *śrāddha*, when one stayed in a city, on festive occasions, in certain *tithis* of certain months (e.g. in full moon in *Pauṣa*), when the cry of an owl was heard.

Some other superstitious practices, according to *Dharma-sūtras*, are as follows : According to *Gautama* (I. 9.23, 24), one should not speak to others about a cow feeding its calf. A rope, with which a calf is tied, should not be crossed over (*Gautama*, I. 9.52). *Āpastamba* prohibits (I. 31.19) the counting of birds in a flock. According to *Viṣṇu* (81. 6-9), the performance of *Śrāddha* should not be seen by a woman in her monthly impurity, dog, pig, and rural cocks. But, it should be shown to a goat.

The *Sūtras* reflect the belief in a number of demons and goblins having peculiar names, e.g. *Ṣaṇḍa, Marka, Ulūkhala, Malimluca, Kiṃvadanta, Śatru, Patrapāṇi, Hantrī-mukha, Sarṣapāruṇa, Keśinī, Śvalomini*, etc. Rites are prescribed to ward them off when they try to possess a new-born baby and its mother. They are supposed to wear variegated garments and walk through the village intent on causing mischief. These night-ranging creatures wear ornaments on breasts and hold lances in their hands, and drink from skulls. Their sisters are believed to peep through the door-joint at night.

Pāṇini And Patañjali

From the *Aṣṭādhyāyi*[4] (IV. 2.14) we come to learn of the practice of food-leaving served in different types of utensils. According to the *Kāśikā*, there were three kinds of food-leavings depending on the particular types of utensils. These were *śārava, māllaka* and *karpara.* The first denotes the leaving in a plate on which food was served, probably given to scavengers. The second referred to the leaving in the pot, from which food was served, meant for the family barber. The third one referred to that left in the cooking pot, meant for the cook.

The words *audarika* (*Pāṇini*, V. 2.67), *ghasmara, admara* (III. 2.160) indicate that gluttony was in vogue.

From *Pāṇini* (IV. 3. 34, 36, 37; VIII. 3.100) we learn that names of persons, derived from those of stars, were widely in use. It appears that star-names of persons were in addition to their *gotra* names. It appears that there was the custom of keeping the star-name a secret.

Pāṇini refers to some curious popular ideas. III.2. 52 and 53 reveal the belief in the fact that physical marks on the body of the husband or wife indicate certain events. Thus, a black mole indicates the wife's death. A particular line on the wife's palm was supposed to indicate the husband's death.

Viprasna (*Pāṇini*, I. 4.39) appears to hint at the practice of asking a soothsayer about the future of a person.

The word *hṛdaya* in *Pāṇini*, IV. 4.96, has been interpreted in the *Kāśikā* to mean a *mantra* meant for *vaśīkaraṇa* (controlling other persons).

We do not know of any noteworthy belief or practice in the *Mahābhāṣya*. The words *Puṇyāha* (V. 4.90) and *Puṇyarātra* (V. 4.47) reflect the belief in the auspiciousness or otherwise of some days and nights. VI. 2. 152 hints at the idea that good and bad actions lead respectively to merit and sin.

Age of Popular Epics

The *Ram* testifies to some popular beliefs. People used to believe that work started at an auspicious moment would be sucessful. Thus, for the entrance to a new house, marriage and journey auspicious time was to be selected. (II. 56. 25, I. 73.9, VI. 3.33). It was believed that , when setting out on a journey the vehicle should face northward (II. 46.34). While entering a hostile country, one was to put one's left foot first (V. 4.3) in order to avoid bad luck. Brimful water-pots and a bull's horn were considered to be indicative of auspiciousness and plentitude (IV. 26. 33-4). Throbbing of eyes or other parts of the body, sight of birds or hearing their voices were supposed to foretell happiness or sorrow (III. 52.2). The inauspicious cry of a crow flying high overhead was supposed to portend evil, but its peaceful cawing, while perched on a tree, indicated a happy event to happen (IV. 1. 55-6). Some portents were supposed to prognosticate death or some other grievous calamity (II. 4.19-20). In war, the following were regarded as ominous :

> Jackals during battle (III. 23.10), a torso dropping before a person in the battle-field (IV. 54.32), sight of a fierce, emaciated tawny male figure with a shaven head peeping into the houses of people (IV. 35. 33-4).

The fall of burning meteors, the wind blowing awry with a thunderous sound, camels, asses and mules, with their hairs standing erect, shedding tears, unnatural birth of animals, e.g. cows bearing asses, mongooses bringing forth mice, etc., the presence of a reptile in a kitchen, birds crying fearfully towards the sun, throbbing of the left arm, depression and restlessness of mind—these are some of the omens portending various evils.

As there were evil omens, so there were some auspicious signs too. All the directions looking pleasant, the wind blowing pleasantly, birds and beasts crying pleasantly, throbbing of the left arm, left eye of a woman, mind delighted without any perceptible reason—these were regarded as indicative of good things.

The omens and portents, referred to in the *Ram,* may be classified as those relating to natural phenomena, behaviour of animals, physical conditions and mental attitudes[4].

There appears to have been a widespread belief in the good and bad things indicated by dreams (II. 4.17, II. 69. 8-16, III. 73.33, V. 27.6, V. 32. 9, VI. 35. 28). The following are some of the sights which, if seen in dream, were supposed to portend misfortune of varying degrees[5] :

> A monkey, thunder from blue sky, flaming meteors, plunging from mountain-top into a cow-dung pool, floating of cow-dung on a pool, diving head on into oil, beating by black and yellow women, speeding towards the south in an ass-cart, wearing a garland of red flowers, strong dark-complexioned women in front of the house seizing furniture, drying up of an ocean, fall of the moon on earth, all-enveloping darkness, breaking into pieces of the king's riding elephant, flaming fire suddenly put out, cracking of the earth, withering of trees, smoke emitted by mountain peaks.

It was a common belief that a person could be possessed by evil spirits which could be warded off by certain incantations and magical rites. Heavy breathing, shaking of the body, loss of vitality or memory, partial loss of consciousness were some of the signs of a person under the control of malevolent spirits (II. 10. 29-30, II. 58.34, II. 60.1).

Some other curious beliefs were that the female mule was killed by its issues as soon as they were born (III. 43.41), that the universe was upheld by eight elephants in the eight quarters and that earthquake was caused when they shook their heads due to fatigue (I. 40.15).

It was a widespread belief that adverse natural phenomena affecting people's happiness, were caused by lapses in the discharge of royal duties. For example, in a country, where the king did not function, there was dearth of moisture required for the growth of crops and plants (II. 67.9). Similarly, drought was supposed to follow maladministration by the king (I. 9.8-9). One is irresistibly reminded of king Duṣyanta's following enquiry to the hermits visiting the royal court in the fifth act of the *Śakuntalā*, verse 9 :

> Is it that the flowering and fructification of creepers have been withheld through my misdeeds ?

That the life span of one hundred years was believed by people in general is proved by the folk-song, referred to in V. 34.6, VI. 126.2, which means – if only one lives, happiness will come to one though after a hundred years. Here, one hundred years may, of course, be taken to mean a very long period.

The following bodily signs of a woman were believed to be auspicious (VI. 48. 7-14) :

> Fine, smooth and black hair, separate eye-brows, round legs which are not hairy, closely set teeth, well-proportioned temples, eyes, hands, feet, ankles, thighs, gradually rounded nails on fingers, plump breasts with deeply set nipples and without a gap in between, deep navel, soft hair on body, complexion like the colour of a valuable stone, standing firm on the toes and soles, lotus-marks on feet.

The following characteristics in a man indicate his beauty and good luck (V. 35.15.20) :

> Broad shoulder, long arm, conch-like neck, attractive countenance, plump throat, reddish eyes, proportionate

limbs, bluish complexion, hard thigh, fist and wrist, long brows and scrotum, high navel, abdomen and breasts, copper-coloured palms and nails, belly and throat, each having three folds of skin, four lines on thumb, high stature, proportionate teeth, elegant gait, fleshy and elevated lips and jaws, long nose, spacious back, high forehead.

From *Vana* 232.7, 8 we learn that, in the *Mbh* age, people used to believe that one person could bring another under control with incantations or drugs. It was also believed that sometimes people were possessed by evil spirits (*Vana*, Chap. 72). The story of king Nala, into whose body Kali is stated to have entered, is well known. *Ādi*, Chap. 76 reveals the belief in certain charms used for reviving a dead person.

There are many instances of curses which were believed to take effect when pronounced by certain persons of great power or by one who has been pained at heart. People used to resort to swearing (*śapatha*) and the breach of promise was believed to result in great harm (*Vana* 252.23, *Udyoga*. 174.16, *Sabha*. 71.14).

In this epic, we find the practice of ordeals like fire, scale, poison, etc. which were believed to declare the guilt or innocence of the accused.

In the *Mbh* there is widespread belief in the doctrine of Karman, the influence of planets on human life etc. People used to select auspicious days or moments for particular kinds of work.

The *Mbh* refers to *śakuna-vidyā* by which people could interpret good signs and evil omens. Deviations of the course of planets and stars, growth of things out of season, some unusual or superhuman incident, the sudden happening of something unthought of, unusual throbbing of limbs, etc. are some of those which portend evil. The cries of jackals by day, cries of fierce birds, sudden blowing of wind at a high speed sometimes scattering dust, fall of a meteor, solar eclipse at a time other than new moon, the sudden fall of flags, the flying of a *Vartakā* bird with one wing, one eye, one leg while vomitting blood towards the sun, fierce look of the sun and the moon, the flow of a river upstream with blood-red water, cry of a jackal with fiery red face turned towards the sun, appearance of fierce looking cloud, horses shedding tears, lack of spirit among horses, lack of radiance of fire, deer crying fiercely at the sun, lack of lustre of sun-rays, thunder and lightning in a cloudless sky, bad dream, the vulture, crane and bees following a person, red, white, green, white colours of the east, south, west and north respectively, simultaneous fall of vultures, crows and cranes over trees, shaking or fall of an image of a deity, the sound of drums which are not beaten, showering of flesh from the sky, a cow bearing an ass, a mare giving birth to a cow-calf, a woman delivering female quadruplets or quintuplets, blood emitted by udders of the cows after delivery, the fall of mountain-peaks, mice fearlessly moving to and fro on streets, cranes imitating the cries of owls, sheep, goats crying like jackals—these are some of the noteworthy omens mentioned in the *Mbh.*

There were some auspicious signs too, e.g. a peacock, swan, crane, etc. following a person, smokeless fire spreading flame to the right, sweet smell of offering in fire, swans, parrots etc. flying around a person, throbbing of certain limbs etc. (e.g. *Bhisma* 3. 65-74).

Some superstitious practices, referred to in the epic, are as follows. On auspicious occasions, the use of flowers, grown on a cremation ground or in the vicinity of a temple, were prohibited (*Anu* 98.33). Eating, bath and study are prohibited in the evening (*Anu* 104.141). The cutting of a tree on a new moon day was regarded as inauspicious (*Anu* 127.3). *Abhiṣeka* for three days with earth touched with the horns of a blue bull was regarded as producing great merit (*Anu* 134. 1-3). The result of bath in all holy places was believed to be achieved by *go-śṛṅgā-bhiṣeka* (*Anu* 130. 10-12). In it one had to bathe a cow's horn with water in which grass had been soaked and then to sprinkle that water on one's own head. Lying down with the head towards the north or west was supposed to be inauspicious (*Anu* 104.48, 49).

Cowdung and cow's urine were looked upon as very pure (*Anu* 69.11, 78.19, 79.5, 146.48). Impurities were supposed to be removed by cowdung. Houses were regularly smeared with it. For purification it used to be smeared over the body before bath. A draught of cow's urine was regarded as purifying.

Cows were looked upon as deities incarnate. It was believed that want of proper care of them caused evil to the owner (*Vana* 2.57). It was customary to salute them in the morning and evening (*Anu* 78.16). Even the sight of cows was believed to be auspicious.

The *Mbh* (*Anu* 141.56, *Udyoga* 18.5) prohibits the sale of certain commodities enumerated under Economic life. There is no apparent reason behind the prohibition which was, perhaps, based on superstition or prejudice. Equally inexplicable is the prohibition of the sale of some of these by *Brāhmaṇas* even in emergency (*Śānti* 78. 4-6).

A popular belief was that each house had a presiding demoness (*Sabhā* 18.2).

From *Bhīṣma* (112.11) we learn that the trembling of images of deities or the shedding of tears by them was considered as extremely ominous.

Bhīṣma (3.2-7) refers to the following births as extremely portentous :

> Women delivering monstrosities, even women of high classes giving birth to eagles, peacocks, mares giving birth to calves, dogs to jackals, women giving birth to female quadruplets or quintuplets, at the same time.

In the age of the *Mahābhārata,* belief in omens appears to have been common from the *Gītā* too (I. 31) in which Arjuna expresses concern at ominous signs.

Omens and portents (*nimitta, utpāta*) of various sorts are mentioned frequently in the *Mahābhārata,* e.g. *Sabhā*. 71.22, 80.28-31, 81. 22-25; *Vana*. 179.41, 223.17-19, 224. 17-18; 39. 4-7, 46. 24-33; *Udyoga*. 73. 39, 83. 23-26, 84. 4-9, 117, 136. 28-30; *Bhīṣma*. 2. 16-33, 3. 1-46, 65-74; 19. 36-38; 99. 21-28; 112.6-12; *Droṇa*. 7. 34-41, 77. 3-7; *Śalya*. 23. 21-24, 56. 8-14, 192. 17-21; *Mausala*. I. 1-5, 2.1-17; *Śānti*. 52.25; *Āśvamedhika*. 53.5 ; *Karṇa*. 72. 12-13.

Some of the interesting ones, besides those stated above, are noted below :

Terrible dream, fall of a meteor, she-jackal howling towards the south, solar eclipse at unusual time, flashes of lightning without cloud, carnivorous birds like vultures falling on temples, spontaneous fire, blood-red water in river, rain without cloud, shower of blood or mud, horses shedding tears, throbbing of the left eye or arm (of males), birds like pigeons and deer weeping with face towards the sun.

The main auspicious signs are cloudless sky, pleasant and cool wind, birds and animals passing by the right side of a man, fire with flames towards the right, shower of flowers, auspicious birds like *Krauñca* and *Mayūra* crying to the right of a person.

Purāṇic Age

The *Vāyu-Purāṇa* (69. 271) refers to a belief that *Piśācas* or goblins haunt an empty house, a house for delivery of babies and a shelter on a cremation ground. In 69. 281-2 it is stated that *Piśācas* haunt a house in connection with which the prescribed rites (*saṃskāras*) are not performed and the inmates wherein are devoid of the code of conduct laid down in *Śāstras*. There is evidence of the belief that *Brahma-Rākṣasas* (i.e. a class of demons) dwelt on the *Śleṣmātaka* tree (69.135).

The *Kālikā-purāṇa,* quoted in several *Smṛti* digests, e.g. *Durgā-bhakti-taraṅgiṇī, Tithi-tattva, Varṣakriyā-kaumudī, Kṛtya-ratnākara*, ordains that, after the immersion of the image of Durgā on the last day of the *Pūja* (i.e. *Daśamītithi*), *Śabarotsav* should be performed. It consists of the people throwing dust and mud at one another, and uttering abusive language mentioning the female and male genital organs. It is stated that one, who does not abuse others or is not abused by others, is cursed by the indignant goddess. The very name of the festival shows that it was borrowed from the aboriginal tribe, called *Śabara*. The details of the festival are also non-Aryan in nature.

Some *Purāṇas* throw light on popular superstitious beliefs and practices. For example, chapter 31 of the *Agnipurāṇa* gives an account of such beliefs current among the common people. In it we find a protective process in which Vāsudeva is invoked to remove all sorts of misery like diseases, evil influence of heavenly bodies, evil spirits etc. The process is called *Mārjana* or *Apamārjana* in which the priest appears to assume the position of Hari who wards off all evils with a piece of *Kuśa* grass fancied as Viṣṇu.

Chapter 315 lays down rules of black magic called *Stambhana, Mohana, Vaśīkaraṇa, Vidveṣaṇa, Uccāṭana, Māraṇa.* The procedure of these acts are briefly as follows. On a birch-leaf the figure of a tortoise is to be drawn and different *mantras* are to be placed on its face and feet. The name of the person intended is to be written on its back. Then the performer will scatter water, and remembering the enemy, strike the ground with his left foot. This will ensure the *stambhana* (paralysing) of the enemy. By putting a mark on the forehead with *rocanā* (a yellow pigment) reciting the *mantra 'Om Namo Bhagavatyai'*, one can enchant the entire world. By putting a mark on the forehead with the *mantra 'Om Pheṃ Hūṃ Phaṭ'*, one can control even kings. By placing under the bed of a person at night the substance, emitted by asses and women in their menstrual flow, as also the placenta of an ass delivered of its calf, etc. one can create enmity with him. One can ensure the destruction of a person by throwing into the latter's house cow's hoof, horn, horse's hoof, serpent's head, etc. The death of a person can be brought about with the root of yellow *Karavī* plant. The blood of serpents and female musk-rats is also useful for the purpose. Bee, crab, scorpion, lizard—these should be pounded together and the powder thrown into oil. By getting it rubbed over the enemy's body he may be caused to be afflicted with leprosy. The death of the enemy can be ensured by writing his name on a birch-leaf and then worshipping it in a funeral ground with the *mantra 'Om Kuñjarī Brahmāṇī'*.

Chapter 140 lays down the herbs, drugs and various other articles supposed to possess mysterious potentialities for making charms, etc. effective. Unguents and collyrium, prepared with them, are also stated. For example, a mark on the forehead with some drugs is believed to enchant the three worlds. There are other means of winning over women, beautifying women, acquiring the ability to play with serpents, ensuring safe delivery, gaining victory in dice-play, getting a male child.

Chapter 142 gives certain incantations for achieving different objects. For example, there are *mantras* for rendering the body proof against injuries caused even by weapons. This incantation is to be put into an amulet to be worn round the neck or the arm. It also averts the influence of evil spirits. A mystic diagram, called *Śānti-cakra*, is described; it is supposed to be able to ascertain the malignant influence of Saturn. We find, in this chapter, a process by which the birth of a male or female child in the womb may be ascertained.

The *Viṣṇudharmottara* and the *Matsya* (243) state that the trembling, dancing, laughing and weeping of god's images forebode great evil.

The *Matsya* (235. 1-3) and the *Viṣṇudharmottara* (II. 140. 1-3) state that a woman, giving birth to monstrosities, or two, three, four and more children at a time, forebodes the destruction of the family or country. The same is the result if delivery takes place long before or after the due time.

Some *Purāṇas*, e.g. *Matsya* (229. 6-9), *Agni* (263. 12-13) divide omens into three classes, *viz.* :

(i) Heavenly—e.g. abnormal condition of plants and stars, eclipse, comets.
(ii) Atmospheric-e.g. unusual clouds, shower of blood-red rain, etc.
(iii) Terrestrial—e.g. earthquake, unusual condition of reservoirs of water, etc.

Some *Purāṇas*, e.g. *Matsya* (228) and *Agni* (263. 7-8), mention eighteen *Śāntis* or rites for appeasing adverse planets and getting rid of other kinds of troubles. For example, *Abhaya Śānti* is performed when a king wishes to be victorious or is attacked by enemies or fears mischief from witchcraft adopted against himself. *Saumya Śānti* is to be done when a man wants to be rid of consumption.

Matsya (229. 14-25) holds that certain happenings, generally regarded as ominous, turn to be auspicious on particular occasions. For example, the following are auspicious in *Caitra* and *Vaiśākha* : meteor, earthquake, etc.

Smṛtiśāstra

Manu (VI. 50) ordains that a *Parivrājaka* should not seek alms from people by explaining to them the results of omens (*Nimitta*). This shows that belief in omens and portents was widespread in those times.

In connection with judicial proceeding, we find some crude practices and naive beliefs which reflect the ideas of common people. We shall deal with divine proofs (*divya*) which were resorted to in the absence of human proofs, *viz.* documentary evidence, possession, witnesses. The different kinds of ordeals are briefly described below.

Tulā or Dhaṭa (Balance)

A sacrificial tree (like *Khadira* or *Udumbara*) is to be cut with the recitation of *Vedic mantras*. Two wooden posts, made of the same tree, should support a transverse beam. Two scales are to be suspended at the two ends of the beam. The accused person is placed on a scale, and weighed against clay, bricks and stones. Then he should get down and pray to the balance to reveal the truth. He again ascends the scale. If he is lighter than the things against which he was formerly weighed, he is declared innocent. If he is heavier, he is guilty.

Agni (Fire)

Nine circles with cowdung are to be drawn, each being meant for a deity beginning with Fire-god. In each circle *Kuśa* grass is to be spread. The accused is to place his feet on them. His hands are covered with leaves of the *Aśvattha* tree. Then a red-hot iron ball is placed in the hands of the accused. He should then walk from the first to the eighth circle slowly, and throw the ball on the ninth circle. Then the Judge should rub rice grains on the hands of the accused. If, at the end of the day, no injury in his palm is found he is declared innocent.

Udaka (Water)

A *toraṇa* (arch), as high as the ear of the accused, should be erected on the bank of a tank. A target is to be fixed 150 cubits away. A post of a sacred tree is to be fixed in the water. An impartial man should stand in navel deep water holding the post. Then the accused will be made to stand in water with the writing containing the charge placed on the head. An army man standing near the *toraṇa* should shoot three arrows at the target. Then a man should run swiftly to the spot where the second arrow struck the ground, and stand there with the arrow in hand. Another fast running man stands near the *toraṇa* whence the arrows were shot. At the third clap of the judge, the accused dives into the water seizing the thighs of the man standing in water. At the same time the man near the *toraṇa* runs at the topmost speed to the place where the second arrow fell. The other man, holding the arrow, starts off at the moment the first runner reaches him and, runs to the *toraṇa*. If he does not see the accused or sees only his head, when he reaches the *toraṇa*, the latter is declared innocent.

Viṣa (Poison)

Poison of a specified nature and of the stated quantity should be administered to the accused in the last watch of the night. Then he will be kept without food throughout the following day. If he does not show any effect of poison, then he will be declared innocent.

Kośa

The accused is made to worship the images of stern deities like Rudra, Durga, etc. and made to bathe the images with water. Then he will drink three handfuls of that water. If, within fourteen days of drinking the water, no serious calamity befalls him, he will be declared innocent.

Taṇḍula (Rice)

On the preceding day, grains of rice are to be husked. The grains, kept in a vessel, should be exposed to the sun. The water with which the image of the sun is bathed, should be poured over the grains and the container kept in that condition for the whole night. The next morning he should swallow the grains thrice. Then it should be spat on a *pippla* or birch-leaf. If blood is found mixed with his saliva, then he will be declared guilty.

Taptamāṣa (Heated Gold)

A fixed quantity of ghee and oil should be poured into a vessel which is to be heated to the boiling point and a piece of gold, weighing one *māṣaka* (= five *guñjās)* is dropped into the mixture. The accused will then take out the golden piece with his thumb, and the next two fingers. If there is no jerky movement of the fingers or no scalded skin, then he will be declared innocent.

Phāla (Ploughshare)

A red hot ploughshare of iron should be licked by the accused once with his tongue. If he is not burnt, he will be declared innocent.

Dharma

Images of *Dharma* and *Adharma* should be made of silver and lead (or iron) respectively. Or, figures of them, white and dark respectively, should be drawn on a leaf or a piece of cloth. Then the images or figures shall be placed in two balls of clay or cowdung. The two balls are to be placed into a new earthen vessel. After invocation to God, the accused shall take out one ball from the vessel. If it is *Dharma*, then he is innocent. There are some literary references to the prevalence of ordeals. The *Mṛcchakaṭika* (IX. 43) mentions the ordeals of poison, water, balance and fire. The drama may have been composed in the early centuries of the Christian era. That the above four were common is attested by their mention by Bāṇabhaṭṭa (7th. cent. A.D.) in his *Kādambarī* (para 47).

It is interesting to note that epigraphical and other evidences also bear out the vogue of trial by ordeal even as late as the eighteenth century or later. For example, the Kittur Pillar Inscription, Silimpur Stone Slab Inscription etc. may be mentioned[6]. It may be added that, even in ancient European countries, trial by ordeal was in vogue[7]. For instance, in early England red-hot iron and boiling water were used for ordeals. The assize of Northampton (1176 A.D.) is known to have ordered the ordeal of water.

Kauṭilīya Arthaśāstra

The work records popular belief in evil spirits. It was believed that they caused various kinds of trouble and that they could be appeased by various offerings including goats at *Caitya* shrines (4.3. 40-41). People appear to have engaged magicians, and those versed in the *Antharvavedic* lore, to ward off these evil spirits. It is interesting to note that these popular beliefs were turned to his advantage by a clever king (5.2.41). From 13.2. 21-35 we learn that, in an enemy capital, the illusion of danger from evil spirits was to be created so that the king concerned would come out for appeasing them. Taking advantage of this situation that king would be slain.

Magical practices of various kinds are recorded by Kauṭilya (5.2.59). Some of these are :

Saṃvadana or *Saṃvanana* –	Practices and potions for winning the love of a man or a woman (4. 4.14., 4.5. 1 etc.).
Akṣaya-hiraṇya Karma –	for acquisition of imperishable wealth.
Rājadvārika –	for gaining royal favour.
Arivyādhikara –	for causing diseases to enemies.
Āyuṣya –	for long life.

Putrīya – for getting a son.

The magical rites for rendering a country free from fear are (5.6.2) *deśapīḍāpaha* (removing danger to the country) and *amitrāpaha* (destroying enemies).

The branch of knowledge, related to such rites, is called *jambhaka-vidyā* which seems to have required the recitation of some *mantras* and the use of certain roots and herbs (4. 4.14).

Another branch, called *mānava-vidyā*, taught rites against dacoits and adulterers, called *mānavas*. It was the power of this *Vidyā* to achieve the following purposes : automatic opening of gates, inducing sleep in other persons, making oneself invisible, winning a woman's love (4.5. 1-6).

The text condemns the use of black magic. *Saṃvadana-vidyā*, referred to above, is also denounced; but its use by the husband or the wife is not banned. It is also permitted to a man seeking control over a girl with a view to marrying her (4.13. 28). Despite the prohibition, the vogue of hostile magic in the society can be inferred.

Some popular practices are recorded as remedies against natural calamities and damages caused by various creatures. In order to avert loss likely to be caused by fire, river, rats, serpents etc. these have to be worshipped on certain occasions (4.3). If rainfall is scarce, Indra, Gaṅgā, mountains, ocean or Varuṇa have to be worshipped.

The worship of mountains on specified occasions was believed to avert the attack of beasts or birds in herds or flocks.

There appears to have been great fear from demons (*rākṣasas*). To get rid of this menace, those, who were experienced in *Atharvavedic* rites and in *Māyāyoga,* were to perform rites designed to destory the evil being. *Caitya-pūjā* or worship of *Rākṣasas* in funeral places, with various offerings, including goats, was also to be performed.

When cattle diseases broke out in an epidemic form, the presiding deities of the respective animals were to be worshipped.

In case of maladies, caused by human agencies, certain magical rites are recommended as remedies. When natural diseases broke out, sages and other holy men were to perform rites for appeasement and expiation. For the prevention of human diseases in epidemic forms, the following practices, *inter alia,* were prescribed : bath by the subjects in holy places, worship of the sea or Varuṇa, milching of cows in funeral places, burning of headless trunks (made of rice and pounded grain) and keeping awake at night on the occasion of the worship of a deity.

Most of the above rites were to be performed at the initiative of the king. Nevertheless, their popular character is evident.

Classical Sanskrit Literature

The *Harṣacarita* of Bāṇabhaṭṭa refers to a number of popular beliefs and practices.

The *Tāntric* practice of *abhicāra* (malevolent magical rites) is referred to in II. p. 23, I. 1. We find mention of *caru* (oblation of rice) offered with red powder sprinkled thereon or even with blood. Several other *Tāntric* beliefs and practices relating to worship and other rites are the use of circles tinged with various colours (III. p. 47. 1.3), drawing of the mystical figure *Svastika* (III. p. 50, 1.26), offer of blood to propitiate goblins called *Vetālas* (III. p. 50, 1.14) supposed to occupy dead bodies, application of collyrium to eyes for attracting people (I. p. 10, 1.2), *mantras* supposed to have wonderful powers like bringing others under control (I. p. 10, 1.22), *mudrās* or poses of fingers (I. p. 8, 1. 24-25), use of white mustard for warding off evil spirits (II. p. 25, last line), use of a yellow pigment called *rocanā* to ward off evil spirits (*Ibid,* last but one line), wearing of a dark thread on the forearm to have magical effects, prayer called *Mahāmāyūrī*[8] for protection against evil spirits (V. p. 21, 1. 27), *Piśācas* haunting trees in a cemetery (VII. p. 65, 1. 12), offering a skull to a *Vetāla* (V. p. 21, 1.6), possession of a person by a *Vetāla* (VII. p. 65, 1.14), flesh offered to *Vetālas* (VIII. p. 86, 1.23), human flesh offered to *Piśācas,* carrying of lamps on the head for propitiating the divine Mothers (V. p. 21, 1.5).

The belief that *Aśoka* plants blossom at the kick of ladies is referred to in (I. p.15, para 2, 1.7, V. p. 28, 1.19). *Bakulas* are stated to blossom when women pour mouthfuls of wine over them (V. p. 28, 1.20).

Certain marks on the body were believed to be auspicious (I. p. 17, 1.24). The mark of a wheel on the palm was regarded as a sign of paramount monarch (IV. p. 5, 1.18). Such signs, seven in number, are referred to (IV p. 6, 1.22). Marks like the lotus, conch etc. on the soles of the feet appear to have been regarded as auspicious (ii. 144).

The *Harśacarita* mentions several omens and portents. Those which indicate good results are as follows :

> Flight of *cāṣa* bird (VII. p. 56, 1.30), cry of crows sitting on a milky tree (*kṣiriṇī* more properly *Kṣī-ri vṛkṣa* – VIII. p. 80, 1.20), wearing corals (IV. 39), flames of fire curving to the right (IV. p.6, 1.31), jars with five fingermarks (II. 115), leaves of mango and *Aśoka* trees (IV. 53).

Those which portend evil are :

> appearance of comets (V. p.27, 1.7; VI. p. 42, 1.21), deer passing by the left side of a man (V. p. 20, 1.21), fierce cry of crows (V. p. 20, 1.23), throbbing of left eye and arm in a man (VI. p. 43, 1.2), images of deities emitting smoke from hair (V. p. 27, 1.20), howling of female jackals (V. p. 27, 1.19), fall of meteors (V. p. 27, 1.19), sight of Jain ascetics (VIII. p. 84, 1.6), breaking of an umbrella.

Some other beliefs and practices are as follows : The wearing of red cotton thread in marriage was regarded as auspicious. Also auspicious were finger-marks on mortar, etc. (IV. 51). It was believed that dreams, seen at the end of night, were fulfilled (I. 67, V. 135). The father, before leaving the house, used to kiss his son on the head. (IV. 48). It was thought that a jar, with spray on its top, if placed at the head of a bed, would ward off evils. On auspicious occasions there was the practice of besmearing a jar with the mark of five fingers, dipped in flour-paste (II. 115). Some jewels, e.g. *rājāvarta*, were looked upon as auspicious. Mango-leaves and saffron were some other auspicious things.

The figure of *Rati* (Cupid's wife) used to be painted on the doors of a bridal chamber (IV. 65). Sandal, used by one, was sent to another as a mark of favour and confidence (VII. 194).

The birth of a daughter was lamented (50). Some other practices are as follows: The bones of the dead consigned to the Ganges (V. 109), an elephant let loose for a dead person (VI. 116), belongings of the dead given to *Brāhmaṇas* (VI. 115), sesame and water offered to the dead (I. 42), human flesh offered to *Piśācas* (V. 72), images of deities washed with milk (II. 114), sale of human flesh (204),[9] putting vermilion on boundary stones (98), offering of human flesh for securing superhuman power (200), a torch carried round an animal in sacrifice (164), vow not to tie the hair until the enemy is extirpated (132), a widow tying her hair in a single knot (108), wearing white garments (108), avoiding collyrium in her eyes (164), offering of blood in black magic (102), application of magic collyrium to attract spectators (54).

The following beliefs of people are also referred to in this work: Some jewels having miraculous power (238), some drugs possessing mysterious power (238), earthquakes are punishments for human lapses (88), serpents having jewels on their heads (118), heroes dying in a battle welcomed by *Apsaras* (101), and taken to heaven in celestial cars (101), mercury making man immortal (162, 222), white mustard affording protection against spirits (36), impurity caused by a solar eclipse (43), jars of various kinds being evil (135. 136), *Kuśa* grass warding off evil (28), right foot, eye and hand auspicious in a male (115), saffron (16), auspicious cry of an osprey distressing to fish (98), curative power of sunshine (23), crossing over sacred things sinful (44), a *Vetāla* believed to do everything for a wizard (202), *Vetālas* believed to roam at night (253), Yama believed to ride a buffalo (71), scratching of earth with fingers or toes inauspicious (121). *Cintāmaṇi* (philosopher's stone) is referred to (135).

The following things are mentioned as kept at the gate of a temple of Caṇḍī: incense, lamp, red cloth, strings of bells white with rice-powder, a lion made of lead with a big iron peg in its mouth, ivory door-bar (*Ka*, p. 738. *Siddhāntavāgīśa*).

In the *Kādambarī*[10] too, we find some popular beliefs and practices. At one place (p. 56), we meet with the custom of offering blood to goddess Caṇḍikā; the blood might be of animals sacrificed on such occasions, and not necessarily of human beings. At pp. 106, 339, use of white mustard as a talisman for children appears to have been in vogue. In the same page there is reference to the use of ghee mixed with ashes (or, charmed ghee) as a means of protecting the child.

An interesting practice was to present a *pūrṇapātra* or a present consisting of a dish filled with valuables, etc. on festive occasions; it was seized by relatives, friends and servants, etc. The *svastika* mark was believed to be auspicious (p. 91).

A popular belief was that the burning of powdered sloughs of serpents and horns of rams, mixed with ghee (of goats), was auspicious (p. 120). *Nimba* tree and other medicinal things, if burnt, were supposed to purify the air and ward off evil spirits (*Ibid*). *Śāntyudaka* (water sanctified with *mantras)* was believed to remove evils from a place where it was sprinkled (*Ibid*).

On a cloth-board (*Mātṛpaṭa*) were drawn the figures of the *Mātṛs* or guardian deities of children (*Ibid*). *Sūtikā-maṅgala-gītikā* was an auspicious song sung for the well-being of a woman in confinement (*Ibid*). *Svastyayana* was a rite with certain *mantras,* believed to remove evil and bring welfare (*Ibid*).

We find the practice of touching water and fire on the part of those who come to visit a newly born baby; this was believed to save the baby from the evil eyes of visitors (p. 121). Rites and ceremonies were performed on the sixth day of the child's birth by people (women) keeping awake through out the night (p. 125).

Certain marks on the body were believed to be auspicious (*Ibid*).

The wives of people, afraid of their husbands' destruction at the hands of enemies, used to give up dressing their hairs which were allowed to hang down to their full length (*Kad,* p. 128).

The *Atharvavedic* or *Tāntric* rite of black magic, designed to cause mischief to enemies, is referred to as *abhicāra-kriyā* (p. 179). There is reference to *Vaśīkaraṇa* (p. 746—*Siddhānta-vāgīśa*).

Human figures (*tṛṇa-puruṣa*), made of grass, appear to have been set up in fields to scare mischievous birds and beasts (*Kad,* p. 333).

People used to believe in the existence of a class of goblins called *Vetālas* (p. 335).

Siddhāñjana appears to have been a collyrium with the miraculous power of healing eyesores, curing blindness, revealing hidden treasures, etc. (p. 338).

Dhūma-raktā-laktakā-Kṣara-tālapatra-kuhaka-tantra-mantra-pustika (p. 338) were manuscripts containing magical spells, mystical formulas and incantations on palm-leaves in letters drawn with red lac and fumigated with smoke (of incense). In this line, we find belief in *Tāntric* and magical rites. *Antardhāna-mantra* (p. 339) is a *Tāntric mantra* believed to be capable of making a person invisible.

References to some omens and portents are found in this work. The eclipse of the sun and the moon was supposed to forebode evil to the world (p. 43). A number of omens is referred to in the work *utpāta-vetāla-vrata* (p. 55). *Digdāha* (p. 184) or preternatural redness of the horizon was believed to forebode danger to the king or general disaster. That the belief in omens and portents was widespread is attested by the existence, in the society, of a class of people called *nimittajña* and *śakuna-jñāna-vids* who were expert in interpretation of auguries.

Certain marks on the body were believed to be auspicious (*Ibid*).

Vyāghranakha (p. 39) or tiger's nails, set in gold and worn round the neck, was supposed to protect a child against the evil eye[11]. The practice of wearing talismans is referred to (p. 228) – *Siddhāntavāgīsa*.

Exorcism is referred to at certain places (*Ka* pp. 217, 745).

The practice of *Śivāvali* (offering food to jackals) is mentioned (*Ka*, p. 229). It prevails even today in some parts of India.

It was the custom among people to report a dream to a *grahācārya* or astrologer (*Ka* 229). A dream, seen at the end of night, was believed to come true (*Ka* 230).

Some auspicious rites are mentioned (e.g. *Ka*, pp. 237, 324, 391). Some protective measures in a house are referred to (p. 237). A *rakṣā-maṇḍala* (protective circle) is mentioned (*Ka* p. 138). Some measures for protecting the foetus are referred to (p. 228).

There was the belief that some herbs were auspicious (*Ka* p. 238).

The use of a camphor lamp and the scattering of white oilseeds were believed to ward off evil spirits (*Ka* p. 239).

Mālatimādhava

In the *Mālatīmādhava* of Bhavabhūti, we find some popular beliefs and practices of a *Tāntric* character. Mādhava, with the object of removing obstacles in the way of his gaining the hand of Mālatī, decides to win the favour of the ghouls of the cemetery by an offering of fresh flesh (*Act* IV). In Act V we find the young Mālatī about to be sacrificed before goddess Cāmuṇḍā. Cāmuṇḍā, a *Tāntric* form of Durgā, was believed to be pleased with a human virgin. The temple of the goddess is in a funeral ground. As Mādhava approaches it, the horrors of the place are being felt by him. The description of the horrors and of Cāmuṇḍā are typically *Tāntric*.

Kathāsaritsāgara

The *Kathāsaritsāgara* is a mine of information regarding popular beliefs and practices. We note below the more prominent among them. Sometimes a particular idea occurs at several places in the different stories. We shall refer to a single context in order to avoid prolixity. References are to the *Ocean of Story* by Tawney, edited by Penzer.

Demons are represented as flying in the air (Vol. II, p. 203) and polluting it (Vol. II, p. 299).

Among the magical beliefs and practices the following are noteworthy.

Magic powers of spells of witches, derived from the eating of human flesh, enable a person to fly in the air (Vol. II, p. 103). Magical charm is employed for gaining the love of a woman (Vol. II, p. 44). Magic can make a person invisible to others (Vol. II, p. 67). A mendicant, performing magical rites on a corpse, can bring it back to life and can use the animated body as he likes (Vol. II, p. 62). Among other things caused by magic, are the creation of delusion (Vol. VIII, p. 43); the mendicant is stated to have been carried by the animated corpse. A Banyan tree in the cemetery, when duly worshipped, can reveal miracles (Vol. II, p. 233). In order to protect a delivery house or birth-chamber, the mother and the baby, against evil influences, the following measures are taken : windows covered with *arka* and śamī plants, various weapons to be kept hanging in the room, burning of jewel-lamps, use of numerous charms and spells and other incantations by conjurers (Vol. II, p. 161). There are charms for appeasing the fire (Vol. II, p. 42), to change the shape of human beings (Vol. II, p. 20), etc. There is a means of propitiating the sea with jewels (Vol. II, p. 72). There are spells to drive away *Rākṣasas.*

A hermit is stated to eat the flesh of children (Vol. II, p. 185). Human flesh is offered to *Vetālas* (Vol. II, p. 235). A heavenly lady purchases human flesh (Vol. II, p. 205).

There are references to tree-worship (Vol. II, p. 97).

The throbbing of the right eye of a man is believed to indicate the coming union with the beloved (Vol. II., p. 144).

A vessel, a stick and the shoes, belonging to *Asura Maya*, are stated to have the following magic powers (Vol. II, p. 22): Whatever food is wished in the vessel it will be available there immediately. Whatever is written with the stick proves to be true. By wearing the shoes one acquires the power of flying through the air. There is reference to spells for breaking walls (Vol. I, p. 136) and chains (Vol. I, p. 137). A charm is said to produce a dream (Vol. I, p. 70). Grains of rice, presented by God's servants, are said to be inexhaustible (Vol. I, p. 75). We meet with a dead fish laughing aloud (Vol. I, p. 46). Again, a magic chariot for roaming through the air meets the eye (Vol. I, p. 80).

We find a popular belief in *Yakṣiṇīs* doing mischief to human beings (Vol. III, p. 187). For instance, we find the mention of one who used to make horns grow on the heads of human beings, lead them into fire and devour their half-burnt bodies.

An interesting belief was that, when a person sneezed, he would die if someone did not say 'God bless you' (Vol. III, p. 30).

An elixir, prepared with the meat of a wild goat, was believed to ensure the birth of a son (Vol. III, p. 218).

It appears that people used to believe in enchanted trees the fruits of which, when taken, led to death (Vol. III, p. 30).

A piece of antelope-skin, with a charm attached, is believed to keep off bees (Vol. VI, p. 114). There are charms also for controlling *Vetālas*, (p. 165), securing long life (p. 6), obtaining a sword (*Ibid*), producing dreams (p. 76, 77, 80).

We find a reference to the custom of sacrificing a human being before a goddess (Vol. I, p. 116).

The kick of a horse (of a special type) to a person was believed to transport him immediately to another place (Vol. VIII, p. 57).

Beef-eating appears to have been resorted to even by *Brāmaṇas* in times of distress (Vol. III, p. 9).

Certain charms are believed to enable a man to lay aside the body (Vol. IV, p. 26).

Some of the evil omens are : a crow sitting on one's left hand, a dog running from the left to right, a snake appearing on the right, throbbing of the left arm and shoulder (Vol. IV, p. 93).

The terrific howl of a jackal was regarded as very ominous (Vol. III, p. 46). The howling of a jackal on one's left side was also supposed to portend evil (Vol. IX. p. 76).

A partridge, appearing on one's right, was regarded as ominous (Vol. IX. p. 76). Some other evil omens were lightning flashes striking the banners, vultures circling overhead, the breaking of State umbrellas (Vol. VIII, p. 156).

Some other evil omens, mentioned in the work, are blowing of terrible wind uprooting trees, tremor of the earth, hills cleft asunder, rumbling in a cloudless sky (Vol. VIII, p. 49).

There are references to protecting herbs (Vol. VIII, p. 56).

It was believed that one's spirits, being elevated or depressed, indicated the approach of good or evil fortune.

In the work, we find the belief in the change of sex (Vol. VIII, p. 46) by means of charms, drugs or by the will of God. Transformation is stated to be effected also by putting a pill into the mouth of the person concerned (*Ibid* p. 42).

There is a reference to a man's capacity for understanding the language of all beasts and birds (Vol. VII, p. 3).

A particular jewel was believed to act as a talisman against old age, disease and demons (Vol. VIII, p; 195).

The *Svapnavāsavadatta* refers (III. p. 24) to the belief that certain herbs prevent widowhood and curb the influence of co-wives.

The *S* states (XV. 96) that the trembling of a woman portends evil. It mentions certain birds as indicating evil (XVI. 19).

Magical practices are referred to in *S* XVI. 64, *K* XII. 37 (*Māyā*) and XIII. 12.

The *Kirātārjunīya* (III. 56) refers to *abhicāra*.

Some women appear to have been engaged for protecting crops (*S* VI. 49, *K* IV. 9, *R* IV. 20)

There was the practice of putting *ātapa* rice on the head of the person to whom blessings were given (*KS* VII. 88, *R* VII. 28).

Birch-bark was used as a writing material (*KS* I. 7). There is mention of palm-leaves also in this connection (*Ka* p. 338).

The *KS* refers (VII. 29) to the practice of tying an auspicious thread in the hand of the bride.

The *Ram* refers (III. 3) to the practice of pregnant women eating burnt earth. It is intersting to note that it prevails even now at least among the rural women of low classes in Bengal.

Middle Indo-Aryan Literature

From the *Brahmajāla Sutta (Dīgha*, I), dealing with *śīlas*, we learn of the following beliefs and practices : divination by means of omens and signs (*nimitta*), fortune-telling by observing marks on the body (*lakkhaṇa*), sophistry (*lokāyata*), occultism (*sālākiya*), auguries from thunderbolts and other celestial portents (*uppāda*), prognostication from dreams, determination whether a site for the house will be lucky or not (*vatthu-vijjā*), warding off ghosts (*bhūta-vijjā*). Some charms and incantations are stated to produce certain effects; some of these resemble the *ābhicārika* practices of *Tantra*. The muttering of a charm is believed to indicate whether a man is well-born or lucky or not. A charm is to be used when living in an earthen house (*bhurivijjā*). There are charms for causing abortion (*viruddha-garbha-karaṇa*). Some incantations are supposed to cause dumbness (*jihvā-nittaddhana*). A charm is believed to keep a person's jaws fixed (*hanusaṃhanana*). The *Dhammapada* commentary refers to a *mantra* (I, pp. 251 f.f.) enabling a man to read the thoughts of people.

The *KKC* refers to some omens and portents. For example, to dream of a delightful elephant was supposed to indicate the future birth of a good son (I. 8).

The Buddha is said to have distinguished between two classes of lower gods called *Khiḍḍā-padosikā* and *Manopadosikā,* in the following way. Those of the former class spend their time laughing, playing and enjoying sexual pleasures. Thus, they lose control over their mind, and fall from high position, and are reborn as human beings. Those of the latter class think too much of one another. So, their mind becomes polluted, and they fall down, and are reborn as men. The Buddha, extremely rational as he was and highly ethical as his teachings were, can hardly have believed in the existence of the above gods. Perhaps to impress upon the common people the doctrine of *Karman* he resorted to this method.

In the *Kevaddha sutta* (*Dīgha*, I, pp. 211-23) there are references to magical practices by which miracles can be performed. There are means by which gods can be visible to a self-concentrated man. The *Valāhassa Jātaka* (Vol. II) tells us that some shipwrecked mariners escaped from a city of goblins with the help of a flying horse. The *Dhammapada* commentary refers (III. pp. 134 f.f.) to flying through air on the back of a wooden Garuḍa bird.

According to the *Campeyya Jātaka* (IV. pp. 454-65), Bodhisatta, born as a serpent-king, could perform miracles by magical power. Another snake-king is said to have had miraculous power (*Śaṃkhapāla Jātaka*, V, pp. 161-77). A *Yakkha* is stated, in the *Dhamma Jātaka* (IV. pp. 100-104), to have possessed such power.

The *Kathāvatthu* (Chap. 21) deals, *inter alia,* with *iddhi* which means super-normal potency. According to the *Milindapañho* (Book IV), *Nibbāṇa* increases *iddhi.*

The *Sumaṅgalavilāsinī* states that the Buddha performed double miracles (*yamaka-pāṭhāriya*) at the gate of *Sāvatthi.* While fire was raging on the upper part of the body, water flowed down the lower part. From the *Dhammapada* commentary (III. pp. 113 f.f.) we learn that the Buddha created a girl of exquisite beauty by his miraculous power.

There are miracles galore in the *Dīpavaṃśa* and the *Mahāvaṃśa.*

People used to believe in many heavens and hells[12]. The torments in hells are referred to at some places, e.g. *Pañcagatidīpana.*

Animistic beliefs are borne out by some Pāli works, e.g. *Mahāsamaya-suttanta (Dīgha,* II, pp. 253-62). The *Papañcasūdanī* on the *Majjhima* refers (p. 119) to the practice of tree-worship; certain trees of rural areas are regarded as worthy of worship.

Belief in demons, *yakkhas,* ghosts and spirits was widespread. The *Nalapāna Jātaka* (Vol. I) refers to a pool haunted by an Ogress. The *Valāhassa Jātaka* (Vol. VI) states that a Nāga King sent a *yakkha* to kill a wise man. The *Jayadissa* (V, pp. 21-36) refers to a demon. The *Dhammapada* commentary (I, pp. 45 f.f.) states that the people of *Sāvatthi* used to worship a *yakkhinī* named *Kālī yakkhini*, who could foretell drought and excessive rainfall. The *BhK* (VI. 4.11) reflects beliefs in spirits, goblins, imps, demons etc.

The *Khettūpamā Peta* (pp. 1-9) of the *Petavatthu* commentary mentions a tree-spirit who stole away a maiden called *Sulasā.*

The slaughter of deer, swine and other animals for offering to goblins was in vogue in Benares (*Jātaka* IV, p. 115).

The *Dhāraṇīs* are an important part of the Mahāyāna literature. These are protective spells designed to secure welfare by destroying evil forces. These consist in incantations, benedictions, cryptic formulae and mystic syllables.

Belief in magic is found in the *Karpūramañjarī*. There are references to the carrying of a person by magic power (I. p. 33), blooming of flowers out of season (II. p. 42), a magic car moving through the air or walls (IV. p. 109).

Belief in miracles is reflected in the *KKC*. For instance, a bamboo-clump is stated (II. 7) to have grown from the eyes on a human skull. The work refers (II. 9) to the art of controlling others.

The *Visākhāyavatthu* of the *Dhammapada* commentary (I) refers to the gift of dowry in marriage. The same work refers to the gift of a village to a girl for purchasing perfumes and other articles required for bath.

The above work contains (I, pp. 397-98) a code of instructions for a girl to be observed in the father-in-law's house. These include secrecy of conversation, prohibition of gift of articles to one who does not return borrowed articles, helping distressed relatives, etiquette before superiors, giving alms to monks etc.

The *SV* (pt. I, pp. 84-87) refers to a South-Indian ceremony called *Dhopana* in which the bones of the dead relatives are dug up, washed and besmeared with scents. On an auspicious day, the people eat various kinds of food, and drink while crying for their departed relatives.

It appears from the account of *Aṅgulimāla* in the *Theragāthā* commentary that garlands were placed round the necks of animals for sacrifice.

The *Karpūramañjarī* refers to the belief that Kālī drinks the blood of the demons from a goblet made of the skull of Parameṣṭhin (IV. 19).

The *Jātakas* are a mine of information about popular beliefs and practices some of which are laid down below. People used to believe in the existence of water-demons or *Yakṣas* (*DDJ, NPJ, TDJ*). The Banyan tree was supposed to be the resort of gods (*AYBJ, Baj, DMJ, SNJ, Paj*). An evil spirit, called *Kālakarṇī,* was believed to cause mischief to people (*LOJ, ALJ*).

There is reference to *preta-pūjā* (worship of the departed) in the cemetery (*ASMJ*). The worship of serpents was in vogue (*Kaj*). Some rites were performed for exorcism. The following method is found in the *ALJ* : at first, a circle is drawn. Then a bed is spread over a corpse. The person, supposed to be possessed, is made to lie down on it. Finally, the person is bathed with 108 pitcherfuls of Ganges water.

The *Mahāmaṅgala-jātaka*(453) mentions the following among other happy auguries :

Sight of an all-white bull, pregnant woman, *Rohita* fish, a full pitcher, fresh ghee, new cloth, *pāyasa*, etc. after getting up in the morning.

The above *Jātaka* (87) states that a person, wearing a rat-bitten cloth, would die with his family.

At some places, in the *Nakṣatra* (49) and *Maṅgala* (87) *Jātakas,* an attitude of disbelief in omens and portents is noticeable.

We find charms and spells connected with magical practices. There is reference to *mṛtakotthāpanamantra* and *prativāhana-mantra* (*SanJ*); the former was supposed to bring a dead person back to life, by the latter the person so revived could be bereft of life. The *Viṣavānta-jātaka* (69) refers to the counteracting of snake venom by charms and drugs. The *Kāmanīta-jātaka* (228) reflects belief in exorcism by charms. By charms the following were believed to be possible : shower of jewels from the sky (*Vedabbha* 48), world-conquest (*Sarvadaṃṣṭra* 241), finding out hidden treasure (*Bṛhacchatra* 336), understanding the language of lower animals (*Kharaputra* 386, *Parantapa* 416).

There is mention (*ABJ*) of *aṅgavidyā* by which a person's future might be forecast by reading his bodily marks.

We have already referred to animal-sacrifice. The animals and birds, commonly used for the purpose, were goat, sheep, boar and fowl.

For ascertaining the real mischief-maker, there was the curious practice of *guṭikāpāta* (*LOJ*). It appears to have been a process in which wooden pieces were used. This method was adopted by sailors when a ship was caught in a storm. It was believed to identify the person through whose misfortune the disaster occurred. Such a person was called *Kālakarṇī.* He was placed on a raft and set adrift in the sea.

The *Garga-jātaka* (155) refers to the practice of uttering *jīva* (may you live) when one sneezed. The Buddha, however, is stated to have disapproved it.

It was regarded as a pious act to provide shelter for birds (*KPJ*). For this purpose, baskets of straw were hung up at places so that the birds might rest there.

The running of *Dharmaśālās* (*KLJ, AJ*) was regarded as an act of piety; seats and water were provided there for people free of charge.

The rich appear to have maintained and educated the poor (*LOJ*).

Village disputes were settled by the village headman, called *Maṇḍala,* who used to impose fine on wrong-doers. (*UBJ*).

The following are some other details about the life of people, available in the *Jātakas.*

For the hunting of deer, people used to catch chameleons (*GJ*). The process was as follows : near the holes of these animals, straw was set on fire, and the hunter with his dogs stood by holding a mace in hand. When the creatures, unable to bear the smoke, came out the hunter killed them.

The use of mortar and pestle as well as winnowing baskets is mentioned (*SJ*).

There was the practice of burying treasure-troves underground (*NJ*).

It appears that domestic refuse used to be put in baskets which were cleared afterwards (*ABJ*).

People used to besmear the floors and fencing of their houses with cowdung (*MLJ*). On festive occasions, there was the practice of smearing the floor with fragrant substances, putting garlands on gates and at other places of the house and burning incense (*TPJ*).

The following utensils appear to have been used while taking meals and serving the same (*KatJ*): dish, cup, glass, a metallic vessel probably meant for washing one's hand and mouth after eating, ladle.

It seems (*ALJ*) that boys and girls were not married before youth. It is clear that one could marry the daughter of one's maternal uncle.

There was the custom of asking *Brāhmaṇas* about the results of dreams seen by people (*MSJ*). Some *Jātakas* (e.g. *Mahāsvapna* 77, *Lauhakumbhī* 314, *Aṣṭaśabda* 418) refer to a sacrifice performed to convert bad dreams into good ones. In the *Lauhakumbhī* we are told that, in such a sacrifice, the meat of four of each of the following classes of creatures had to be offered: elephant, horse, bull, human being, sparrow. The *JC* (II.

14) reflects the belief that the effect of an evil dream can be counteracted by offering living beings to the goddess. The *BhK* (I. 14) refers to the belief in dreams.

The vogue of human sacrifice is attested also by the *Khaṇḍahāla-jātaka* (542); a king's son and his wife were also to be offered to ensure his passage to heaven. The *Tarkāri-jātaka* (481) provides that the blood of a *Brāhmaṇa* of pure conduct, tawny-complexioned, toothless and belonging to one's paternal or maternal side, should be offered, and his dead body interred at the place over which the southern gate of the capital was to be built.

Some *Jātakas* refer to popular modes of treatment of patients. For example, the partaking of curd was prescribed in jaundice (*Dadhi-vāhana* 186). In case of poisoning, the person concerned had to be made to vomit and after that he was asked to take ghee, honey, sugar, water mixed with *Peepul* (*Lipta* 91, *Śālittaka* 107).

From some *Jātakas* we learn that, in times of epidemics, people used to leave their houses, even their villages. The disease, called *ahivāta* in *Kacchapa* (178) and *Āmra* (474) *Jātakas* was perhaps identical with modern plague. There was the superstitious belief that one could avoid this fell malady by escaping through a tunnel dug through the wall.

Blankets appear to have been used daily (*SNJ*); probably it was the practice in cold climate only.

Young students appear to have used wooden pieces as slates for writing on them (*Kat J*).

For ascertaining the guilt of the accused the fire-ordeal was in vogue (*ABJ*).

Animals for drawing carts, and those for sacrifice were decorated with garlands and *Pañcāṅguli* (*NVJ*, *BJ*). *Pañcāṅguli* is explained by some as a handful of grains, while others take it to mean coloured marks put on the animal's body with one's five fingers.

The *ABJ* refers to the popular belief that the recitation of a particular incantation led to victory in dice-playing.

The following additional information, available in *Jātakas,* is recorded by T.W.R. Davids in *Buddhist India*, Calcutta, 1950.

There was the practice of tying leaves in the field to scare away animals (No. 12-*Banyan-deer birth-story*). Human sacrifice was offered to trees (5.472, 474, 488). Trees were regarded as oracles, and requested for wealth and sons (No. 98, 109, 307, 493). Tree-spirits were supposed to injure those who injured them (4. 210, 353). Trees are said to have been pleased with the offer of garlands, lamps and food (3. 23, 4. 153). Tree-gods are mentioned also in *Jātaka* 48.

A popular superstition among women was that the shedding of tears over a light was ominous (*GS* III. 22). The throbbing of the left eye of a woman was regarded as auspicious (*Ibid* II. 37). Women were sometimes believed to come under the evil influence of a planet (*Ibid* IV. 86).

The *GS* refers (VII. 16) to the custom of women not to talk with their husbands in presence of their superiors. Women were debarred from crossing the threshold of the house (VI. 25). Women appear (VI. 13) to have expressed anger by laughing reproof, show of excessive affection and decoration with tears. Housewives used to relieve the suffering of their distressed relatives (VII. 6). Verse V. 72 refers to the practice of a woman asking her husband for a favourite article during her pregnancy.

The wives of men, gone abroad, used to abjure the decoration of the body (*GS* I. 33). Such women used to write on the wall the date of termination of their husbands' stay abroad.

A woman, in monthly impurity, appears (VI. 29) to have been debarred from sexual relation. During such periods women used to besmear their faces with ghee mixed with turmeric powder (I. 22, III. 89, VI. 19.28). But, even at such times their husbands used to kiss and fondle them amorously (I. 22, VI. 28). At the end of the period of impurity, women used turmeric for bath (I. 8). The cloth of a woman, in her first menstruation, was called *ānanda-paṭa* (V. 57).

The society was not free from beggars. The *GS* (II. 62) refers to beggars. The begging bowl was called *Karaṅka* and the vessel, out of which alms were given, was known as *caṭuka*.

There are other references to poverty. The *GS* (VII. 10) refers to the unfulfilled wishes of the poor. Verse IV. 29 mentions scanty and tattered clothes of the destitute in winter.

The undertaking of a journey, on certain inauspicious days, was believed to be ominous (*GS* III. 61).

There are references to the wife following her dead husband on the funeral pyre. Verse VII. 33 of the *GS* states that the wife, ready for the purpose, was dressed as a widow. Verse V. 7 states that the wife had to embrace the corpse of her husband. If a man died leaving many wives, all of them had to be dressed like a Suttee.

From the *KKC* (I. 17) we learn that there was the practice of keeping the bodies of thieves and adulterers pierced with spikes in the cemetery. Strips of rags appear to have been tied to posts at such a place. The motive was, perhaps, to impress upon the people the reprehensible nature of the crime.

If fire broke out in a village, it was proclaimed by beat of drums (*GS* VI. 35); it was probably meant for warning people and calling them for help .

Trial by ordeal (*divya*) appears to have been in vogue in law-courts. *GS* V. 48 refers to the *Kośa* ordeal undergone by Śiva for pleasing Pārvatī. It may be added that, in law-books like the *Yājñavalkya-smṛti,* ordeals are prescribed in the absence of the human proofs, *viz*. document, possession, witness.

Kāpālika women used to besmear their body with ashes from the funeral place (*GS* V. 8). *Kāpālika* males had trident-marks on their foreheads (*JC* I. 19).

Fatalism among the people is referred to in *GS* (e.g. II. 32, III. 7, VII. 56). Some people used to believe in human effort (*Ibid* I. 42).

People appear to have believed in reward and punishment as a result of good and bad deeds respectively (*GS* I. 99, II. 74, IV. 84, VI. 75 etc.). There are references to lurking fear caused by sinful deeds (e.g. *GS* II. 83).

Belief in the other world and re-birth is reflected at several places (e.g. *GS* V. 41. VII. 8).

The *GS* refers to certain practices supposed to be conducive to welfare. On the day on which the cultivation of cotton-fields was commenced, the cultivator's wife used to put auspicious decorative designs on the plough (II. 65). On the occasion of auspicious rites, pitchers filled with water, used to be placed at the gate of the house (II. 40). Welcome-garlands (*Vandana-mālika*) were placed at the gate (III. 62). At the time of a person leaving the home for a journey a water-pitcher with mango-leaves used to be placed at the gate (II. 43).

The *JC* mentions (II. 7) the custom of offering cooked rice to goddess Kātyāyanī. Such an offering in the month of *Caitra* was regarded as especially auspicious. Buffalo was among the animals offered to the goddess (III. 8). From III. 10 buffallo-meat appears to have been used by some as food. The following are some of the animals whose meat was edible: deer, pig, goat. The hind legs of a goat appear to have been a delicacy.

The *JC* refers (II. 2) to the practice of keeping a dark spot in the threshing ground of a field as a sign for preventing bad omens spoiling the harvest.

The work refers to auspicious bodily signs (I. 17).

Leprosy appears to have been a common disease. A leper was debarred from invitation to a *Śrāddha* ceremony (*JC* III. 9).

The *GV* mentions (1071) *ahicāra* (Skt. *abhicāra*) or magic designed to cause mischief to others. The prevalence of *Tāntric* rites is borne out by references to *kaula* women (319); *Kaulas* were a sect of *Tāntric* devotees. They are described as witnessing the sacrifice of a *mahāpaśu* (human being) in honour of goddess Vindhyavāsinī.

The *NKC* reveals people's firm belief in the prophecies made by ascetics. Being told that his sons were destined to serve somebody, the king of Mathurā renounced the kingdom (IV. 5-6). Believing a prophecy the deity *Sudarśana* and the *Rākṣasa* kept the valuables for a long time in the forest for *Nāgakumāra* (VI. 1-8). In accordance with the wish of a sage, *Vanarāja* received *Nāgakumāra*, and married his daughter to him (VI. 8). For the same reason, the two princes, Acheya and Abheya, took up service under him (VI. 16-17).

The *BhK* (III. 17.7) refers to the practice of putting curd, grass and fried rice on the head of a person who was given a farewell before proceeding on a journey.

In *Bhk* (I. 15) we find faith in the prediction by astrologers. An astrologer was *kokkāviu sunimittu viyakkhaṇu* (expert about omens). I. 16 refers to the festivities on the occasion of child-birth. After a month from birth, a male child was taken to a Jaina temple for being christened. The custom was to utter the name of the Jina into the ears of the child.

Bhk (VI. 6) refers to the practice of causing a crow to fly away after a dear one had gone on a journey. The idea was, perhaps, that the crow would return with the man gone abroad.

REFERENCES

1. Seven rivers, according to Sāyaṇa.

2. *tatroddhṛtam amatrebhyaḥuddhāṛt* means *bhukto-cchiṣṭa* or *Ujjhita*.
3. These have been exhaustively dealt with in the present author's *Dharma Sūtras-a study* etc., pp. 184 f.
4. For details, see S.N. Vyas, *India in the Rāmāyaṇa Age*, pp. 148 ff.
5. For details, see *Ibid.*
6. See D.C. Sircar, *The Successors of the Sātavāhanas,* App., Calcutta, 1939.
7. Vide Stephens, *History of Criminal Law of England,* Vol. I.
8. According to Buddhists, name of an amulet and of a tutelary goddess.
9. These and the following references to the *Harṣacarita* are to the pages of the notes. The reader has to look up both parts of the notes which are divided as *Ucchvāsas* I-III, IV-VIII. The first part ends with p. 231.
10. Ed. M.R. Kale, Bombay, 1928.
11. The page numbers, which follow, refer to Siddhāntavāgīśa's ed.
12. Vide B.C. Law, *Heaven and Hell in Buddhist Perspective.*

3

POPULAR CULTS AND CREEDS

Vedic Age

IN the remote *Ṛgvedic* age, we find people assuming gods behind the natural phenomena. Water and fire, the two most useful things, have been deified. Agricultural implements have been regarded as gods. *Sunāsira*, probably personifications of the share and the plough, which are indispensable for agriculture, is supposed to refer to two deities helping the growth of crops. The cow and the dog, which are extremely useful in life, are also looked upon as gods. The hawk (*śyena*) is regarded as a connecting link between heaven and earth; it is deified. Divinity is attributed to bows, arrows, chariots, the musical instruments like *Dundubhi*. A sense of gratitude and fear appear to underlie the deification of certain things.

The characteristic names of the following deities reveal the popular ideas underlying their conception :

Alakṣmīghna-devatā (X. 155)	— deity removing adversity.
Rājayakṣmaghna devatā (X. 161)	— deity healing the fatal disease called *Rājayakṣmā* (Pulmonary consumption).
Duhsvapna-nāśana-devatā (I. 120. 12)	— deity removing bad dreams.
Sapatnī-dhāvana-devatā (X. 145)	— deity driving away the co-wife.

A popular element in the theology of the *RV* is that human traits are attributed to gods. Like men they are described as taking food, carrying weapons and riding chariots, etc. Like the humans again they are fond of drinks. Even some human frailties are ascribed to gods. For example, the incestuous impulse is demonstrated in the love overtures of Yamī to her brother, Yama. God Pūṣan is conceived as a paramour of goddess Uṣas.

God Rudra is a glowing example of the typically folkish deity. Rudra (lit. the roarer) personifies all that a cattle-rearer dreads—storm and plague, Marut, his sons, are the hurricanes coming down from the mountains where Rudra lives. He is believed to possess remedies against pests let loose by himself.

Besides anthropomorphism, we find also theriomorphism in certain deities. Some of them are conceived as birds and beasts.

A folk element is noticeable in the fact that gods are warned against merchant-like conduct. To ask for the price of a thing delivered is befitting a merchant. But, a god should not be merchant-like in asking for the price of things bestowed on devotees.

The *AV* mentions some deities unknown in the *RV*. One such is *Ap'vā*, the spirit of panic, which causes confusion in the enemy's plans, attacks him and destroys him. Popular ideas are at the root of the conception of certain deities. For example, Susan is appeased for ensuring the safe delivery of a child. The spirit, *Uttuda*, is prayed to for rousing love in a girl. The *AV* is quite familiar with serpent-deities. It is interesting to note that even *Vrātyas*, who were perhaps a class of wanderers not conforming to *Vedic* authority, were deified in this *Veda* perhaps out of a desire to appease these arrogant and powerful people. The *Ṛgvedic* Rudra has undergone a considerable change in the *AV*. He has bow and arrows as well as a mace in his hand. He is Sarva, Bhava, Paśupati, Bhūtapati, etc. He is accompanied by a fierce looking roaring dog. He can afflict people with diseases which can be cured by him.

Both the *RV* and *AV* mention some minor goddesses the most noteworthy of whom are Kṛtyā and Nirṛti who are believed to be intent on mischief.

As an example of purely popular religious faith, distinguished from the hierartic one, noticeable in the *RV*, we may mention Phallus-worship (*RV* VIII. 21. 5, X. 99.3). The fear of and contempt for this practice have been voiced in the hymns. Thus, it seems that this was in vogue among the non-Aryans. The

Aryans were seeking divine help against the Phallus-worshippers, the *Śiśnadevas*[1] as they were called.

Age of Brāhmaṇas

The ritualistic elaboration, found in the *Brāhmaṇas*, gradually led to the speculative matters of the *Upaniṣads* through the *Āraṇyakas*. In the *Brāhmaṇas* themselves, we find importance attached to the element of devotion or reverence as essential in sacrifice. The external practices, connected with sacrifice, began to be subordinated to the subjective element of *Śraddhā*; this seems to be the significance of the following observation of the *Śatapatha* (9.1.1.16)—*Yajño vai namaḥ* i.e. sacrifice is supplication. This attitude appears to contain the germ of the *Bhakti* cult which deeply influenced the *Bhagavadgītā*, the *Purāṇic* religion, Vaiṣṇavism and Tāntricism.

In several other spheres of popular religion, the *Brāhmaṇas* were the precursors.

Vedic Viṣṇu and Rudra gave rise to several popular myths and legends. In the *Ṛgveda*, Viṣṇu represents a form of the sun. The midday sun, the smallest but the most scorching, led to the origin of the Vāmana or Dwarf legend of the *Purāṇas*. The sun, rising in the east, touching the zenith at midday and setting in the west to rise in the following morning, has been represented as Vāmana striding over the three regions. The *Taittirīya Brāhmaṇa* (1.2.5.5.) itself identifies Viṣṇu with Vāmana. The *Śatapatha* (7.4.1.14) goes so far as to declare the identity of the Sun (Viṣṇu) with *Brahman*, the Supreme Being. It is, therefore, evident that the Viṣṇu cult, so popular now-a-days, originated in the remote age of *Brāhmaṇas*.

Vedic Rudra is a prominent deity. He is the god of storm and thunder. He is the killer of cows and human beings and the destroyer of vegetation (e.g. *RV* 1.114.10). Sometimes he is referred to as *Paśupa* (*RV* 1.114.9) or protector of cattle, healer of diseases (*RV* 1.43.4) and as the best physician (*RV* II. 33.4). But, these epithets do not bring out his benevolent aspect. It is always with a sense of horror that he is invoked to protect animals which are the victims of his oppression, to grant freedom from diseases with which he afflicts people. The very name Rudra (lit. one who makes all cry) reflects the attitude of the people towards this fierce deity. His malignant form is also clear from the *Atharvaveda* (11.2.22).

It is in the *Vājasaneyī Saṃhitā* (*Śatarudriya* hymns) of the *Yajurveda* that we find both the benevolent and malevolent aspects of Rudra side by side. We hear, for the first time, of the *Śiva-tanu* (benign body) and *aghora* (non-fierce) form. Rudra is the protector of thieves and robbers, but is also the healer of diseases, the slayer of venomous serpents and female demons. He is also represented as lord of directions, fields, paths, nourishment, food, trees, assemblies, talented people, etc. He is also the presiding deity of ministers and merchants.

The popular nature of Rudra is evident from his association with thieves and robbers, etc., as stated above. He is also represented in the *Vājasaneyī Saṃhitā* as revealing Himself in the low class people, e.g. carpenters, potters, *Niṣādas*, etc. The familiar appellations of Rudra or Śiva, occurring in the *Purāṇas*, *viz.* Śitikaṇṭha, Gaṇapati, Bhava, Sarva, etc. are all found in the above *Saṃhita*. Thus, the transformation of the malignant Rudra into the benignant Śiva began as early as the later *Vedic* age, and culminated in the Epic and *Purāṇic* age. The *Śatapatha* (I. 7.3.8) knows Sarva, Bhava as popular in the *Prācya* (eastern) region and *Vāhlīka* land respectively.

The Gaṇapati and Senānī aspects of Śiva, mentioned in the later *Vedic* age, led to the emergence of later Gaṇeśa and Kārtikeya who are represented as sons of Śiva. The mount of Rudra is the *ākhu* (rat) in the *Brāhmaṇas* (e.g. *Śatapatha,* 2.6.2.10; *Taittirīya*, 1.6.10.2.). But, in the later age, the mount of the father was transferred to his son, Gaṇeśa who came to be invoked for protecting the crops from the ravages of rats. Kārtikeya became the Commander-in-Chief of Gods. Ambikā, Rudra's sister in the *Brāhmaṇas* (e.g. *Śatapatha*, 2.6.2.9), and connected with autumn (*Taittirīya*, 1.6.10) became Śiva's consort in the later times, and began to be worshipped in autumn.

In the later *Vedic* age, the influence of the non-Aryans on some popular cults cannot, perhaps, be entirely ruled out. We have seen above how Rudra was associated with the anti-social elements and the low class people. It is possible that the vanquished non-Aryans influenced the victorious Aryans in the conception of Rudra. In human history, the reciprocal influence of the conquerors and the conquered is not unknown. It is interesting to note that, even today, robbers in their hideouts worship *Kāla Bhairava*, the terrific aspect of Śiva and Kālī either with their booty or before proceeding to commit their dangerous crimes. They believe these deities to be their protectors.

The phallic worship of the non-Aryans, the *Śiśnadevas*, appears to have had an impact on the *Aśvamedha* sacrifice of the later *Vedic* age. A part of the sacrifice is that when a male horse is slain, the Chief Queen lies beside it under a cover. She grasps the horse's genital organ, and puts it into her own invoking the virile animal to discharge its semen. At that time, the priests indulge in indecent talks (*Śatapatha*, 13.5. 2; *Taittirīya*, 3-9). These practices appear to be too indecorous and obscene in rites performed by the Aryans whose life and activities reveal good taste and refined civilisation.

Similar indecent practices are noticeable in the *Mahāvrata* sacrifice. A part of it consists in the use of abusive language pertaining to fertilisation, between a student and a courtesan. Then there is actual sexual intercourse between the two.

In the *Gosava* sacrifice (*Jaiminīya Brāhmaṇa*, 2.113), the sacrificer praises the bull for fertilising all cows related to it. Then he attempts to imitate the bull's sexual activities, and besides having sexual union with the femle relatives, he goes so far as to indulge in incestuous relations with his mother and sister. Such practices violate the basic principles of civilised people, and we cannot account for them among the highly cultured Aryans unless we presume that these infiltrated into the Aryan society from the aboriginals living side by side with them.

Kalpasūtras

The importance of Rudra, as a deity, continues in the *Sūtras* too. In the *Gṛhyasūtras*, we find many names of Rudra some of which occur in the *Vājasaneyī Saṃhitā* and *Brāhmaṇas*, while others are new, e.g. *Nara*, *Mṛḍa*, *Śaṃkara*, etc. In the *Sūtras* (e.g. *Baudhāyana Gṛhya*, 1.1.9), there is provision for the *Sulagava* sacrifice in honour of Rudra. The significance of the name is controversial. According to some, it is so called as in it the substances, derived from the cow (*gavya)*, are cooked on spits (*śūla)*. According to others, its name signifies that it was offered to Rudra, the bearer of *Śūla* (trident). From some sources it is so called as a bull is sacrificed in it. Earthly happiness of all kinds is believed to be the result of this rite. In it Rudra's wife, variously called Rudrāṇī, Sarvāmī and Bhavānī, also gets offerings.

Viṣṇu also continues to be a prominent deity in this age. He is also called Nārāyaṇa.

Several other popular deities, who emerge in this period, are Dhanvantari, Vaiśravaṇa (or, Kubera), Anumati, Śrī Bhadrakālī, Takṣaka, Vaisaleya, the last two appearing as names of serpents in epics and *Purāṇas*. Some uncommon deities, mentioned in the *Sūtras*, are Sulvana, Śatruñjaya, Kṣatraṇa, Mṛtyuñjaya, Martyava, Saka, Jañjabhu.

Sītā (furrow) appears as an agricultural deity. Among goddesses are Hrī, Śrī, Lakṣmī, Puṣṭi, Kālī, Ṣaṣṭhi, Mahiṣikā.

In the *Sūtras*, four Vināyakas appear; they are supposed to possess people resulting in their mental disease and adverse fate. In later times, Vināyaka is found as a name of Gaṇeśa.

Besides *Sītā-yajña* (sacrifice for the furrow) and *Khala-yajña* (sacrifice for the threshing floor), we find a number of religious ceremonies in connection with the various agricultural operations such as yoking the plough, commencement of ploughing, harvesting crops, carrying the corn to the barn, etc. *Gobhila Gṛhya* (*IV* 4.26-30) records the interesting custom of presenting offerings to *Ākhurāja* (king of moles) at mole-hills presumably to appease these creatures who damage the crops.

Some *Gṛhya Sūtras* (e.g. *Āśvalāyana*, II. 1.9; *Pāraskara*, II. 14.9) prescribe serpent-worship obviously to propitiate this venomous creature which may not bite the worshipper. According to the *Kauśika-sūtra* (74.8-10), offerings should be made to the prominent serpents Vāsuki, Çitrasena, Citraratha, Takṣa and Upatakṣa. Śveta, son of Vidarva, probably a quadruped, is prayed to for subduing the serpents. According to some, Śveta is a snake-killing horse; such white horse is mentioned in the *RV* (I. 118.9).

There are references, in some *Gṛhyasūtras*, to tree-worship. According to *Sāṅkhāyana* (1.15-16) and *Kauṣītakī* (1.9.12), a man, passing with his newly wedded wife by a huge tree, should recite a *mantra* to it. The worship of a *Palāśa* tree is a must in the *medhājanana* ceremony. *Bharadvāja Gṛhya* (II. 31: 65.1) provides the recitation of a *mantra* at the sight of an uncommon tree and pouring water, before noon, on *Nyagrodha* and other milk-exuding trees. The Maruts are supposed to reside on *Aśvattha* trees.

Bath in holy rivers and at other holy places (*tīrthas*) is regarded in the *Gṛhyasūtras* as capable of washing off sins and conferring merit. According to *Dharmasūtras* (e.g. *Gautama*, XIX. 15; *Baudhāyana*, III. 10.10.13; *Vasiṣṭha*, XXII. 12), all rivers, sacred lakes, places of pilgrimage, abodes of sages, cowsheds and temples remove sins.

The cow, held in veneration since the age of *Saṃhitās*, appears to have enjoyed high esteem in the age of *Sūtras* too. Cow-slaughter is mentioned in connection with many rites e.g. *Aṣṃakā, Śūlagava, Argha, Madhuparka*-offering, cremation rite etc. But, a close study reveals the tendency of gradual elimination of this practice. For instance, there is option in the use of cow-meat and provision for alternative substances, in *Aṣṭakā*, *Śūlagava*, cremation-rites, etc. The reverence to the cow can be gauged from the facts that the sight of a bull during *Veda-vratas* is regarded as auspicious. Even cowdung is a sacred thing with which the sacrificial place should be smeared. Some *Dharmasūtras* (e.g. *Gautama*, XXII. 20; *Baudhāyana*, I. 10.19, 3-6) provide for expiation to wash off the sin of cow-slaughter.

In the *Kauśika-sūtra* (56.13), besides some later deities, the *Gandharvas Hāhāhūlarū* are also mentioned.

Among popular religious practices, mentioned in the *Sūtras*, mention may be made also of *Agrayaṇa* or offering the first fruits of the season to the deity. It is also called *Navaprāśana* or *Nava-yajña*, and reminds one of the present-day *Navānna* ceremony performed in many regions of India.

According to *Mānava Gṛhya* (II. 12.17), offering should be made, *inter alia,* to *pipīlikās, piśācas*, *Apsaras, Gandharvas* each of which is regarded as divine.

Pāṇini and Patañjali

Among the post-*Vedic* deities, the most popular in Pāṇini's time appears to be Pārvaṭī. She is known as Bhavānī, Sarvāṇī, Rudrāṇī and Mṛdānnī (*Pan* IV. 1.49). A noticeable feature about popular religious practices, referred to in the *Aṣṭādhyāyī*, is that months, years, seasons and stars are deified. (*Pan* IV. 2.31, 34, 35; IV. 3.34, 36, 37 etc.) *Māsika* was the deity of *Māsa* (month), *Sāṃvatsarika* of *saṃvatsara* (year). *Ṛtu* itself is regarded as a deity. *Proṣṭhapada* (*Bhādrapada*), a *nakṣatra*, is mentioned as a deity. Names like Varuṇadatta, Aryamādātta appear from *Pan* VI 2.148 to indicate the belief in the blessings of the deities concerned. Thus, reference to the popular *Bhakti* cult is obvious. Devotion to Vāsudeva is obvious from IV. 3.98. IV. 3.97 refers to *bhakti* towards *Mahārāja* or *Kubera*. That *bhakti* was very popular in this age seems to be hinted at by the fact that only this word has been used by Pāṇini (IV. 3.95) as a leading rule. In the Pāṇiniyan school, this word has been used not merely in the abstract sense of devotion, but also as the object of devotion; e.g. *bhavānī bhaktirasya* (*bhavānī* is his object of devotion). The word Vāsudeva, mentioned above, appears to hint at the popular Kṛṣṇa cult.

Pāṇini (V. 3.96, V. 2.101) leaves no doubt about the use of images of deities, these being called *pratikṛti* or *arcā*. Pāṇini's rule *Jīvikārthe cāpaṇye* (V. 3.99) indicates that images were used as a means of livelihood as well as articles for sale.

Besides mentioning some earlier demons, Pāṇini refers (III 2.35) to *Rāhu* as an enemy of the moon. In V. 3.84, Pāṇini mentions, *inter alia*, *Śevala*, *Supari* and Viśāla which were, perhaps, names of Yakṣas, a class of semidivine beings.

Besides genuine ascetics, Pāṇini mentions (V. 2.76) a class of hypocritical ascetics called *daṇḍājinekas* (those masquerading as ascetics merely by the outward sign of staff and deer-skin). Another class of sham ascetics appears to be the *ayaḥśūlikas* (V. 2.76) who pierced their tongues or arms or some other limbs with iron spikes so as to draw sympathy, admiration or devotion of the people.

Pāṇini mentions *Maskarin* as a wandering mendicant (VI. 1.154). It is supposed to be the name of *Maskari* (Makkhali) *Gosāla*, a contemporary of the Buddha, and founder of the heretical *Ājīvika* sect.

Besides the *Āstikas* (theists or believers in the other world) Pāṇini refers (IV. 4.60) to *Nāstikas* and *Daiṣṭikas*. *Nāstikas* were the annihilationists who were followers of the great teacher, Ajita Kesakambalin, belonging to the materialistic *Lokāyata* school. *Daiṣṭikas* were the followers of *Makkhali Gosāla* mentioned above.

The popularity of Buddhism in Pāṇini's age is evident from certain references in the *Aṣṭādhyāyī*, besides those mentioned above. For example, the word *Śramaṇa*, meaning a Buddhist monk, is mentioned in II. 1.70; the existence of Buddhist nuns too in the society is clearly implied. The word *Cīvara* (garment of a

Buddhist monk) is mentioned in III 1.20. The term *arhat,* referred to in III. 2.133, generally denotes a venerable Buddhist.

In the *Ukthādigaṇa* of the *Aṣṭādhyāyī* (IV. 2.60) a teacher and a student of the materialistic doctrine are called *Lokāyatika.*

The word *dharma,* as used by Pāṇini (IV. 4.47, VI. 2.65), does not mean religion, but custom or usage. Thus, Pāṇini appears to have recognised the principle that clear proof of usage outweighs the written text of the law or even if there was no written law on a particular matter, it would be valid if it was in consonance with the local usage.

Patānjali mentions some post-*Vedic* gods of whom the most prominent is Kṛṣṇa (I. 1.4). Supernatural beings, classed as *Nilimpa*, are mentioned (III. 1.138). Besides the Viṣṇu cult, Śaivism appears to be popular in this period; *Bhava, Sarva, Girīśa, Mahādeva, Tryambaka*, as different designations of Śiva, reflect the various aspects of this deity. The popular deity, Skanda is mentioned (V. 3.99). The female deities Lakṣmī (I. 4.3) and Suparṇī (iv. 1.44) are mentioned.

From Patañjali's comment of *Pān* II 2.34, it appears that there were festive gatherings in temples where musical instruments used to be played. In this connection, the deities mentioned are Dhanapati (Kubera), Rāma and Keśava who thus seem to have been popular; the last two are identified with Balarāma and Kṛṣṇa respectively. The popularity of the worship of the lower divinities like *Yakṣas* and *Nāgas*, in this period, can be inferred from the many statues of them and their figures carved at Bharhut and Sānchi.

A noteworthy feature of the popular religious beliefs of this age is that charity was sincerely believed to lead the donor to heaven in due course (III. 3.7).

The wide vogue of images of deities, in this age, is borne out by various references in the *Mahābhāṣya*. From Pāṇini's rule *Jīvikārthe cāpaṇye* (V. 3.99), and the remarks of Patañjali it seems that there were at least three classes of images – for livelihood, for sale and for worship. It appears that a class of people used to earn livelihood by roving about with images of certain deities.

The idea of *Bhakti*, mentioned by Pāṇini, got a fillip in this age. Patañjali mentions (VI. 3.5) Kṛṣṇa and Janārdana as synonyms of Vāsudeva. *Vāsudeva-bhaktas* are referred to (III. 1.26). There are references also to the dramas *Bali-bandha* and *Kaṃsa-vadha,* both extolling the Viṣṇu-Kṛṣṇa cult. Kṛṣṇa and his group are mentioned (VI. 3.5.). All this leads to the conclusion that the Kṛṣṇa cult gripped the imagination of the people at large. The identification of the *Vedic* Viṣṇu with Vāsudeva, Nārāyaṇa, Kṛṣṇa, the association of Balarāma and Vāsudeva with the Vṛṣṇis, the place given to the group of Vāsudeva in the pantheon, the divine dignity of *Saṃkarṣaṇa*, like that of Vāsudeva or Viṣṇu, indicate the southward and northward expansion of a localised faith and a syncretism of different creeds.

Śaivism appears to have been a popular cult in Patañjali's time. We find, in his commentary references to *Śiva Bhāgavata* (V.2.76) and *Śiva Vaiśravaṇau* (VI. 3.26). It appears that there were two kinds of devotees of Śiva—one class carried an iron trident and, perhaps, resorted to harsh practices to achieve their end while another simply propitiated the deity with devotion and offerings.

Among the ascetic orders, mentioned by Patañjali, there is one called *Maskarin* who advocated inaction, and resembled the heretical *Ājīvikas*. Patañjali mentions also *Daiṣṭikas* (IV. 4.60) who were probably followers of *Makkhali Gosāla*, the preacher of the doctrine of the futility of *karman* as a means to the attainment of the desired end. The term, *Śramaṇa*, denoting a non-Brahmanical order in feud with the *Brāhmaṇas*, is also mentioned.

Though there is no direct reference to Buddhism and Jainism in the *Mahābhāṣya*, monuments and epigraphic evidence testify to their prevalence in the society.

Patañjali mentions (VII. 3.45) the materialistic *Lokāyata* school and *Bhāguri*, a noted exponent of this school.

From certain references (e.g. I. 1.1, I. 4.59, III. 1.26), it is clear that the ethical and moral principles of *Śraddhā* (faith), *tyāga* (sacrifice) and self-restraint were highly prized in the society.

The Age of Popular Epics

The *Ram* testifies (II 55.25-6) to the vogue of tree worship. The *Nyagrodha* (Indian fig) tree was regarded as particularly sacred. Belief in the doctrine of animism is also evidenced by the invocation of mountains, lakes, seasons, sky, air, etc. (II 25). Forests were believed to be guarded by sylvan deities (I. 31.14).

Another popular practice was the worship of demi-gods and malevolent spirits, called *bhūtas* which were believed to haunt the forests (II. 25.43, III. 25.43, V. 1.8). Fear-complex was also at the root of looking upon savages, particularly the cannibals (II. 25.20) with respect.

The *Mbh* refers (*Vana* 31.5, *Anu* 162.62) to hypocrites (*dharma-vāṇijakas*) who used *dharma* as a tool for earning money, and condemns them. We hear also of the oppressive stronger section of the people making the weaker section take *adharma* as *dharma* (*Āśrama* 30.24, *Sabha* 69.15).

It appears (e.g. *Śānti* 135. 13-24, 136.7) that even a section of robbers used to observe the basic principles of religion current among the upper classes.

A popular faith was that each house had a presiding demoness who was worshipped with various good articles (*Sabhā* 18.2).

The Skanda cult, found in the *Mbh*, reveals popular beliefs and practices to a considerable extent. It should be noted that Skanda or Kārtikeya does not appear in the *Vedic* pantheon. We meet with this deity, for the first time, in the *Chāndogya Upaniṣad* (VII. 26.2).

Connected stories about Skanda occur in the following places of the *Mbh* (Cr, ed, Poona) :

Āraṇyakaparvan—*Mbh* III, Chaps. 213-21.
Śalyaparvan—*Mbh* IX, Chaps. 43-45.
Anuśāsana—*Mbh* XIII, Chaps. 83, 84, 86.

The salient folk-elements in the stories are as follows. *Agni* assumed a goat's head, and played with son, Skanda, as though pleasing him with toys (*Mbh* II. 215. 23). The retinue of Skanda included people of all classes in the society (*Mbh* III. 214-29). Malevolent spirits, both male and female, carry out the command of the deity (*Mbh* III. 219. 42). The cock is closely associated with Skanda; this seems to indicate that he was connected with the religion of the common people. Among the hosts of his troops are people speaking various regional dialects (IX. 44.97), various kinds of tribal people (*Mbh* IX. 44.101) and people wearing different kinds of dress (*Mbh* IX. 45.56-91). The god was surrounded by mother-goddesses who were grotesque, multiformed and had limbs resembling those of various kinds of birds and beasts (*Āraṇyaka* III. 217-18). Some of them appear to have been malevolent. His followers and soldiers bear names showing their weird and ugly forms (*Śalyaparvan* IX. 44. 52-101).

From the above it seems that Skanda was orginally a non-Aryan deity believed in by naive village people and tribal folk. He was probably absorbed by the Hindu pantheon as a result of close association of the upper classes with the common people. The hypothesis is, to some extent, corroborated by the fact that, in the *Mṛcchakaṭika* (III), Skanda is mentioned as the tutelary deity of thieves.

Though the religious sects like *Śākta, Śaiva, Vaiṣṇava* etc. are not dealt with as such, yet a study of the epic reveals the creeds professed by them.

That heretics existed in the society is proved by the fact that some spies, in the guise of heretics, were engaged by the king to ascertain the attitudes of the public (*Śānti* 149.40). The precise nature of the views, held by the heretics, is not known. The existence of a section of the people, belonging to heterodox schools, is also proved by references to the discussion among adherents of the orthodox and heterodox schools of philosophy in the court of Mithilā, (*Śānti* 218.4). The word *Cārvāka* is mentioned at some places (e.g. *Śalya* 64.32, *Śānti*, Chap. 38). It is significant that, in the *Śāntiparvan*, there is a reference to the refutation, by *Brāhmaṇas*, of unorthodox views. In the court of Mithilā, those *Brāhmaṇas*, who successfully combatted the heretical views, were held in high esteem. Cārvāka is the traditional exponent of the materialistic school. Nīlakaṇṭha takes (comm. on *Śalya* 64.32) Cārvāka to refer to a demon in the guise of a *Brāhmaṇa*; the demon may be a figurative appellation of one who demolished the traditional orthodox views. Heretical views are referred to in various contexts and mostly with an attitude of disapproval; e.g. *Śānti* 318.5, 218.23, 24, 25, 27, 28, 29; *Aśva* 49.2; *Vana* 30. 30-43. Draupadī, having expressed some materialistic views, Yuddiṣṭhira said (*Vana* 31.1) that her words were apparently agreeable, but really conveyed ideas contrary to the orthodox views. It may be noted that *Cārvāka* is taken by some not as the name of an individual, but as one whose words are pleasant to hear (*cāru vāk*), but devoid of truth. The hedonistic attitude of the materialists is referred to in *Aśva* 49.9. The strong denunciation of the non-believers (e.g. *Aśva* 50.4) tends to prove that the materialists had a powerful hold on a section of the society, and that the traditionalists had to take pains to combat their views, and disabuse the minds of those who were led astray.

The *Mbh* contains a good number of references[2] to Buddhistic views like nihilism, placing the relics of a great man inside pillars, etc. disbelief in the caste-orders and four stages of life, denunciation of rites requiring animal-sacrifice, upholding non-violence as the sublime ideal, etc. It may be argued that these were the views of a class of non-conformists within the orthodox fold. But, the Buddhists are clearly referred to by such words as *Kṣapaṇaka* (*Ādi* 3.126) explained by Nīlakaṇṭha as *Pāṣaṇḍa bhikṣu*.

Purāṇic Age

Śaivism appears to have been very popular in the *Purāṇic* age. The *Vāyupurāṇa* contains many references to Śiva, and the practice of Śaivism. Variously designated as Maheśvara, Rudra, Paśupati, Bhūtapati, Nīlakaṇṭha, etc., Śiva is regarded as the Supreme God, the creator, preserver and destroyer of the universe.

In his Rudra aspect, he is represented as the god of death and the destroyer of death itself (24.128). Fond of the cremation ground and the funeral ashes (30.201), he moves about skull in hand. He is identified with the fierce *Kāla* (32.8. ff.). He is often characterised by uncomplimentary descriptions which hint at his malevolent and horrible activities. These are *sughora, bhīma, krūra, mṛtyu, duhsaha*, etc. At one place, Śiva is referred to as a drinker of *surā* (*surāpa*). *Rudra* appears also as the designation of a class of his associates, the other classes being *Bhūtas* (41.32-6), *Asuras*, *Rākṣasas*, *Daityas* (24.109, 30.317, 55.65-8 and so on), *Piśācas*, *Yakṣas, Gandharvas*, etc. An entire chapter of this *Purāṇa* (55) is devoted to the origin and glory of *Śivaliṅga*, thus testifying to the popularity of the *Liṅga* cult or Phallus-worship. There is, however, an opinion that there is no clear reference to Phallus-worship in this *Purāṇa*; the description of the *Liṅga*, referred to above, does not show its connection with *Yoni*, such a union being regarded as the symbol of creation.

Though there are references in it to Skanda and Gaṇeśa, of the existence of cults related to them there is no clear evidence.

Kauṭilīya Arthaśāstra

This work bears out the existence of heretics in the society. They are referred to by the contemptuous terms *Vṛṣala, Pāṣaṇḍa*. Among the heretics, mentioned by name, are *Śākyas* or Buddhists and the *Ājīvakas* (or, *Ājīvikas*). In III. 20.16 there is provision of punishment for feeding them at the rites in honour of gods and manes. This shows the derogatory position of these people in the society.

Kauṭilya refers (I.2) to *Ānvīkṣiki* as a must among the subjects to be learnt by a king. This term includes *Sāṃkhya Yoga* and *Lokāyata*. Thus, it is clear that he treats *Lokāyata*, i.e. materialistic or hedonistic philosophy on a par with the two orthodox systems of philosophy. This shows that he did not attach the opprobrium, found in later times, to this system which perhaps, gripped the society.

Smṛtiśāstra

Manu mentions heretics who are designated as *Nāstika* (II. 11) or *Pāṣaṇḍa* (IV. 30). *Nāstika* is stated as one who reviles the *Veda*. *Pāṣaṇḍā* is explained by Kullūka as one who performs religious acts opposed to the *Veda*. In the same context is mentioned *haituka* who, as Kullūka says, indulges in arguments opposed to the *Veda*.

Yājñavalkya mentions *Pākhaṇḍins* (II. 5.70) who, according to the *Mitākṣarā*, were *nirgranthas* probably meaning thereby Buddhist or Jaina monks. *Vīramotrodaya* and *Aparārka*, however, take the word to mean those who deny *Vedic* authority.

Thus, we see that, though *Varṇāśrama-dharma* predominated, yet heretics were there in the society, and some people boldly questioned th authority of the *Veda*.

Classical Sanskrit Literature

Harṣacarita

The *Harṣacarita* mentions adherents of the heretical faiths of Jainism and Buddhism. The word *maskarin* (V. p. 35, 1.2) appears to denote a Buddhist mendicant. *Pāṇḍurabhikṣu* (VIII. p. 73, 1.3) perhaps refers to those Buddhist monks who abandoned red robes peculiar to them, and adopted white ones. The word *Saugata* 1. 17 (VII. p. 65) clearly refers to the follower of Buddhism. *Arthaśūnya vijñapati* (*Ibid*) appears to hint at the Buddhist school of Vijñāvādins.

Ārhata (1.3, VIII. p. 73) appears to refer to Jain philosophers.

Śvetapaṭa (*Ibid*) perhaps denotes the *Śvetāmbara* (white-robed) sect of the Jainas. The term *Jaina* itself is mentioned (VIII. p. 73, 1.4). Jainas are described as having pulled out their hair (*Keśāluñcana*). The term *Kṣapaṇaka*, denoting a Bauddha or Jaina mendicant, occurs in this work (II. 100); he is described as dirty.

The other popular faiths, referred to in the work, are *Bhāgavatism* (1.4, VIII. p. 73), *Śaivism* (1.5, VIII. p. 73), *Pāśupata* sect of the Śaivas (122) *Pancarātra* (*Ibid*), *Lokāyata* (VIII. p. 73, 1.4).

The following religious rites and practices are mentioned in the *Harṣacarita* (references are to pages of notes in Kane's ed; 1918): *Rājasūya* (VII. 196), *Kukkuṭa-vrata* (I. 84-85), propitiation of stars (II. 115). There are reference to the washing of Śiva's image with milk (V. 73), use of *mudrā* in worship (I. 46), *Nīrājanā* (I. 34) or waving lights before deities as an act of adoration, animal sacrifice (I. 95), a circle drawn on the ground in worship (III. 201), propitiation of the *Mātṛs* (V. 71), sacrifice of buffaloes before Durgā (VIII. 218), human flesh offered to Śakti (III. 200).

The *Siśupālavadha* refers (XIV. 6) to *Rājasūya* sacrifice.

The *Kādambarī* (*Ka*) refers to the following :

> Worship of Kālī with human flesh (*Ka* p. 11), offerings of flowers, incense, cosmetics, cakes, meat, *Pāyasa* and *toya* in *Durgāpūja* (*Ka* p. 227), *Tripuṇḍraka* mark on the foreheads of *Brāhmaṇas* in worship (*Ka* p. 275). This work mentions the deity Caṇḍī also (*Ka* pp. 735, 742).
>
> The *Kirātārjunīya* mentions (III. 4) *Agnihotra*. *Aśvamedha* is mentioned in the *Naiṣadha-carita* (V. 21).

From the *Kādambarī* (*Kad*) we learn of the existence of the religious sects other than the followers of the traditional *Veda*-based religion. The words, throwing light in this respect, are as follows :

Kṣapaṇaka (p. 57)-	Jaina mendicant.
Sarvāstivāda (p.87)-	The *Vaibhāṣīka* school of Buddhists. It may also refer to the *Mādhyamika* school (*sarvasya astiḥnirāsah tasya*

	vādaḥ).
Jinadharma (p. 87)-	Jainism.
Vihārabhūṣaṇa (p. 74)-	*Vihāras* were Buddhist or Jain monasteries.
Vinayānurāgī (p. 155)-	appears to refer to people devoted to the precepts laid down in the *Vinaya-piṭaka* of the Buddhists.
Raktapaṭa (p. 155, 313)-	a sect of Buddhists wearing red robes.
Pāśupata (p. 155)-	worshipper of Śiva-*paśupati*.
Nirālambanā Bauddha-buddhi (p. 213)-	doctrine of the Bauddhas, acc. to which there is no permanent soul, but only self-subsistent cognition.
Monks (*Ka* p. 227)-	There is a reference to naked Buddhists.
Śvetapaṭa-vyañjana (p. 313)-	*Śvetāmbara* Jainas.
Āryāvilokiteśvara or *Āryāvalokiteśvara* (p. 313)-	A Bodhi-sattva.
Arhat (p. 313)-	Chief Bauddha or Jain saint. A superior divinity of the Jainas.
Kārpaṭịka (p. 333)-	Buddhist mendicant.
Śramaṇa (p. 338)-	Buddhist ascetic. It may also denote a religious mendicant.

The cult of *Ṣaṣṭhī* is referred to elsewhere in the book. She is the goddess presiding over the sixth day of the birth of a child, and is prayed to for giving the child strength and protecting it throughout life. She is stated to be wearing a cloth dyed with liquid turmeric.

Mālatīmādhaba

The *Tāntric* basis of the scene in Act. IV of the *Mālatīmādhava* where Mādhava decides to seek the aid of ghouls in his attempt to gain Mālatī, is obvious. In Act V, preparations for offering Mālatī to goddess Cāmuṇḍā, also bespeak the prevalence of *Tāntric* modes of worship. The scene is laid in a burning place. The description of the horrors of a cemetery and of the goddess is imbued with *Tāntric* spirit.

Mṛcchakaṭika

In the *Mṛcchakaṭika* (act III), Skanda or Kārtikeya appears as the patron-deity of thieves. As we have seen before in connection with the *Mahābhārata*, this non-Aryan deity, originating among rural and tribal people, was gradually elevated to the Hindu pantheon.

Kathāsaritsāgara

In the *Kathāsaritsāgara* we find many references to Śaivas. The skull-bearing Śaiva ascetic, wandering about, is a common sight (Penzer, II, p. 196). Besmeared with white ashes and wearing matted hair, he appears to be like the moon-crested God Himself. We are told of hypocritical ascetics (*Ibid* pp. 4-5). It is interesting to note that a swan is found to be offered to Śiva (Vol. VI, p. 20) – an unusal practice. While Śiva appears to have been a popular deity, Buddhism was of wide prevalence. We find also Buddhist nuns, e.g. *Yogakaraṇḍikā* (Penzer I, p. 156). Hypocritical female ascetics are also met with (Vol. III. p. 101).

Pāśupatas also appear in the society reflected in this work. They are stated to have practised magic (Vol. III. pp. 186-87) and resorted to treacherous practices (Vol. IV. p. 235).

The *Tāntric* goddess, Cāmuṇḍā, with whom human sacrifice is often associated, appears at some places (Vol. IV. p. 149). She is adorned with a garland of skulls, and is described as terrible. Goddess Kālī is described as skull-bearing and wearing skeletons (Vol. p. 197).

A goddess Sārikā is worshipped (Vol. VI. 0. 109).

A rite for averting evil spirits from all quarters consists in waving the hand round the head (*Ibid*).

Kāpālikas are mentioned in the work (Vol. IX, pp. 12-14). A *Kāpālika* is described by Moniter Williams as a Śiva-worshipper of the left-hand order, carrying human skulls from which they eat and drink. A *Kāpālika* is represented as hypocritical, and intent on carrying away another man's wife. He is also stated as worshipping a corpse in a cemetery, resorting to certain *Tāntric* practices including the use of charms and spells for mastering others and the performance of rites in circles.

The Buddhist nun, as a match-maker or rather a go-between, is often met with in Indian stories. In the *Daśakumāracarita*, she helps the meeting of *Apahāravarman* and *Kāmamañjarī,* Ratnāvalī in getting back her husband and *Kalahakaṇṭha* to prepare plans for winning Nimbavatī. In the *Mālatīmādhava*, she (*Kāmandaki*) helps the promotion of the love of the couple partly out of affection and partly in remembrance of her friendship with their fathers.

The *Deśopadeśa* refers to the *Śaiva* sect.

The *Śiśupālavadha* refers (II. 28) to Buddhism.

Kṛṣṇa Cult

Kṛṣṇa and his exploits in Vṛndāvana and Mathurā, particularly in the former, gripped the imagination of common people. Many of the works, dealing with Kṛṣṇa-Rādhā, breathe a folkish atmosphere; in them there is no pretension to the exposition of deep Vaiṣṇava philosophy nor any propagandist attempt to propagate Vaiṣṇava faith among the people. The authors of such works appear to describe the activities of Kṛṣṇa solely for the purpose of delectation and aesthetic pleasure not only on their own part but also to cater the same among the readers. The devout Vaiṣṇava may read high philosophical ideas and deep symbolism into the simple sports of Kṛṣṇa; but from the literary point of view we must observe that here is genuine folk element presented in a highly stylised and sensuous manner which at once provides us with literary relish and an idyllic charm.

We shall quote below a few typical verses from some of the well-known works.

iha vatsān samacārayad iha naḥ svāmī jagau vaṃśīm /
iti sāsraṃ gadato me yamunātīre dinaṃ yāyāt //
(*Padyāvalī,* No. 87)

[Here he grazed the calves, here our lord played the flute. May my days be spent while I keep on saying this in tears on the bank of the Yamuna.]

nītaṃ nava-navanītaṃ kiyaditi kṛṣṇo yaśodayā pṛṣṭaḥ /
iyad iti gurujana-savidhe vidhṛta-dhaniṣṭhā-payodharaḥ //
pāyāt (*Ibid*, 138)

[How much of fresh butter h... ...n taken by you—thus being

asked by Yaśodā, Kṛṣṇa said "this much", in presence of his superior. May he, holding the breasts of Dhaniṣṭhā, protect (us)!]

yāvad gopā madhura-muralī-nādamattā mukundam
mandaspandairahaha sakalair locanair āpibanti /
gāvastāvan masṛṇa-yavasa-grāsa-lubdhā vidūram
yātā govardhana-girl-darī-droṇikābhyantareṣu //
(*Ibid* ,153)

[Oh, while the cowherds, enraptured on hearing the sweet notes of the flute, are as if drinking Kṛṣṇa to the lees with winkless eyes, the cows, tempted by soft grass, going very far, have entered into the water-vessels in the cave of the Govardhana mountain.]

jīrṇā tariḥ sarid atīva gabhīra-nīrā
bālā vayaṃ sakalam ithham anarthahetuḥ /
nistārabījam idam eva kṛśodarīṇāṃ
yanmādhava tvam asi saṃprati karṇadhāraḥ //
(*Ibid*, 271)

[The boat is dilapidated, the river is very deep, we are girls; thus, everything is the source of mischief. The only redeeming feature is that, 'O Mādhava', you are now the boatman.]

vṛndāraṇye pramada-sadane mallikā-puṣpa-mode
śrīśubhrāṃśoḥ kiraṇa-rucire kokilādyair manojñe /
rātrau citre paśupa-vanitā-citta-dehā-pahāri
kaṃṣārāter madhura-muralī-vādya-rājo rarāja //
(*Ibid*, 285)

[The masterly instrument of the sweet flute of the enemy of Kaṃsa, attracting the heart and bodies of the wives of cowherds, shone at night in the pleasure-garden of Vṛndāvana, fragrant with Mallikā flowers, charming by the beams of the moon and attracted by cuckoos and the like.]

jalakeli-tarala-karatala-mukta-
punaḥ-pihita-rādhikā-vadanaḥ /

jagad avatu koka-yūnor-
vighaṭana-saṃghaṭana-kautukī kṛṣṇaḥ //
(*Padyāvalī*, 301).

[May Kṛṣṇa, who again covered the face of Rādhā after releasing it with his hands, restless in water-sports, who takes delight in uniting and disuniting the young couple of ruddy goose, protect the world !]

tāmbūlaṃ svamukhārdha-carvitam itah ko me mukhe nikṣiped
unmārga-prasṛtaṃ ca cāṭuvacanaih ko māṃ vaśe sthāpayet /
ehyehīti vidūra-sāritabhujaḥ svāṃke nidhāyādhunā
keli-srasta-śikhaṇḍakaṃ mama punarvyādhūya badhnātu kaḥ //
(*Ibid*, p. 338)

[Kṛṣṇa at Mathurā remembering Yaśodā—Here who will put into (my) mouth betel-leaf half-chewed in her own mouth, who will control me with conciliatory words when I go astray, who will now, with arms stretched far, place me in her own lap, and fix my chaplet after shaking it when it drops in sport ?]

The entire setting of the *Gīta-govinda* is idyllic. An atmosphere of folk-life permeates the poem. The love-sports of Kṛṣṇa and Rādhā, on the bank of the Yamunā, in the bowers, on beds of flowers and foliage—all this conjures up a picture of rural life and the youthful enjoyments of common people. The very opening verse of the poem, quoted below, makes the reader visualise the rural background of the sports of the lovers.

meghair meduram ambaraṃ vanabhuvaḥ śyāmāstamāla- drumāḥ
naktaṃ bhīrurayaṃ tvameva tadimaṃ rādhe gṛhaṃ prāpaya
ittham nanda-nideśatas-calitayoḥ pratyadhvakuñja drumaṃ
rādhā-mādhavayor jayanti yamunākūle rahaḥ kelayaḥ

[The sky is overcast with clouds, the forest-grounds are dark with *Tamāla* trees, it is night, he is timid; so you alone escort him home. Victorious are the secret sports of Rādhā and Kṛṣṇa, thus proceeding towards the bower-trees on the way at the direction of Nanda, on the bank of the Yamunā.]

The songs, introduced at intervals in the poem, are in the form of the utterances of Kṛṣṇa, Rādhā and her friends. In each song there is a personal feeling. A few such songs are quoted below :

ratisukhasāre gatambhisāre madanamanoharaveśaṃ.
na kuru nitambinī gamana-vilambam anusara taṃ hṛdayeśam
dhīra-samīre yamunātīre vasati vane vanamālī
gopī-pīna-payodhara-mardana-cañcala-kara-yuga-śālī

[O lady with heavy buttocks, do not delay, follow him, the lord of your heart, who, dressed beautifully like Cupid, has gone to the place of assignation in which the essence is the pleasure of sexual intercourse. On the bank of the Yamunā, with gentle breeze, lives Kṛṣṇa (lit. one having a garland of wild flowers), possessed of palm restless in rubbing the plump breasts of the cowherd women]

Kathitasamaye'pi harir ahaha na yayau vanaṃ
mama viphalam idam amalarūpamapi yauvanaṃ /
yāmi he kamiha śaraṇaṃ sakhījana—vacana-vañcitā //

[Hari, alas, did not go to the forest even at the stipulated time. This youth of mine, though of spotless beauty, is futile. Deceived by the words of friends, with whom, 'O tell me, shall I seek refuge' ?]

samuditamadane ramaṇīvadane cumbanavalitādhare /
mṛga-mada-tilakaṃ likhati sapulakaṃ mṛgamiva rajanīkare //
ramate yamunā-pulinavane vijayī murāriradhunā //

[At present, the victorious Kṛṣṇa enjoys himself in the forest on the bank of Yamunā. On the woman's face, in which Cupid has been fully delighted, (or, in which the signs of love are manifest) and in which the lower lip has been projected for kiss, he gleefully puts the mark of musk like the spot on the moon.]

It should be added that the musical *padāvalīs,* forming a vital element of the poem, resemble, in their form and content, the vernacular poems. The very term, *Padāvalī,* in the sense in which it is used, appears to have been borrowed from folk poetry. Such features led some scholars to postulate the existence of an Apabhraṃśa original of Jayadeva's poem.

A remarkable characteristic of the influence of the Kṛṣṇa cult on Sanskrit literature is this : Erotic verses, depicting various aspects of love, have been current in India from remote antiquity. Love in union (*sambhoga śṛṅgāra*) formed the subject-matter of many poems and stray verses. The tremendous popularity of the Kṛṣṇa-Rādhā and Kṛṣṇa-Gopī legends tinged a large number of the current verses of erotic content with a Vaiṣṇavite colour. What was spoken of ordinary man and woman was adapted to describe Rādhā-Kṛṣṇa or Gopī-Kṛṣṇa. In doing so, the natural impulse of ordinary mortals was sometimes spiritualised. In such Vaiṣṇavite verses, love in separation figures more prominently than love in union. Thus, pathos was infused to make the poetical pieces more poignant in feeling and sweeter in relish. We quote some instances below.

The famous stanza *yaḥ kaumāraharaḥ*, etc., fully quoted elsewhere in this work, has been mentioned in the *Padyāvalī* (382) as a remark of Rādhā to a friend in solitude. How this verse, quoted in anthologies sometimes anonymously and sometimes as composed by Śīlābhaṭṭārikā, came to be a Vaiṣṇavite one in the Bengal school is evidenced by the fact that Caitanya is stated, in the *Caitanya-caritāmṛta* (*Madhya*, 1 and 13 paricchedas) of Kṛṣṇa-dāsa, to have attached deep significance to it; he is said to have recited it in emotional ecstasy. It may be added that the stanza is included among verses on unchaste women so that its genesis is earthly and has nothing spiritual in it as it depicts the ordinary feelings of an ordinary heart, and points to a common frailty of human nature. In the *Gopālacampū* of Jīva Gosvāmin, this verse is put into the mouth of Rādhā. Kṛṣṇa, hearing it in solitude, changed the fourth line which runs as *kṛṣṇārodhasi tatra kuñjasadane*, etc.

The following verse depicts a man, attached to another woman, trying desperately to please his offended wife and the wife cleverly reproving him :

kiṃ pādānte luṭhasi vimanāḥ svāmino hi svatantrāḥ
kaṃ cit kālaṃ kvacid abhiratas tatra kaste' parādhaḥ /
āgaskāriṇy-ahamiha mayā jīvitaṃ tvad viyoge
bhartṛprāṇāḥ striya it nanu tvaṃ mayaivānunevaḥ //

[Why do you, being demented, roll beside my feet : husbands, indeed, are independent. You have enjoyed yourself somewhere for sometime, for it what is your offence ? I am the wrong-doer, because, in your separation, I have survived. Wives, indeed, have husbands as their lives so that it is you who should be coaxed by me.]

This verse, appearing in the anthologies under the name *Vākkūṭa* or *Bhāvadevī* stated to be the utterance of a woman of offended vanity (*māninī)*, is shown in the *Padyāvalī* (381) as Rādhā's remarks in order to please Kṛṣṇa.

Instances of the appropriation of ordinary love poems by the Vaiṣṇavas in order to apply the same to Rādhā-Kṛṣṇa, may be multiplied. Various conditions of lovers and the beloved, depicted in such well-known works as the *Amaru-śataka, Mālatī-mādhava, Uttara-rāmacarita,* etc., are represented, in the *Padyāvalī*, as those of Rādhā and Kṛṣṇa in the self-same verses, sometimes quoted verbatim or with some variations. Verses have been borrowed also from poets like Kṣemendra, Trivikrama, etc. Some such verses are *Padyāvalī, 230, 238, 318, 384, etc., Vidagdha-mādhava,* Act. V (*Kaṛmāte na* etc.).

A noteworthy work, inspired by the Kṛṣṇa cult, is the highly sensuous and devotional poem, entitled *Kṛṣṇakarṇāmṛta* of Līlāśuka. The verses have a rural setting against which Kṛṣṇa is described with deep devotional fervour. We quote below a few verses bearing the stamp of folk element.

barhottaṃsa-vilāsa-kuntala-bhāraṃ mādhurya-magnānanaṃ
pronmīlan nava-yauvanaṃ pravilasd-veṇu-praṇādāmṛtam /
āpīna-stana-kuḍmalābhir-abhito gopībhir-ārādhitaṃ
jyoti ścetasi naścakāstu jagatām ekābhirāmādbhūtam //

[May the single and peculiar lustre in the world, in which the mass of hair is decked with a chaplet of peacock's plumes, the face is steeped in charm, fresh youth is being manifested, wherein the nectar is the sound of the beautiful flute, worshipped by the cowherd women with very plump budding breasts shine in our heart !]

bālośyam ālola-vilocanena
vaktreṇa citrīkṛta-diṅmukhena /
Veśena ghoṣocita-bhūṣaṇena
mughena dugdhe nayanotsavaṃ naḥ //

[This boy, with his beautiful face having restless eyes and decorating the directions, and with his dress containing ornaments befitting cowherds, is producing a feast to our eyes.]

paśupāla-bāla-pariṣad-vibhūṣaṇaḥ
śiśureṣa śītala-vilola-locanaḥ /
mṛdula-smitārdra-vadanendu-sampadā
madayan madīyahṛdayaṃ vigāhate //

[This boy, the ornament of the assembly of the cowherd boys, enters my heart while delighting it with the wealth of the charm of his face-moon endowed with the grace of soft smile.]

The following three dramas by Rūpa Gosvāmin are permeated by folk elements based on the Rādhākṛṣṇa legend : *Vidagdha-mādhava, Lalita-mādhava* and *Dānakeli kaumuḍī.* The *Vṛndāvana-līlā* of Kṛṣṇa forms the principal theme of these works : this *līlā,* set against the background of the forest and fields of the place, breathe a rural atomosphere. Some incidents of these dramas and verses quoted from them, will testify to their typically folk character. In the *Dānakeli-kaumudī,* Kṛṣṇa obstructs the way of Rādhā, accompanied by other cowherd girls. He says that he is the master of the place, and cannot allow them to proceed unless they pay toll. A friend of Rādhā proposed her as the toll. Rādhā remonstrated in the following verse :

bhramyatyeṣa gireḥ kuraṅgakuhare kṛṣṇa bhujaṅgāgraṇīḥ
spṛṣṭo yena janaḥ prayāti viṣamaṃ kāmapy-asādhyāṃ daśām /
nābhadraṃ na ca bhadraṃ ākalayituṃ śaktāsmi dṛṣṭi-cchaṭā
mātreṇāsya hatāham icchasī kutaḥ prakṣeptum atrāpi māṣem // 96

[In the mountain-cave wanders this foremost black serpent (or, the gallant Kṛṣṇa) being touched by whom a person is reduced to a dangerous state which has no remedy. Struck by the mere flash of his glance, I fail to understand good or evil. Why do you wish to cast me to him ?]

The following is a part of a speech of Rādhā, agitated by the notes of Kṛṣṇa's flute :

sūtiste dhanuṣaśca vaṃśavarato vande tayorantimaṃ

viddha yena janastanuṃ viharayan nāntaściraṃ tāmyat /
viddhāhaṃ hṛdi mārapatri-viṣamair dhvāneṣubhir nas tvayā
krūre vaṃśi najīvanaṃ na ca mṛtir ghorāvirāsīddaśā //
Vidagha-mādhava (VI. 12).

[Your birth as well as that of the bow is from the best bamboo. Of these, I salute the latter; struck by it a man dies, and does not suffer agony forever. 'O cruel flute, hit in the heart by you with the arrow in the form of sound, more fierce than Cupid's shaft, we can neither survive nor die. (Thus) a horrible condition has befallen us'.]

Many other Vaiṣṇava poets owe their inspiration to the Kṛṣṇa legend. Kṛṣṇ's exploits, particularly those in Vṛndāvana, figure prominently in their works. The prominent among these works are the *Saṃkalpakalpadruma, Mādhava-Mahotsava, Gopāla-virudāvalī*, all by Jīva, the *Kṛṣṇāhnika-kaumudī* and *Ānanda-vṛndāvana-campū* of Kavi Karṇapūra, the *Saṃgītamādhava* of Prabodhānanda. The interspersed songs, in the form of *Padyāvalī*, betray a greater folk-element. Among such works are the *Dānakelicintāmaṇī* and *Muktācaritra* of Raghunātha.

Middle Indo-Aryan

The practice of worshipping *cetiyas* (Skt. *Caityas*) arose among the Buddhists after the demise of the Buddha. These were holy trees, stones or spots supposed to be haunted by good or evil spirits. Under the *Mahāparinibbānasutta*, the *Dīgha-nikāya* (ii. pp. 102-3, 118, 123, 126, 160-61) mentions several *cetiyas*. These existed even at the time of the Buddha, as is borne out by the *Vinaya* (i. p. 35, ii. p. 172).

Stūpas (mounds) were also worshipped by the people. The Master himself says in the *Mahāparinbbānasutta* that these should be built on the relics of the following persons : Tathāgata Paccekabuddha *Tathāgata-sāvaka*, Cakkavatti (Monarch).[3] The practice appears to have prevailed even before the Buddha. After his passing away, his own relics like the tooth, hair, etc. came to be buried in mounds which were worshipped. The most convenient site for the erection of *stūpas* was a crossing of four highways. These were worshipped with garlands, scents or coloured powder. It is stated that such worship is intended for the lay devotees alone, e.g. *Brāhmaṇas*, *Kṣatriyas* and *gahapatis* or householders in general (*Dīgha*, ii, p. 141). The great popularity of *stūpa*-worship is attested by Aśoka's earnestness in collecting relics and building *stūpas* over them.

The idea of visiting holy places seems to have arisen among the people after the Buddha's demise. It might originate from the Brāhmaṇical belief in the acquisition of merit accruing from such visits. The following four places were regarded as holy; the places where the Buddha was born, attained *bodhi,* promulgated the *dhamma cakka* and breathed his last. This practice became particularly popular among the lay devotees.

The Buddha taught rigorous practices for attaining perfection in *śīla, citta* and *paññā* (Skt. *Prajñā)* as a prerequisite for reaching the goal. In the post-Buddha period, easier means were conceived and propagated. *Saddhā* (faith) and perfection in the *brahmavihāras*[4] were considered (*Vatthupama-satta, Majjhima,* I. pp. 36 f.) to be the means to the highest end.

In the period, following the demise of the Lord, he was deified (e.g. *Mahāvastu*, I, pp. 167-8). The deification became very popular among the masses. In course of time, regular images of the Buddha came to be worshipped, as is borne out by the *Divyāvadāna* and the *Mahāvaṃśa.* Thus, image-worship came into vogue sometime before the 4th century A.D., the approximate time of composition of these two works.

The existence of the two large religous sects, viz. *Brāhmaṇas* and *Samaṇas*, in north India is attested by the *Suttanipāta*. The *Samaṇas* were divided into four classes, viz. *Maggajivins*, *Maggadesakas, Maggijīvins* and *Maggadūṣins*. The Brāhmaṇas were divided into three classes, viz. *Titthiyas*, *Ājivikas* and *Nigaṇṭhas*.[5] They are stated to have killed cows in sacrifices. The *Niddesa* informs (I. p. 89) us that some *Samaṇas* and *Brāhmaṇas* used to worship the following : elephant, horse, cow, dog, crow, fire, serpent, goblin, demon, four directions, a kind of fairy-bird, etc. besides Brahmā, Indra, Kṛṣṇa, etc.

The *Dhammapada* commentary refers (e.g. III, pp. 65 ff.) to the jealousy of the heretics towards Buddhism. Of the heretical teachers, mention is made of the following : Makkhali Gosāla, Ajita Kesakambalī, Pakudha Kaccāyana, Sañjaya Belatthiputta, Nigaṇṭha Nāthaputta *(Vinaya,* III, p. 79). Their pupils and followers too must have been heretical.

The *Karpūramañjarī* appears to refer to the worship of Kālī

(IV. 19), Gaurī (IV. p. 103), Cāmuṇḍa (IV, pp. 105-07).

The worship of the goddesses, variously named as Caṇḍamārī, Kātyāyanī etc., appears to have been very popular (e.g. *JC*. I. 16, II. 7).

The Trinity, Brahmā, Viṣṇu and Maheśa, are mentioned but once in the above work (III 34).

The Jainas were formidable rivals of the Bauddhas. Nigaṇṭha Nātaputta enlisted a large number of Jaina adherents whom the Buddha could not win over. While Buddhism emphasised the control of mind, Jainism stressed self-mortification.

The *GS* (II. 85) mentions a *vrata* called *Śyāma-śabala*. In it, the devotee was to enter at first into fire and then into water.

This work refers to the Kṛṣṇa cult which was obviously popular in the South where the work originated. Verse I. 89 mentions Krṣna and Rādhā, and refers to Kṛsna's sports with her and other women. In verse II. 14 we find Kṛṣṇa dancing with Gopīs, and clever Gopīs kissing his reflection on their foreheads. Verse II. 12 describes how Yaśodā always looks upon Dāmodara as a boy, and how the women of *Vraja* secretly laugh on looking at the face of Kṛṣṇa. Stanza II. 17 is a poetical description of the physical charm of Kṛṣṇa. The river Yamunā, the sporting place of Kṛṣṇa and the Gopīs, is mentioned in VII. 69. The popularity of the Kṛṣṇa cult is borne out also by the *KKC* (VII. 7).

The popularity of the Viṣṇu cult is indicated by references to Viṣṇu particularly in his Dwarf-incarnation, and his exploits (II. 51, V. I, 6, 25). The Fish-incarnation is referred to in the *KKC* (VII. 9).

Śiva and Pārvatī are referred to in the initial and final verses of the *GS*. They seem to have been popular deities; in V. 55 the sexual union of the deities is described. It is stated that, when the cloth of Pārvatī was removed by Rudra, She, out of shame, covered his two eyes with her hands and began to kiss his third eye.

From the *GS* (II. 90) there appear to have been temples in villages. Verse II. 73 seems to hint at the worship of many deities. Verse IV. 32 refers to the practice of *Jekkāra* which perhaps, means *jayakāra* (loud cry of glory), at the time of worshipping a deity. Verse III. 27 appears to indicate the performance of sacrifice in fire.

Verse IV. 8 refers to the worship of the Buddha by the *Buddhist*

Samaha. According to an old commentator, the verse reflects contempt for the Buddhists. It seems that Buddhism was on the wane when the *GS* was composed.

Verse II. 72 mentions *āryagṛha* which is explained as the temple of Caṇḍī. She seems to have been a popular deity. There is a reference (II. 94) to *nagara-gṛha-devatā* which probably means the presiding deity of a town.

The *JC* refers (I. 19) to *Kāpālikas*, *Tāntric* devotees. It also mentions a sect of (Jaina ?) ascetics, called *Kṣullakas*. They are described as wearing only one white garment and a loin-cloth, carrying a gourd, the begging bowl and fully shaving their heads (IV. 15).

REFERENCES

1. Some take the word to mean a class of people worshipping the phallus as a symbol of creation. But, it has also been explained as people given to sensual pleasures (*Śiśnaih dīvyanti krīdanti iti*).
2. *Śānti* 218. 32-34, 264.8, Chap. 271, 276.32, 33 *Aśva* 49.3, *Vana* 134.8, 190. 65-67 etc.
3. This runs counter to the spirit of the Buddha's teaching (e.g. *Dīgha*, II, p. 138) which forbids worship, and insists on self-restraint and self-improvement as the means of reaching the goal (Vide *Mahāvastu*, X, p. 334) and the verse *ātmā hi ātmano nāttah* etc. quoted in the *Bodhicaryāvatāra* p. 483. The direction in the above *Sutta* may be an interpolation.
4. Viz. *Maitrī* (friendship), *Karuṇā* (compassion), *Muditā* (delight at others' happiness) and *upekṣā* (equanimity).
5. This term usually denoted the Jains.

4

IDEAS, MANNERS AND CUSTOMS

THE literary works in Sanskrit, right from the *Vedic* times down to the classical, reveal the manners, customs and aspirations of the common people. Some of these may appear to be quaint to the sophisticated modern man. Nevertheless, these afford us a glimpse of the proletarian mind and plebeian life of the masses through the ages. It is not possible to lay down.all the details in our present study. So, we shall refer broadly to matters in this connection.

The Vedic Age

In the *RV*, the prayers reveal a desire for wordly happiness consisting of long life, prosperity, wealth of cattle, brave sons, freedom from diseases, victory over enemies, spacious houses, etc. Beautiful women were coveted. Women are keen upon their husbands' love. There are charms and practices for controlling the husband and curbing the co-wife. Separation from the husband by the latter's absence or death is dreaded. Women, running after paramours, are detested. Clandestine love between men and women, though looked down upon, is widely found. Women are sometimes characterised as hard-hearted. Their sphere of activity was not confined to the harem alone; they are found even to climb mountains.

In the marriage ceremony, both the bride and the groom were adorned with ornaments and beautiful garments (*RV* X. 78.7). The custom of the girls' self-choice of husbands is attested by *RV* X. 27.12; negotiated marriage was, however, common (*RV* X. 68.2). No particular age restriction appears to have applied to girls for the purpose of marriage. Instances are found of girls' living in their fathers' houses even upto an advanced age without being married probably for want of a suitable match. Again, even an aged woman used to be married to a man if found suitable. We find the custom of the father giving presents to his daughter while proceeding to her husband's house. Long conjugal life was a great desideratum (*RV* X. 85.36). The position of the wife is exalted in her husband's home. Men's fight against women is regarded as unfair.

The *RV* presents the picture of a happy home where the mother is ever vigilant about her child, the child moves with tottering steps, and the father walks with the baby in his arms, the mother anxiously tries to make her daughter look beautiful, the husband affectionately calls the wife who is always eager to please him. A henpecked husband is, however, an object of contempt (*RV* IV. 32.16). *RV* VIII. 47.10 contains a prayer for a comfortable home. Guests are entertained with pleasure.

Among the human qualities, uprightness, liberality and benevolence are praised, while crookedness and miserliness are denounced. There are, however, tendencies among people for craving more and more money. (e.g. *RV* X. 117.8). The amassing of money, as the sole aim of life, has been condemned. Too avaricious usurers, who count interest day by day, instead of performing sacrifices, have been denounced. Deceitful addiction to intoxicating drinks, etc. have been condemned. In the *RV* I. 109.2, we find the custom of maintaining the son-in-law or brother-in-law unable to earn livelihood.

Listening to the advice of experienced persons appears to have been a virtue.

Of the various acts of omission and commission, believed to give rise to sin, were lack of worship and defiance of gods. Inadvertence, intoxication, anger, gambling with dice and lack of discrimination between the good and the evil, incest, etc. were regarded as some of the causes of sin. *RV* X. 5.6 states seven misdeeds of a sinful nature without naming them. The effect of sin was believed to be removed by salutation to gods and sprinkling water on the head.

Quarrels appear to have been frequent in *Vedic* society. The apples of discord were cows, fertile land, water, a house full of attendants, etc. Use of abusive language and shouting were common features in wordy combats. We find prayers for non-involvement in feuds.

Common causes of fear among the people were wolves and wells; fall into the latter of not only men, but also of cattle was dreaded.

Friendship with people appears to have been very much prized, a friend having been looked upon as a guide through the tortuous ways of life.

The dog was regarded as a very helpful animal not only for protection against attacks, but also for carrying loads.

Curse was a common feature; the objects of curse were those who were responsible for family discord or harm to a married couple, unchaste women and proud fellows. The revengeful attitude of the people appears to have been directed against the following persons; atheists, those who decry the *Veda* or do not perform religious rites, the rebellious, crooked, malicious, slanderers, the harsh-tongued, the hostile, etc.

The following crude methods of punishment are found in the *RV* :

> Throwing the offender into a dark room (*RV* I. 116.8), death with froth in the mouth, tearing the body into pieces, decapitation, severance of other limbs, demolition of the offender's house.

Some queer customs are noticeable in connection with the disposal of the dead body. From *RV* X. 16.7 we learn that it was covered with a cow's skin and fat. Passages like *RV* X. 18.10-13 lead us to think that the corpse was buried, while others (e.g. *RV* X. 15.14) tend to show that it was burnt. The sinners were believed to be consigned to a dark and bottomless abyss (*vavra*) beneath the three regions.

Among the means of transport were horses and chariots drawn by horses or asses. Elephants and camels appear to have been used for carrying fighters in war. Besides mules, camels also were used as beasts of burden.

Boats (*nau*) propelled by oars (*aritra*) are frequently mentioned (e.g. *RV* I. 116.3, V. 59.2 etc.). There are explicit or implied references to sea-going vessles (e.g. *RV* I. 46.8, II. 116.5 etc.). *RV* III. 32.14 seems to refer to ferry-boats. *RV* I. 116.5 mentions a boat with as many as one hundred oars.

So far as civil law is concerned, we find, in the *Ṛgveda*, that an unmarried girl, living with her parents throughout her life, will get a share of the patrimony (II. 17. 7). The *aurasa*[1] son's duty is to give his sister in marriage, but not any share of the father's property to her. *RV* X. 185.3 seems to show that a *ksetraja* son, i.e. a son begotten by one person on the wife of another, is also recognised. That *putrikāputra* is recognised is evident from *RV* III. 31. It is explained by commentators on *Smṛti* literature in two ways, *viz*., a daughter appointed by a sonless man to act like his son, or the son of a daughter of such a person so appointed.

We note below a few interesting matters found in the *AV*.

The birth of a male child is hailed (I. 11.6, III. 23.2), while that of a daughter is deprecated (VI. 11.2). A brotherless girl is condemned for marriage. The following are regarded as inauspicious signs of a marriageable girl : a spot on the forehead, uncouth limbs, fierceness of look, etc. (I. 18). *K* 37.7-12 refers to an interesting method applied for ascertaining the disposition of a girl for marriage. She is to be given eight or nine clods of earth collected from different spots. The particular one, held by her, is supposed to indicate her mental attitude depending on the nature of the place from which the earth concerned was collected.

The *AV* contains prayers and charms for the safety and security of cattle. A charm for protection against worms occurs in II. 32 (*K* 27.21.26). A shepherd's charm is found in IV. 3; it is meant for protection against tigers, wolves and robbers.

AV III. 17 contains a prayer to *Sītā* (furrow) for bumper crops. VI. 50 appears to have been used to drive away creatures harmful to crops.

In connection with diseases, some curious ideas are found. The frog was used for curing fever (*K* 32.17) which was believed to be transferred to it. Yellow birds were believed to cure jaundice (*K* 26.18). It was also believed that this disease could be transferred to such birds. An insect was used (*K* 29.11) to counteract the effect of poison. *K* 26.13 reflects the belief that insanity was transferable to birds. The use of amulets for curing diseases is well known.

Age of Brāhmanas

We find some curious customs in the *Brāhmaṇas*, relating to the disposal of the dead bodies of human beings. In the case of a householder, who kept *Gārhapatya agni* (household fire), if his dead body was untraced, the following procedure was adopted. The effigy of such a man, made of the stalks of a *Palāśa* tree, used to be cremated (*Aitareya*, 6.32.1).

Along with other forms of marriage, *svayaṃvara* (self-choice, i.e. choice of the bridegroom by the girl herself), after attaining puberty and maturity was in vogue. From certain references (e.g. *Aitareya*, 7.33) polygamy appears to have been common. At many places (e.g. *Aitareya*, 3.12.12; *Gopatha*, 3.20) polyandry is prohibited.

Intercaste marriage was prevalent in society (e.g. *Śatapatha*, 4.1.5.9), though marriage within the same caste was regarded as the best. In intercaste marriage, generally the husband was of a higher caste and the wife of a lower one.

Certain practices in family life are interesting. A wife is not to take her meals before her husband (*Śatapatha*, 1.9.2.12). The husband, desiring valiant sons, is not allowed to have food in presence of the wife (*Śatapatha*, 10.5.2.9). The husband is to lie on the right side of the wife (*Śatapatha*, 7.5.1.6). The daughter-in-law should show great respect to her father-in-law and should not be forward in his presence, but should remain beyond his sight (*Aitareya*, 3.12.1).

Women are regarded as fickle-minded and hard-hearted with whom friendship is impossible (*Śatapatha*, 3.2.5.6; 11.5.1.9 etc.).

Kalpasūtras

So far as marriage is concerned, the general attitude is that marriage within the caste is good. But, intercaste marriage also is allowed (e.g. *Pāraskara Gṛhya*, 1.4.8-11; *Baudhāyana Dharma*, 1.8.16.2-5), provided the husband is of a caste higher than that of the wife. *Vaśiṣṭha Dharmasūtra* (I. 26-27), which probably belonged to a later age, forbids the *Āryas* (*Dvijas*) to marry *Śūdrā* girls.

As regards the form of marriage, the people of this age believed that the quality of the progeny depended on it. The *Gāndharva* form, which happens by mutual love, is condemned by some authorities (e.g. *Baudhāyana Gṛhya*, 1.11.20.10-15) for *Brāhmaṇas*. It is however, allowed to all by others (e.g. *Bhāradvāja Gṛhya*, 1.11; 11.12; *Āpastamba Gṛhya*, 1.3.20); even *Baudhāyana* refers to the views of some who allow it for all castes.

The *Sūtras* mention the usual eight forms of marriage, but vehemently condemn the *Rākṣasas* and *Piśācas* forms. In the former, the bride is captured by force, while in the latter she is seduced. The fact that these two forms are stated, and strongly denounced seem to point to their prevalence in the society. The girls, who fell as victims to these two types of oppressive acts, were allowed by certain authorities (e.g. *Vaśiṣṭha Dharma,* XVIII. 73; *Baudhāyana Dharma*, IV. 1.1.17) to be married to other men. Āpastamba makes it clear that connubial relationship arises through *dharma.* Thus, the implication is that force cannot create marital relationship. From the attitude of *Kalpasūtras* it seems that, if such a marriage was not desired to be annulled, it would be recognised according to the principle of *factum valet*. It was, perhaps, designed to give social status to a girl so married, who would otherwise have no *locus standi.*

Baudhāyana Dharma (1.1.2.2-3) appears to hint at the custom of marrying the daughter of maternal uncle or paternal aunt prevailing in the south. Such a marriage is, however, condemned.

As regards the age of the bride, the general rule is that she must be younger than the groom. But, the exact age is a matter of controversy. From the provision of *Caturthīkarman* in the *Gṛhyasūtras*, marking the consummation of marriage, it may seem that the bride had attained puberty before marriage. Some *Sūtras* (e.g. *Gobhila Gṛhya*, III. 4.5; *Vaikhānasa Gṛhya*, III. 2; *Vaśiṣṭha Dharma*, XVII. 70) prescribe *nagnikā* as the best girl for marriage. About the meaning of the word the authorities differ. The following meanings are suggested—

(i) One whose menstural flow is imminent, i.e. who is fit for sexual union.
(ii) One who has not attained womanhood and has not experienced the impulse of youth.
(iii) One who looks beautiful without dress.
(iv) One whose menstural flow has not yet commenced and whose breasts are not yet developed.

It is curious that the *Jaiminī Gṛhya* recommends (1.20) a girl, who is not a *nagnikā*, for this purpose. From the *Kāṭhaka Gṛhya* (19.2) twelve years is the highest age-limit upto which a girl could remain unmarried.

Excessive sleep, too much fondness for games, crying, squint in eyes, having many friends, having a beautiful younger sister, wandering about—these were regarded as some of the disqualifications in a bride.

As regards the time, propitious for marriage, authorities differ. From the custom of showing the sun to the bride one may infer that marriage was celebrated at daytime. From *Bhāradvāja Gṛhya* (1.12) it seems that the ceremony could be performed in the morning, midday or afternoon. The custom of the bridegroom showing the polestar to the bride appears to indicate that it took place at night also. *Āpastamba Gṛhya* (1.4.2) refers to the view of some who approve marriage at any time. The months *Āṣādha, Māgha, Phālguna, Caitra* and the star *Citrā* are condemned by some for this purpose. According to the *Kauśikaśutra* (75.1-5), any time after the full moon of *Kārtika* up to the full moon of *Vaiśākha* is suitable for marriage.

Some practices, relating to marriage, are interesting. According to the *Mānava Gṛhya* (1.12.1-7), the bridegroom has to part the hair of the bride with a porcupine-quill with three spots or with a blade of *Darbha* grass with roots. Then he has to rub oil on her hair which has to be braided with a piece of thread made of the wool of a living shep. Then the couple has to take curd and honey together. The ceremony over, the persons present have to shower grains on the couple; this symbolises the shower of blessings of God (*Hiraṇyakeśī Gṛhya*, 1.21.6).

After reaching the husband's native place, the wife should spend the first night at the house of an old *Brāhamaṇa* lady who has her husband and children alive.

Among the various practices, at the husband's house after the bride reaches it, there is the custom of placing a boy on her lap (e.g. *Āpastamba Gṛhya*, II. 6.11). According to some authorities, the boy must be the son of a woman who has only sons and no daughters, and whose sons are all alive. This is believed to ensure the birth of a male child to the wife. It is clear that daughters were unwanted.

A woman, in her monthly course, was regarded as impure and unfit for her normal duties including dressing herself and keeping clean. On the fourth night of the commencement of menstruation it was incumbent upon the husband to meet her. According to *Baudhāyana Gṛhya* (I. 7.45-46) and *Āpastamba Gṛhya* (III. 9.1), for the progeny of good quality, from the fourth to the sixteenth night, each succeeding even night was considered better than each preceding one for sexual union .

Pāṇini and Patañjali

From Pāṇini (III. 3.161) we learn that there were two modes of invitation for feasts, viz *nimantraṇa* and *āmantraṇa*. The former appears to have been confined to invitation in connection with sacrifices and *Śrāddhas*. The latter appears to denote invitation in general.

From the *Aṣṭādhyāyī* (e.g. IV. 2.14) we learn that there was the custom of having domestic servants and family barbers.

From certain references in the *Mahābhāṣya* (e.g. II. 2.25 – one enquiring about the number of another's wives) polygamy appears to have been in vogue in the society of Patañjali. In this society, the birth of a male child was welcome (III. 2.5). It is implied that the birth of a daughter was not hailed.

Age of Popular Epics

The *Ram* mentions a ceremony at the end of autumn, when harvesting was over. In it the people gathered together and partook of the first harvested grains after offering the same to gods and the manes (III. 16.6).

In the *Ram* we get a few instances of popular belief. We have noted, in the chapter on Popular Cults and Creeds, that the people used to believe in evil spirits (*bhūtas*), the sacredness and life of trees, the sylvan deities guarding the forest, etc. Another noticeable feature of folk-life was the veneration of cows. Grave sin was believed to be committed by killing cows (IV. 17.36). Touching the cow with one's foot, milking it excessively thus depriving the calf of its due were regarded as sinful (II. 75.22, 54). The gift of a cow was considered to lead to great merit (e.g. I. 18.20, I. 72.21-31).

Some of the salient features of the *Mahābhārata* society are as follows : Draupadī's five husbands hint at the existence of polyandry. Of the forms of marriage, *Gāndharva* was very common. The epic reflects a more warlike society than that of the *Rāmāyaṇa*. An atmosphere of fight surcharges the entire epic. The hero-mother, *Vidulā* exhorts her weak son, unwilling to fight, to take up arms. Kṛṣṇa boosts the morale of Arjuna perplexed at the sight of relatives on the other side. Religiosity and devotion are stressed throughout the voluminous work. Vidura is poor, but his devotion pleases Kṛṣṇa. In many respects, the epic is a precursor of the later *Smṛti* all the branches of which, *viz. Ācāra, Prāyaścitta, Vyavahāra* and *Rājadharma,* appear to have been influenced by ideas laid down in the *Mbh.* Women were highly honoured. Husbands are advised not to use harsh words to wives, because they are, indeed, Lakṣmīs incarnate and on them depend men's pleasure, fame and love. One's wife is the only friend of a dying man. The wife should look to the comfort of her husband, and never act contrary to his wish.

What has been stated under the epics substantially holds good in the case of *Purāṇas*, *Smṛti* and classical Sanskrit. Other ideas, custom, etc., mentioned in these branches of literature, will be found under *Purāṇic* age in the different chapters. So, we do not repeat them here.

A few more customs, referred to in different works of classical Sanskrit literature, are noted here. The *Naiṣadhacarita* (XIV. 70) records the practice of the bride's eating fish and rice in a marriage ceremony.

We can gather the following customs from the same poem: *Ulūlu-dhvani*[2] (a sound made by women wagging their tongues within their mouths) in a marriage ceremony (XIV. 51), the bridegroom holding a crown and mirror (XV. 60,70), conch-shell bangles worn by a married woman (XII. 35).

Some scholars think that the work was written by a Bengali poet. If the conjecture is correct, then those customs should be taken to have prevailed in Bengal.

The *Śiśupalavadha* refers to the following customs : welcoming guests with water, betel-leaves etc. (V. 27), greeting juniors with embrace (XII. 14), a woman following her dead husband on the funeral pyre is mentioned in (XV. 93), proclamation by *dundubhi* (a kind of drum) (VI. 67), conch-shells sounded for fighters to get ready (XV. 72).

The following were the practices in mourning (V. III. 116, 118): avoiding betel-leaves, fasting, leaving the beard unshaved, use of slight bedding.

The *Harṣacarita* refers (V. 69) to the custom of holding a sword to the head by way of salute. It mentions (I. 25) the practice of announcing royal proclamations by drums. It refers (VIII. 90,

247) also to the custom of announcing royal march in a similar way.

The *Kādambarī* (*Siddhāntavāgīśa's* ed.) refers to the following customs :

> Playing of some musical instruments to indicate the dissolution of an assembly (p. 44), sound of conch-shells indicating the advent of noon (p. 44), and the time of bath (p. 53), some men, stick in hand, showing the king the place of bath (p. 49).

Benevolent people appear to have made a gift of the following for public welfare (p. 177) : orphanage, well, house containing drinking water, pleasure-garden, temple, dam or bridge (*setu*), machine for raising water (*jalayantra*).

The *Deśopadeśa* describes the conduct of students from *Gauḍa* studying in Kashmir. They walk along the streets avoiding the touch of others. They are lacking in the capacity for disputation, and are very prejudiced. Extremely irascible as they are, they do not hesitate to stab their fellow-students. They buy things without paying the proper price, and abuse others. They frequently visit brothels, drink wine and take to gambling.

The *Narmamālā* depicts the despicable character of *kāyasthas* who used to hold high offices under the government. They destroy temples, and curtail expenses for the fodder for cows.

The *Gṛhakṛtyādhipati* (Chief Executive Officer of the internal administration) is a hypocritical devotee of Śiva, and persecutes *Brāhmaṇas*. The *Paripālaka* (Provincial Governor) ravages temples and villages, terrorises villagers and is up to any crime including murder of *Brāhmaṇas* and slaughter of cows. The *Lekhakopādhyāya* (Head clerk) is in the habit of receiving illegal gratification. Similar is the *Gañjadivira* (Accountant General) who fills his pocket with unclean money. The *Niyogin* (Supervisor of villages and *parganās*) amasses a fortune by resorting to unfair means. He is a veritable crane intent on devouring the village-fish. He persecutes the villagers, imprisons and canes them. Under him there is the *Grāma-divira* who can forge signatures, wipe out old letters, and insert new ones. The author describes *Āsthana-diviras* (Court-clerks) as unscrupulous taking bribe, drinking wine and visiting public houses.

The *Kalāvilāsa* states (canto v) that crafty scribes (*kāyasthas*) deceive others by their crooked writings. The author describes (canto vii) the tricks played by the travelling singer, bard, dancer and actor to rob people of their money. The goldsmith is described (canto viii) as resorting to subtle tricks in order to deceive people. In the next canto, the author describes the wiles of wicked persons like the astrologer, the quack passing off as a physician, and the merchant.

Middle Indo-Aryan Literature

Section vii of the *Bhikkhu-pātimokkha* asks a monk not to enter into a sick-room with shoes on (rules 61,62). Rules 74, 75 forbid him to commit nuisance on green grass and water. These rules for monks reflect the manners of people in the society.

Regarding the conduct of women in domestic life, we have referred to some rules under popular beliefs and practices.

The *GS* refers to some manners and ethical behaviour. From verse I. 32 we learn that straightforward dealing was looked upon with respect. It was regarded as improper to divulge a secret, heard by a man, even in a quarrel (IV. 21). A good-mannered man controls his anger. Even if angry, he does not think of unbecoming treatment, he does not express it. If he expresses it, he feels ashamed (III. 50). A dignified person, following an undesirable one, has his countenance unchanged (III. 65).

The *GS* throws some light on the relation between the husband and the wife. Depending upon his lineage, a man used to treat his wife (I. 24). The wife of a person, conscious of his high lineage, but living in a distressed condition, is stated to have been annoyed at the arrival of relatives to help him; it was considered to be dishonourable to the husband (I 38). Polygamy prevailed not only among the upper classes (I. 79, II. 6, VI. 28 etc.), but also among common men (II. 73). Some village headmen appear to have had many wives (V. 49). The youth of a junior co-wife was the object of jealousy of the senior one (IV. 82). There was the usual rivalry between co-wives. The first wife of a person appears to have carved out a permanent niche in his heart (II. 22). Young wives appear to have disclosed their love-secrets to their female relatives like aunt, paternal or maternal, and to the wife of the maternal uncle (I. 93, 97, II. 24, III. 4,46, 64, 94; VII. 48 etc.).

The re-marriage of a woman, whose husband was missing,

appears to have been in vogue. From the *Cendrakinnara-jātaka* (485) we learn that, after Siddhārtha's departure from home, many people sought the hand of his wife. The *Utsaṅga-jātaka* (67) also hints at this practice. The *Kuṇala-jātaka* (536) refers to polyandry.

It was the duty of a woman to look after the welfare of all the inmates of the house (*GS* VI. 12). It was improper for a woman to speak to her husband in presence of superiors.

The popular Brahmanical epics, the *Rāmāyaṇa* and the *Mahābhārata*, appear to have been adopted by the Buddhists and Jains to propagate their respective doctrines. The ideals in these epics appear to have inspired the non-Brahmanical people also. They modified the stories to suit their own purpose. The Pāli *Daśaratha-jātaka* and the Prākrit *Paüma-cariya* may be mentioned as instances. *GS* (I. 35) mentions the ideal characters of Sītā and Lakṣmaṇa. From this work we learn that the lives of Rāma, Lakṣmaṇa, etc. were written or painted on the walls of the house. Verse IV. 11 refers to the demons of Laṅkā. Verse V. 43 refers to Bhīma kicking Duryodhana with the help of Mādhava (Kṛṣṇa).

REFERENCES

1. It is one of the twleve kinds of sons recognised in the *Yājñavalkya-smṛti*. (II. 8.128).
2. Perhaps the first literary reference to this custom occurs in the *Atharvaveda* (31.9.6). This custome is also referred to in the *Chāndogya Upaniṣad* (III. 19.3) and *Naiṣadhacarita* (XIV. 49). For a discussion on this custom, see K.K. Handiqui's introduction to his English translation of the *Naiṣadhacarita*.

5

FOOD, DRINK, DRESS AND DECORATION

The Vedic Age

THE *Vedic* literature throws considerable light on the food and drink of the people, their garments and ornaments.

Among the foodgrains, the *RV* repeatedly mentions barley (*yava*), particularly fried barley. Of frequent occurrence is the word *anna* which may not necessarily mean rice; it denotes food in general. *Dhānya* has also been mentioned, *saktu* (pulverised grain) was commonly used. *Kṣīrapakva anna* (*RV* VIII. 77. 10-foodgrain boiled in milk), *apūpa* (cake) appear to have been delicacies. Crushed grain, mixed with curd, was also relished. *Puroḍāśa* (a kind of cake) was used in sacrificial offerings.

Among drinks are mentioned wine and *somarasa*; the latter was, perhaps, used by the upper classes, particularly in sacrifices. *Dadhimantha* (*RV* X. 86. 15) perhaps means liquefied curd or clarified butter.

Milk (*kṣīra*), curd (*dadhi*) and ghee are mentioned.

From I. 162. II ff., 164. 43, IV. 18.13, VI. 17,11, X. 27.2, 17, X. 79.6, 86.14, etc. the use of the meat of bulls, horses, buffaloes and even of dogs is proved.

RV VII. 6 18, bears out the use of fish.

Besides the foodgrains, mentioned in the *RV*, the *AV* names *godhūma*[1] (wheat) *vrīhi*[2] (paddy) (*AV* VI. 140.2), the cereals and pulses *māṣa, masūra, mudga, tila* (sesamum), *sarṣapa* (mustard) etc. Besides ghee, butter (*navanīta)* was used. *Madhu* (honey) appears to have been used as an article of food in this age. A preparation of fried rice, called *lāja,* is mentioned. *Māṃsa, saktu, apūpa, puroḍāśa, kṣāra, dadhi,* etc. are mentioned in *AV* too. This *Veda* also testifies to the wide prevalence of drinking wine.

From the *Vedic* literature we get an idea of the people's dress and decorations.

As regards garments, the *RV* contains the following terms : *adhivastra* (VIII. 26.13), *kurīra* (X. 85.8) and *pratidhi* (VIII. 85.8). The first denotes an outer cover or veil. The second was, perhaps, a head-dress or head-ornament. The last one may denote a part of a woman's dress. Linen and wool seem to have been used in making clothes.

Gold was widely used for making ornaments (*RV* I. 35.4, IV. 60.4). *Niṣka, rukma* were the names of certain ornaments. The neck and the ear were the parts usually decorated.

Baldness appears to have been regarded as a blot on one's appearance. Cure of it is prayed for (*RV* VIII. 91).

From a study of the *AV* it seems that one's garments consisted of an inner cover, an outer cover and a chest-cover. Besides *kurīra* and *pratidhi,* already occurring in the *RV,* we find in the *AV* also *nīvi, upavāsana,. vavri, uṣṇīṣa, kumba, tirīṭa.* These appear to denote respectively underwear, veil, upper garment, head-dress, (the last three denoting kinds of head-dress). The last three are taken by some to mean different sorts of head-ornament. Footwear (*upānaha*) and blanket (*kambala*) are also mentioned. Besides linen and wool, silk and *śaṇa* (hemp) were also used as materials for dress.

Besides gold, *maṇi* (jewel) is also mentioned in the *AV* as an ornament.

Cosmetics and *lākṣā* (lac-dye) appear to have been used as beautifying aids.

The people were very particular about their hair.

Baldness was hated, and medicines were applied for the growth of hair. There are prayers for the growth of thick hair. A thorny thing seems to have been used as a comb. The barbers used to shave hair and beard

Age of Brāhmaṇas

In the age of *Brāhmaṇas,* rice and wheat appear to have been the staple food. Different products of barley and rice, mentioned in the *Aitareya* (2.8.5), are : *dhānā, karambha, parivāpa, puroḍāśa* and *payasyā.* These were as follows respectively : fried barley cooked with butter, powder of *dhānā* fried with butter, parched rice fried in butter, rice-cake, mixture of curd and milk. The following kinds of paddy and products of rice and barley are known from references in the *Śatapatha* (12.7.2.9) and *Taittirīya* (3.8.15) :

Lāja –	puffed rice looking like flowers.
Masūsya –	a variety of well known north Indian paddy.
Priyaṅgu-taṇḍula –	a kind of paddy, golden in colour.
Pṛthuka –	flattened rice (generally called *cipiṭaka* ; *cūḍā* in Hindī).
Saktu –	pulverised rice or barley.
Saṣpāṇi –	matted rice.
Tokmāni –	matted barley.
Yavāgu –	rice gruel.

Milk and various milk products are mentioned. These are : *ājya* (clarified butter), *āmikṣā* (curdled milk), *dadhi* (curd), *vājin* (whey), *karambha* (porridge), *ghṛta* (unmelted butter ?), *navanīta* (cream or fresh butter), *sānnāyya* (mixture of curd and milk), mixture of milk and *soma, çaru* (milk, curd, honey, butter etc. mixed together), *śrita* (boiled milk), *sara* (thickened surface of milk), etc.

Meat was not only eaten, but was also regarded as the best kind of food (*Śatapatha*, 11.7.2.1). The meat of barren cows and sterile ox, goat and sheep was a delicacy. From the *Śatapatha* (3.1.2.21; 3.4.1.2; 7.5.2.42) and *Aitareya* (1.3.4) the vogue of beef-eating is undoubted; it used to be served to a king or other highly respectable guests.

Some of the appliances and utensils, connected with the preparation of food, are mentioned in certain *Brāhmaṇas*; e.g. mortar and pestle (*ulūkhala-musala, Śatapatha* I. 1.4.7), winnowing basket (*śūrpa, Ibid*, I. 1.4.8), plate (*śarāva)*, pot (*kumbhī*), utensils made of bell-metal (*Aitareya,* VIII. 37.4). The *Śatapatha* (VI. 5.1.6) mentions oven (*ukhā*) and the mode of making it. The oven appears to have been made of a mixture of clay, sand of gravel, stone and iron dust.

Udumbara (sacrificial fig), jujube and berries are some of the edible fruits mentioned in the *Brāhmaṇas; SB* 5.2.2.2 speaks very highly of *Udumbara*. *Śatapatha* (3.4.1.18) mentions sugarcane. *Aitareya* (7.35.4) mentions shoots of Banyan trees and fruits of fig. *Plakṣa* (*Ficus infectoria*) and *Aśvattha* (*Ficus religiosa*) are mentioned as suitable food for *Kṣatriyas*.

Among the drinks are mentioned *soma, surā,* honey, milk and fruit-juice. *Soma* appears to have been confined to the priestly class. *Surā* or spirituous liquor is condemned *(e.g. Śatapatha* 5.12.10; 12.7.3.20; 12.8.1.5). It is specifically prohibited for *Brāhmaṇas*. The *Taittirīya*, however, mentions, *surā* as the best; it is extracted from certain herbs or fermented from rice. *Parisrut* appears to have been a semi-fermented liquor condemned for *Brāhmaṇas* (c.f. *Śatapatha*, 5.1.2.14; 12. 9.1.1). *Surākaṃsam* or wine-goblet is mentioned in the *Aitareya* (VII. 35.4).

In the age of *Brāhmaṇas*, people appear to have attached great importance to dress and decoration. Knitting, sewing and weaving were known. Garments were made of wool, cotton and silk. Generally, the dress consisted of three parts—*vāsa* (main portion), *adhivāsa* (outer or over-garment) and *nīvi* (under-garment). The term *peśa* (e.g. *Aitareya,* 2.11.10) appears to mean ornamentation or embroidery. The skin of a black antelope (*kṛṣṇājina*) appears to have been the cover of the body of a student.

From certain *Brāhmaṇas* (e.g. *Śatapatha*, 12.8.3.11, 13.2.2.18 etc.) gold and silver ornaments appear to have been in use. Necklaces made of gold or pearls (e.g. *Śatapatha*, 13.2.6.8) are mentioned.

Kalpasūtras

In the *Kalpasūtras*[3] we find the use of various foodgrains, *viz*. rice, barley, wheat, millet, sesame and pulses. Salt and sugar appear to have been added to food for adding to the taste. *Lohita-lavaṇa* (*Kauśika-sūtra*, 31.17) appears to have denoted rock-salt (*saindhava lavaṇa*).

Among the condiments, *Pippali* (long pepper) and *marīca* (black pepper) are mentioned.

Two kinds of cakes, made of ground corn, are mentioned. Of these *puroḍāśa* was offered chiefly in sacrifices and *apūpa* was generally eaten by the people, (c.f. *Khadira Gṛhyasūtra*. III. 2.29 and *Kauṣītaki Śrautasūtra*, 20.7, etc.); it was also used on ceremonial occasions like *Apūpāṣṭaka*. *Tailāpūpa* (cake prepared with oil) is mentioned in *Kāṭhaka Gṛhya* (70.1), but it appears to have been intended as an offer in sacrifice.

Among the preparations of rice are mentioned *odana* (cooked with water) and *pāyasa* or *kṣīraudana* (cooked with milk), *sthālīpāka* (rice or barley cooked with milk or water) appears to have been a special dish meant for ceremonial occasions. *Yavāgu* (gruel of rice or barley), and *Yāvaka* (a barley product) are also mentioned (e.g. *Gautama Dharma-sūtra*, XIX. 14, *Kātyāyana Srauta-sūtra,* VII. 4.25, *Kāṭhaka Gṛhya-sūtra*, 6.3. etc.). *Āmikṣā* was a sort of coagulated curd. *Kṛsara* (*Gobhila Gṛhya-sūtra*, II. 9.5) was a mixture of cooked rice and sesame. *Saktu* (pulverised grain) and *lāja* (a preparation from fried rice) also find mention in the *Sūtras*. Cooked rice, mixed with curd, *odana* and ghee appear to have been favourite dishes. A curious practice was that certain articles, including a preparation of ground rice, barley or sugarcane-juice, were offered to serpents. *Karambha* (*Āpastamba Dharma-sūtra*. I. 5.17.19) seems to have been a popular food; it may mean a sort of gruel made with flour and curd or a sort of porridge prepared with unhusked, parched and kneaded barley grains.

Of the fruits, mango seems to have been common; because *Āpastamba Dhama-sūtra* mentions it (I. 7.20.3) as a familiar example. Other fruits mentioned in the *Sūtras* are *kharjūra* (dates), variety of jujube called *Badara, Karkandhu* and *Kuvala* (*Āpastamba Śrauta-sūtra*, XIX. 26; XIX. 2.10 etc.).

Among utensils, mention is made, in the *Sūtras,* of those made of metal, wood, stone and clay (e.g. *Kātyāyana Śrauta-sūtra,* II. 3.5; *Baudhāyana Dharma-sūtra*, I. 6.14. 1-9). Among the metals in common use were, perhaps, bell-metal, copper and iron. Gold and silver utensils also are mentioned, but these seem to have been confined to the well-to-do class, particularly for use in certain expensive *Śrauta* rites. Cooking pots, pitchers and plates of earth appear to have been popular. *Baudhāyana Śrauta-sūtra* (XV. 16) refers to leather-bags used for storing ghee, oil, honey and grains.

The *Śūtras* bear clear testimony to the vogue of meat-eating in the society. Meat, both roasted on spits and cooked in pots, appears to have been in use (*Gobhila Gṛhya*, III. 10.29, IV. 1.6 etc.). It was an essential element in *madhuparka* offered to distinguished guests. It was also an offering in feasts connected with *Śrāddha* and in *Aṣṭakā*.

The *Dharmasūtras* shed considerable light on the meat permitted and prohibited in that age. One-hoofed (*eka-śapha*) animals are categorically banned (e.g. *Gautama*, II. 8.28). Of the two-hoofed ones (*dvikhurī*), *Kuluṅga* is forbidden (*Baudhāyana*, I. 12.6). *Baudhāyana* (I. 12.6) allows the following two-hoofed animals: *ṛṣya, hariṇa, pṛṣata* all of which appear to indicate different species of the deer, *mahiṣa* and *varāha*. The last one seems to be different from *Śūkara*, and there is no distinction between a rural or a wild *varāha*, as we find in the case of *śūkara*. Regarding the beasts of the *Pañcanakha* (five-toed) class, *Baudhāyana* (I. 12.5) prohibits *khaḍga* (rhinoceros), *kacchapa, śvāvit, śaraka, śaśa, pūtikhaṣa*. *Gautama* (II. 8.27) agrees with Āpastamba, but omits *pūtikhaṣa*. Vaśiṣṭha (XIV. 39) allows all in Āpastamba's list, but omits *khaḍga* and *pūtikhaṣa*. Regarding animals of the *Ubhayatodat* (having teeth in both the upper and lower jaws) class, Gautama (II. 8.28) bans all. As a general rule, Gautama prohibits the animals which are *keśī* (having hair, excessive hair according to commentator Haradatta, *e.g. Camarī*, etc.) and *aloma* (devoid of hair). Among the animals of the village, *Baudhāyana* (I. 12.1.4) excludes all excepting goats and sheep. *Baudhāyana* (1.12.3), *Āpastamba* (I. 17.29), *Gautama* (XVII. 27) and *Vaśiṣṭha* (XXIII. 30) prohibit the village boar. By implication therefore, the meat of a wild boar appears to have been edible. *Vaśiṣṭha* (XIV. 47) refers to the difference of opinion about a wild boar. Forbidden (*Āpastamba*, I. 17.29, V. XIV. 43) is the meat of the animals called *gavaya* and *śarabha*.

The question of beef-eating in this age is interesting[4]. While Gautama provides for the atonement of the sin arising from cow-slaughter, *Baudhāyana* (I. 12.1) also has a similar provision. But, *Āpastamba* (I. 17.30.31) clearly permits beef-eating. *Vaśiṣṭha* (XIV. 46) follows suit.

As regards bird-meat[5], the *Dharmasūtras* mention many birds permitted or prohibited. Among those of the *Vikira* or *Viṣkira* class *Ap*. (I. 17.32) prohibits *kukkuṭa*; commentator Haradatta observes that the prohibition relates to only village *kukkuṭa*, but not to wild ones. This bird is also prohibited by *Gautama* (II. 8.29) and *Baudhāyana* (I.12.3). Of such birds, *vāraṇa* is forbidden by *Baudhāyana*. Among the *pratuda* class, *Gautama* (II. 9.35) allows all, but *Āpastamba* (I. 17.33) prohibits *plava*. Categorically prohibited by *Āpastamba* (I. 17.34) are the creatures of the carnivorous (*kravyāda*) class. The flesh of *rakta-pāda* (*pārāvata*, according to others) and *rakta-tuṇḍa (cakora* etc., according to some; aquatic birds with red beaks, according to others) is forbidden. *Gautama* (XVII. 33) allows the flesh of the birds of the *Jālapāda* (web-footed) class.

So far as fish is concerned, the following are prohibited:

Vikṛta-rūpa –	misshaped.
Sarpaśīrṣa –	having heads like those of snakes.
Manuṣya-śīrṣa –	having heads like those of human beings. *Jala-manuṣya,* according to Haradatta.
Kravyāda –	Carnivorous.

Also prohibited are the aquatic creatures called porpoise, *nakra, kulīra, mṛdura (makara,* according to Haradatta), *ceṭa, gavaya.*

The following varieties are unanimously permitted *bṛhacchirorama-śakarī, cilicima, rājīva, rohita, śapharī, sahasra-daṃṣṭra, varmī. Śatavalī* is considered by Āpastamba as a very delicious fish.

Of the vegetables and juicy substances, prohibited are *karañja* (red garlic), *kisalaya* (sprouts), *kyāku* (mushroom), *laśuna* (garlic), *niryāsa* (substances exuding from trees; *hiṅgu,* etc., according to Haradatta under *Gautama*, II. 8.33), *parārīka* (leek), *vraścana*(red juice issuing from incisions on trees), *palāṇḍu*(onion), *gṛñjana* (turnip) and *śleṣmāntaka or śleṣmātaka* (a kind of fruit, according to M. Wms.).

Among the sweet substances, used as food according to the *Sūtras*, we find *phāṇita* (sugarcane-juice ? *Āpastamba Dharmasūtra*, I. 5.17.19), *modaka* (ball-shaped sweetmeat), *svastika* and *nandyāvarta*, the last two being explained in many ways. Honey appears to have been widely used.

The following drinks appear to have been in vogue in the age of *Sūtras,* besides milk:

Takra (butter-milk mixed with water). See *Baudhāyana Dharmasūtra*, IV. 5.22.

Mantha – (a preparation of parched barley meal stirred in milk, curd, water or malted butter).

Of *mantha*, the following varieties are prescribed for different castes :

Ājyamantha–	prepared with malted butter. For *Brāhmaṇas.*
Payomantha–	prepared with milk. For *Kṣatriyas.*
Dadhimantha–	prepared with curd. For *Vaiśyas.*
Udamantha–	prepared with water. For Śūdras. See *Āpastamba Śrautasūtra*, XIX. 13.12, XXII. 26.1.
Māsara–	(*Kātyāyana Śrautasūtra,* XIX. 1.18-20).

A mixture of the following :

Germinated rice called *śaṣpa*, barley (*tokman*), fried grains (*lāja*), *nagnahu* (generic name of certain roots, herbs, spices etc.) serving as yeast, these are all powdered. With it are mixed two gruels of rice and millet (*śyāmāka*), boiled in water.

As regards intoxicating drinks, *surā* is the commonest. Other such drinks are *madhu* and *maireya*. *Surā* appears to have been a very popular drink, especially at marriage and certain other rites. Female dancers drinking wine are mentioned (c.f. *Sāṅkhāyana Gṛhyasūtra*, I. 11.5). From certain *sūtras* (e.g. *Kātyāyana Śrautasūtra*, XIX. I. 20-27, *Āpastamba Śrauta-sūtra*, XIX. 5.7-11 etc.) we learn that it was prepared from the fermentation of germinated rice, barley and parched grains and some plants and herbs used for yeast. *Surā*-drinking is prohibited in *Dharmasūtras* for the twice-born, particularly *Brāhmaṇas* drinking it intentionally. Vaśiṣṭha forbids the drinking of water collected at the bottom of a boat (XIV. 36).

People of the *Sūtra* age appear to have worn garments made of cotton, wool, flax, hemp, animal skin, silk, *kuśa* grass and bark; the last two kinds were probably used exclusively at religious rites and sacrifices. *Kṣauma* and *Kauśeya* are the words used to denote clothes made of linen and silk respectively. An upper garment and a lower one were, perhaps, usual. On certain occasions, the turban (*uṣṇīṣa*) was also used. *Adhivāsa* is the term used to denote an upper garment. *Prāvaraṇa* is also found to indicate a wrapper or an outer cover. The word *tārpya* (*Baudhāyana Śrautasūtra,* XXV. 34; *Baudhāyana Dharmasūtra,* I. 6. 13.12; *Kātyāyana Śrautasūtra,* XV. 5.7-10) has been variously explained as a cloth, soaked with ghee, a cloth made of a material obtained from the *Tṛpa* tree, a silk garment or under-garment, a linen garment, a cloth made of yarn thrice dipped in water before weaving. *Kātyāyana Śrautasūtra*(XV. 5.7-13) mentions a garment called *Pāṇḍva*. Both weaving and sewing appear to have been in vogue. *Kumba-kurīra* (*Āpastamba Śrautasūtra*, X. 9.7, *Baudhāyana Śrautasūtra*, VI. 4) appear to have been golden ornaments attached to the head-dress (or veil ?) of the sacrificer's wife; some however, take it to mean a hair-net. *Śāmūla* (v.l. *Śāmūlya, Śāmūla, Śyāmūla*) is explained as a woollen garment or a sort of blanket (*AP Śraustasūtra*, VI. 29. 3, X. 17.9; *Baudhāyana Śrautasūtra*, XVIII. 48; *Lāṭyāyana Śrautasūtra*, IX. 7 etc.).

Blankets of wool (*Kambala*) and of the hair of mountain goats (*Kutapa*) were used (*Āpastamba Dharmasūtra*, I. 1.3. 8; *Baudhāyana*, I. 5.8.34).

As regards ornaments, both males and females of the *Sūtra* age appear to have worn them. Apart from earring and other ornaments of gold and silver, used at the *Aśvamedha* sacrifice and by *snātakas,* we hear of *niṣka* or necklace worn round the neck, made mostly of gold and sometimes also of silver; it appears to have been used by both men and women (e.g. *Kāt. Śrautaśūtra*, XIV. 3.30; *Āśvalāyana Śrautasūtra*, III. 9; *Sāṅkhāyana Gṛhyasūtra*, III. 1.7 etc.). *Rukma* (*Kātyāyana Śrautasūtra,* XVI. 5.1; *Āpastamba*, XX. 2.5; *Baudhāyana*, X. 57), made of gold or silver, seems to have been a round ornament, with 21 studs sewn in a strap of deer-skin and strung on a three-fold hempen cord, worn round the neck and hanging over the breast.

The use of flowers and flower-garlands, especially in marriage and other ceremonial occasions and by *Snātakas*, is attested by several references (e.g. *Sāṅkhāyana Gṛhyasūtra*, I. 12.9; *Hiraṇyakeśī Gṛhyasūtra*, I. 11.4; *Pāraskara Gṛhyasūtra*, II. 6.23-24 etc.).

Other aids to beauty included mirror, collyrium (*añjana*) and fragrant unguents (e.g. *Sāṅkhāyana Gṛhyasūtra*, I. 12.5; *Kātyāyana Śrautasūtra*, VII. 2.31; *Hiraṇyakeśī Gṛhyasūtra*, I. 10. 4 etc.).

Various forms of hair-style were obviously in vogue. In the *Cūḍākaraṇa* rite (tonsure), hair on the head was arranged in varying forms depending on the practice in the family concerned, e.g. a plait on the right side of the head, braids on both sides, top-knots (*Kāṭhaka Gṛhya*, 40.2-8):

Shaving the head and beard was necessary on certain occasions, e.g. *Śrauta* sacrifices and at the end of the period of mourning (*aśauca*) consequent upon the death of close relatives. It appears that, as a means of beautifying oneself too, this was done.

Women sometimes used to keep two locks of hair, one on each side (*Āp Gṛhyasūtra*, I. 7. 16-18). In the *Sīmantonnayana* ceremony, performed after a certain period from the first pregnancy, the husband was to part the wife's hair upwards beginning from the middle. A porcupine quill (*śalali*) or a *Kaṅkata* was used as a comb (*Pāraskara Gṛhya,* II. 14.15; *Kauśika sūtra,* 76.5 etc.).

Pāṇini and Patañjali

Articles of food, according to Pāṇini, can be divided into four classes :

I. *Bhojya* – food in general.
II. *Bhakṣya* and *Miśrīkaraṇa* – comprising *palala* (meat), *sūpa, śāka* (vegetables), *guḍa, tila, ghṛta* etc. are *miśra* articles. *Sūpa* may denote broth, soup, a sauce or condiment.
III. *Vyañjana* and *Upasikta* – *Vyañjana* denotes articles to be added to the taste of the food; e.g. curd, butter etc.
IV. *Saṃskṛta* – articles ready for eating directly from the place of the preparation, e.g. groats ground in hand-mill. Curd, butter-milk, milk, etc. are given by Pāṇini as examples of this kind of food.

Various articles of food are stated below :

I. Cereals – *Śāli* (a kind of rice growing in winter and transplanted), *mahāvrīhi* (a main kind of rice), *hāyana* (a kind of paddy growing in the rains), *yāvaka* (a variety of rice), *ṣaṣṭika* (a kind of paddy ripening in 60 days), *nīvāra* (wild rice).
II. Pulse – *Mudga māṣa, kulattha.*
III. Miscellaneous – *Yava* (barley), *yavānī* (inferior barley), *aṇu* (a kind of small grain), *gavedhūka* (Hindī *gadheruā,* boiled with rice or barley), *tila.* Cooked food (*kṛtānna*) comprises –

Odana –	boiled rice.
Yavāgu –	barley gruel.
Yāvaka –	according to Patañjali, barley, made free of chaff by pounding and then boiling its grain in milk or water with sugar added to it.
Piṣṭaka –	Cakes made of powdered grain, particularly rice.
Saṃyāva –	according to Kullūka on *Manu*, V. 7, a sweet preparation of ghee, milk, *guḍa* and wheat flour.
Apūpa –	Sweet cake made of wheat flour.
Saktu –	pulverised grain.
Kulmāṣa –	perhaps a thick gruel made by stewing beans, maize or any other inferior grain, with water, *guḍa* and oil. Appears to have been used by the poor.
Palala –	a sweetmeat prepared from powdered sesamum and sugar or molasses.
Cūrṇa –	fried wheat flour mixed with ghee and sugar.

Among the sweets, Pāṇini mentions *madhu* (e.g. V. 2. 107), *guḍa*(V. 4. 103), *phāṇita* (VII. 2.18), the last one meaning juice of sugarcane boiled down to a thick form from which sugar is crystallised. *Śarkarā* (granulated sugar from sugarcane) is also mentioned.

Among milk products, Pāṇini mentions curd, buttermilk (II. 4.14, IV. 2.18). *Phāṇṭha* of *Pāṇini* (VII. 2.18) may mean a hot drink or butter made from the cream of the day's milk. *Haiyaṅgavīna* (V. 2.23) appears to mean ghee produced from the previous day's milk.

Of the prevalence of intoxicating drinks at the time of Pāṇini, there is ample evidence (e.g. II. 4.25, III. 1.100, IV. 3.76, V. 2.112 etc.). Two kinds of drink, not found in *Vedic* literature, but mentioned by Pāṇini, are *maireya* and *kāpiśāyana*. *Maireya* (VI. 2.70) appears from the *Arthaśastra* (II. 25) to have been made with the following ingredients – *meṣaśṛṅgi* bark, *guḍa*, powdered *pippal* (long pepper) and black pepper (*marica*); powdered *triphalā* may or may not be added. *Kapiśāyana* (IV. 2.29) appears to have been prepared from grapes grown in Kapiśī, a region in north Afghanistan. Pāṇini refers (VI. 2.10) also to the decoctions, called *Kāṣāyas*, of which there appear to have been several varieties.

The *Gaṇapāṭha* of V. 4.3 mentions *kālikā* and *avadātikā* as special kinds of wine. Do these mean black and white drinks respectively ? *Avadātikā* might be the *śveta-surā* of the *Arthaśāstra*. Kātyāyana mentions *sīdhu* in the *vārtika* on II. 2.8.

Other articles of food, according to Pāṇini, are *śāka* (leafy vegetables), *bhājī* (cooked vegetables – IV. 1.42, also called *śrāṇā*, IV. 4.67), *sūpa* (soup of boild pulses, VI. 2.128). *Upadaṃśa* (III. 4.47) probably means things like radish, ginger, etc. munched with the main food.

Of the fruits, *āmra* or mango (VIII. 4.5) and *jambū* or rose-apple (IV. 3.165) are mentioned.

Regarding the culinary art, the practice of roasting on spikes seems to be indicated by the word *śūlākaroti* (V. 4.65), the thing roasted having been called *śūlya* (IV. 2.17).

Pāṇini mentions (IV. 2.129) *deva-sūda* and *bhājī-sūda* which appear to mean two kinds of cooks – the first working in temples and the second cooking vegetables at other places. *Āḍhaka, ācita* or *pātra* (V. 1.53), *droṇa* (V. 1.52) appear to have been particular measures of food cooked by different kinds of cooks who were, perhaps, classed in accordance with the same. *Drauṇī* or *drauṇikī* (V. 1.52), *dvyāḍhakī* etc. (V. 1.55) probably referred to female cooks cooking food of the respective quantities. *Prāsthika, kauḍavika, khārika* appear to refer to vessels in which particular quantities of food, indicated in their respective names, could be cooked (c.f. III, 2.33).

The different kinds of fabric, used for making garments, are the following according to Pāṇini : *Kauśeya* (IV. 3.42) meaning silk cloth, *auma* or *aumaka* (IV. 3.157) made from the yarn of flax (*Umā*) and hemp (*bhaṅgā*) plants, *ūrṇā* (IV. 3.158) or wool and *Kārpāsa* (IV. 3.143) or cotton. Some of the garments were *antarīya* (I. 1.36), *prāvāra* (referred to in III. 3.54) and *bṛhatikā* (V. 4.6). *Antarīya* appears to denote cloth directly covering the body. *Prāvāra* seems to have been a wrapper. *Bṛhatikā* was, perhaps, an upper garment thrown over the shoulders, and hanging down to the knees. *Raṅku* in IV. 2.100 seems to denote the material for *rāṅkava*, found in ancient literature, which probably meant a costly wrapper.

Several kinds of blankets appear to be referred to by Pāṇini, Kātyāyana and Patañjali. Pāṇini mentions (V. 2.42) *paṇya-kambala* or blankets sold in a market. In a *vārtika* under VII. 3.45, Kātyāyana mentions *varṇaka; Varṇaka*, according to the *Arthaśāstra* (II. 11), denotes a kind of woollen blanket. Patañjali mentions (I. 406; II. 1.69) *kutapa* or *thulma*; the former means a Nepalese blanket.

Beautifying the body with ornaments and various kinds of decoration in the Pāṇiniyan age are indicated by such words as *subhagaṃkaraṇa* (III. 2.56), *alaṃkāra* (IV. 3. 64), *keśaveśa* (IV. 1.43) etc.; *aṅgulīya* (IV. 3.62), *karṇikā* (IV. 3.65), *lalāṭikā* (IV. 3.65), *graiveyaka* (IV. 2.96) are some of the ornaments mentioned by Pāṇini. *Kumbā* (III. 3.105) perhaps denotes an ornament used by the females in hair-dressing. *Kabarī* (IV. 1.42) as a coiffure is also mentioned.

Mention is made of the following aids to beauty and requisites for decoration :

Darpaṇa (mirror), *añjana* (collyrium), *mālā* (garland), *gandha* (perfume), *daṇḍa* (stick), *asi* (sword), *upānah* (shoes), the last three appear to have been used by males.

Among the foodgrains and cereals, Patañjali mentions[6] *śāli* (a kind of rice of ten varieties), *hāyana* (a type of red rice), *yava* (barley), *ṣaṣṭika* (the variety of paddy ripening in 60 days), *yavānī* (an inferior type of barley), *gavedhuka* (mixture of rice and barley boiled together), *tila* (sesamum). The pulses include *mudga, rājamāṣa, māṣa*. Things like ground groats were designated as *saṃskṛta* (lit. refined), so called as these did not require further processing before being eaten.

Miśrīkaraṇa (mixing), *vyañjana* (use of something for preparing food) appear to have been two processes of adding to the taste of the food, (*Mahābhāṣya*, II. 1.34-35). *Dadhi* (curd) appears to have been sprinkled over the food (II. 1.35). Tamarind, *palāla* (ground sesamum), *sūpa* (pulse-soup) and *śāka* (vegetables) appear to have been mixed with other edible articles. Radish (*mūlaka*, IV. 1.48) and bottle-gourd (*alābu*, VI. 3.61) appear to have been vegetables in common use.

The following were some of the popular vegetarian dishes :

Odana or *bhakta* (I. 1.1, III. 1.26) – boiled rice. It appears (II. 3.13) to have been occasionally cooked with meat.

Yavāgu (II. 1.36) –	rice gruel.
Sūpa (I. 2.51) –	thin curry.

Light food or snacks included the following :

Kṛsara (VIII. 3.59) –	mixture of sesamum and rice, with some peas and spices.
Saktu (I. 1.57) –	groats with molasses or curd. Sweetmeats included.
Śaṣkuli (I. 1.47) –	ground rice, sugar and sesamum cooked in oil.
Pūpa or *apūpa* (I.1.1., I. 2.45) –	cake of rice or barley prepared with ghee.
Piṣṭapiṇḍī (II. 1.57) –	flour-cake.
Palāla (I. 1.1) –	made of *guḍa*, *tila* and sugar cooked together.
Modaka (V. 1.119) –	sweet balls.

Besides *guḍa* and *śarkarā* (sugar), honey (I. 1.1) also appears to have been used as a sweetening medium.

Guḍodaka (I. 4.3) appears to have been a mixture of water and molasses, used as a soothing drink. *Māthitika* (V. 3.93) appears to have been the designation of a person selling *mathita* or whey. *Haiyaṃgavīna* (V. 2.23) is also mentioned; it means clarified butter made from the milk of the previous day.

Of the animals, whose meat was allowed as food in the time of Patañjali, mention is made of five-toed ones (*pañcanakhāh*) and other animals are expressly prohibited (*anye abhakṣyāḥ)* From I. 1.1 we learn that boars and cocks, bred in the village, were also prohibited; the implication is that the wild ones of these species were allowed. Taboo was attached also to these two bred in cities (VII. 3.14).

The meat of the *Śāraṅga* bird appears to have been eaten (II. 2.36). *Māṃsaudana* (rice mixed with meat) appears to have been a favourite dish for which deer-meat was used (II. 3.1). From II. 2.36 the eating of onions seems to have been in vogue. I. 2.39 reveals the practice of eating fish after removing the scales and bones.

Among the fruits, Patañjali mentions *bimba* (*Momordica monadelpha*, I. 1.58), *dādima* (pomegranate, I. 1.9), *mṛdvikā* (reddish grapes, VI. 3.42) and *kuvali* (jujube fruit, IV. 3.170).

The various kinds of intoxicating drinks, mentioned by Patañjali (I. 2.62, IV. 1.52, V. 3.66, VI. 4.194), are :

Surā –	prepared from molasses.
Prasannā –	distilled from rice and described as very oily.
Śuṇḍā –	besides denoting a kind of alcoholic drink, it also meant a place where it was available.
Āsuti –	a drink used in religious rites. III. 2.29 refers to the practice of drinking from a vessel and with a pipe of reed. III. 2.8 strictly forbids a *Brāhmaṇa* woman to drink *surā*.

From the *Mahābhāṣya* we can gather the following items of dress.

Śāṭaka (I.1.1) –	Cloth or garment in general used mainly to cover the body.
Śāṭī (II. 2.5) –	Cloth for a female, white in colour.
Upasaṃvyāna (I. 1.36) –	Lower garment which was generally white (I. 1.11).
Paṭa (I.4.21) –	Upper cloth for covering the shoulders, white in colour.
Uṣṇīṣa (I. 1.27) –	Head-dress, red in colour, used by a priest.

Kārpāsa (cotton) and *ūrṇā* (wool) are mentioned in the *Mahābhāṣya* (IV. 1.55 and V. 1.3).

V. 1.2 attests the use of footwear made of leather (*carma*) and *dāru* (wood).

IV. 2.2 appears to refer to the practice of dyeing garments, the common colours having been blue, yellow, green, brown-red, red.

The following ornaments, made of gold, are mentioned in the *Mahābhāṣya* (I. 1.1) :

Rūcaka –	necklace (?).
Kaṭaka –	bracelet.
Svastika –	?

Kuṇḍala – ear-ring.

Two hair-styles are mentioned by *Patañjali* (II. 2.24) – locks gathered at the back with braids hanging down or tied as a knot at the back. From I. 1.2, we learn of people with shaven heads (*muṇḍa*), with matted locks (*jaṭī*) and others with a tuft of hair on the crown of the head (*śikhī*). I. 3.1 and VI. 1.9 refer to the practice of cutting hair and shaving beard. *Tanukeśyaḥ striyaḥ* (VI. 3.34) or women with scanty hair are mentioned.

Age of The Popular Epics

In the *Rāmāyaṇa* we find that the Aryans were accustomed to both vegetarian and non-vegetarian food. The *vānaras* (monkeys) were used to vegetarian food alone, their food having been fruits, roots and leaves. The *Rākṣasas* were carnivorous.

The following were used by the Aryan people as food-stuff : rice (*taṇḍula* I.5.17), barley (*yava* III. 16.6), wheat (*godhūma*, III. 16.6), pulses called *mudga*, *caṇaka*, *kulattha* and *māṣa* (VII. 91.19.20).

Boiled rice appears to have been the most popular food. From II. 91.20 we learn that rice of excellent quality was offered, along with other articles of food, to the army of Bharata. Refined rice, mixed with curd and milk, was a favourite dish (II. 3.14.6). II. 61.5 reveals that rice with curry was looked upon as a very agreeable food :

haviṣyānna (III. 56.14) – or rice boiled in clarified butter.
lāja – parched and puffed rice.
kṛsara (II. 75.30, 20.18) – mixture of sesamum and rice.
modaka (II. 20.17) – pellet of rice, sugar and pulses.
mīṣṭānna (I. 53.3) – a tasty preparation of rice.
pāyasa (II. 75.30) – rice boiled in milk with sweet substances.

Among milk products, the following are noteworthy : curd (*dadhi* e.g. I. 53.3), curd mixed with sugar (*rasāla* II. 91.73), ghee (II. 20.17, III. 73.14, 72.3).

Oil has been referred to as *sneha* (VII. 91.20), *taila* (V. 53.8), *lavaṇa* (VII. 91.20) is also mentioned. *Amla-rasa* (V. 11.18) perhaps denotes a sort of vinegar used for adding a sour taste to food.

or by an intruder.

Corporal punishment is prescribed for theft and some other offences like entering a fort without permission, deceitful gambling, sale of human flesh, etc. In all cases of physical punishment, excepting death, payment of fine is the alternative (4.4.10). Corporal punishments included, *inter alia,* the cutting of certain limbs, the breaking of the neck, the blinding of eyes. Fines were generally of three kinds, *viz. prathama-sāhasa* (first amercement), *madhyama-sāhasa* (middle amercement) and *uttama-sāhasa*(highest amercement). Death penalty appears to have been of two kinds, *viz. Śuddha-vadha* (simple killing), *Citra-vadha* (killing by torture). Death by causing the offender to be put on a spike (*śūla*) appears to have been common. Death by torture was of various kinds, e.g. drowning, putting fire on the skinned head, putting burning substances on palms and on the head, kicks by bulls, burning with fire, piercing with arrow, etc. The principle of an eye for an eye, a tooth for a tooth appears to have been followed, to a certain extent, in awarding punishments to criminals. For example, for cutting the genital organ and testicles of a person the offender was to undergo similar punishment. For cutting off a limb of parents or certain other relatives, the offender was to lose the very same limb of himself.

Death penalty is prescribed for murder, the modes of death differing according to the nature of the crime. These are – flaying the head before setting fire to it for the murder of one's parents and some other very respectable persons, tearing by bullocks for a woman killing her husband or some other superior, drowning for poisoning one to death (4.4.11).

It is interesting to note that the work provides for post-mortem examination of the bodies of *āśumṛtakas* or those who died all of a sudden (4.4). Suicide is regarded as a sin. The body of a person so dead is to be dragged by a *Caṇḍāla*, and no obsequial rites are allowed for such a person.

Offences relating to sex are dealt with in the section called *Kanyā-prakarma*. The actual criminal and his abettor suffer the same corporal punishment which can be avoided by paying the prescribed amount (4.4.12).

The last chapter of this Book deals with *aticāras* or acts of misconduct. These include a variety of offences, e.g. approaching an elder's wife for adultery, sexual union with a woman of the prohibited caste, making a person eat and drink what is inedible and undrinkable respectively, trespass into another's house, felling a tree, unleashing an untamed animal, throwing a stone, etc. without warning to the persons likely to be affected, injury by a cart, etc. (4.4.13).

A person may be arrested on any of the three grounds, *viz.* *Śaṅkā* (on suspicion of a crime likely to be committed), *rūpa* (for possession of stolen goods) and *Karma* (in consideration of the circumstances). Suspicion may arise from a variety of circumstances, e.g. spending money in an extravagant manner, addicted to wine, woman or gambling, getting wounds treated secretly, moving about stealthily at night, going about in disguise, evading the notice of officers, repeated enquiries about the wives, houses and properties of other persons (4.6.2).

A noticeable feature of the work is that it does not appear to provide for imprisonment as a mode of punishment. Two kinds of houses for confinement (*bandhanāgāra*) are, however, mentioned (2.5.5), *viz. dharmasthīya* and *mahāmātriya*. The former was, perhaps, meant for restraining a defendant during the pendency of the suit against him and appears to have been like the modern lock-up. It might also be for keeping a guilty person confined for a certain period for non-payment of fine. It may be noted that fines could be paid either in cash or by doing the prescribed work for the State (2.23.2, 2.24.2). The other one was, perhaps, intended for criminals unable to pay the fines. The differences in the names of the two kinds were, perhaps, due to the fact that the former was for those committed by judge (*dharmastha*) and the other for the people punished by other royal officers.

Sedition was a grave offence. People entertaining seditious thoughts were to be won over through secret agents (1.13.2-13). Other means of getting rid of them are also prescribed, particularly when prominent men among the subjects were involved (1.13.15-21).

A list of the subjects of dispute, stated in the work (Book Three), which is slightly different from the usual eighteen *vivādapadas* of *Dharmaśāstra*, will show the matters giving rise to litigation in those times. These are :

(i) *Vivāha-saṃyukta* - matters relating to mariage.
(ii) *Dāya-vibhāga* - partition of inheritance.

(iii) *Vāstuka* - disputes relating to property.
(iv) *Saṁayasyā-napākarma* - breach of contract.
(v) *Ṛṇādāna* - non-payment of debt.
(vi) *Aupaniṣadika* - relating to deposits.
(vii) *Dāsakarmakara-kalpa* - matters relating to slaves and labourers.
(viii) *Sambhūya samutthāna* - partnership business.
(ix) *Vikrīta-kritānuśaya* - revocation of sale and purchase.
(x) *Dattasyā-napākarma* - non-conveyance of gifts.
(xi) *Asvāmi-vikraya* - sale without ownership.
(xii) *Svasvāmi-sambandha* - matters relating to possession.
(xiii) *Sāhasa* - violent or aggressive criminal act.
(xiv) *Vāk-pāruṣya* - abuse.
(xv) *Daṇḍa-pāruṣya* - too severe punishment.
(xvi) *Dyuta-samāhvaya* - gambling and animal betting.
(xvii) *Prakīrṇaka* - miscellaneous.

Classical Sanskrit Literature

That drinking was common in the society is proved by the fact that the *Nāmalingānuśāsana* gives as many as twenty-nine synonyms of *madya*, each conveying a particular characteristic of the drink. Some of these words are noted below with their respective connotations :

Hālā (that which causes shame to be cast off).
Parisrūt (that which is distilled).
Gandhottamā (having a highly agreeable smell).
Mārdvika (prepared from *mṛdvikā* or grapes).
Maireya (produced in the country of Mirā).

Besides the above, a few other names are found in various Sanskrit works. These are :

Sauvīraka (produced in the *Suvīra* country).
Kairātaka (produced or drunk by *Kīratas* ?).
Avadātikā (white wine ? Is it the same as the *Śvetasurā* of the *Arthaśāstra* ?)
Kālikā (does it mean that which is produced or consumed within a time-limit ?)
Āsuti (that which is presssed out or extracted ?)

Ariṣṭa (that which cures diseases ?).

That India has a very ancient tradition of drinking is proved by references to this practice since *Vedic* times.

Both Caraka and Suśruta, the oldest authorities on medicine and surgery respectively advise drinking in the proper manner and to a limited extent. According to them, wine is invigorating, digestive and clarifies intellect. Drinking for health is recommended in winter, not in summer and the rains (Cakrapāṇi on *Caraka-sūtra*, 13, 23; *Suśrutā -sūtra*, 46, 378, 382. Also *Carakasūtra*, 27. 191-195. 27. 191-195).

Bāṇabhaṭṭa, in his *Kādambarī* (Kale's ed., 1928, p. 39) refers to the vogue of drinking in the society. The word *pānabhūmi* seems to refer to a liquor shop or bar. *Madhukoṣaka* probably denotes wine glass. The word *mattā* clearly shows that even women used to drink wine. *Nānāsava-pātra* (p. 149) seems to indicate that various kinds of vessels were used for drinking it. One of the meanings of the word *Kādambarī* is wine which may have been intended by the author.

The subject of drinking will be discussed also in the chapter on Food, Drink etc.

Kathāsaritsagara

Theft is of common occurrence according to the *Kathāsaritsāgra*. There are several thieving stories, e.g. that of Śiva and Mādhava (Penzer, Vol. II). The body of a thief is stated to be dragged through streets (Vol. V, p. 268, 282) and hung from the wall (p. 247). A form of punishment of thieves is the cutting off of his hands and tongue (*Ibid*., p. 61). Thieves are found to break through walls (Vol. V., p. 142). At one place (*Ibid*. p. 248), it appears that a king stationed his daughter in a brothel to catch a thief. Assassins are found to be bribed (Vol. I, p. 22). Adultery is frequently met with in the work. For instance, Devadāsa's wife is addicted to it (Penzer, II. pp. 86 f.f.). An adulterous fellow is punished with the confiscation of all his property by the king (*Ibid,* p. 88). The husband of an adulterous wife is found to cut off her nose; this shows the gravity of the offence in ancient Indian society. There are references to adultery in several works (e.g. *Ka*, p. 378).

The vices of gambling (Vol. VII. p. 72) and hunting (*Ibid*. p. 90) are mentioned in the work.

Theft[4]

Of all the different crimes, mentioned in Sanskrit literature, theft merits a separate treatment. It has been looked upon as a serious crime ever since *Vedic* times. In some cases of theft, e.g. stealing of gold belonging to a *Brāhmaṇa*, the only punishment is death as it is looked upon as one of the gravest sins. Stories of theft in some form or other abound in poems, dramas, tales and romances. Theft is not confined to articles; we meet with cases where a man or a woman is bodily lifted e.g. abduction of Sītā by Rāvaṇa. Theft of cows has been quite common since *Vedic* age. Even gods are found to stoop to this heinous practice. We find even the lover approaching the beloved like a thief, because he was debarred access openly. The wide prevalence of theft in various forms is attested also by about a dozen words denoting this practice. These are : *stena, taskara* (doing that heinous act which cannot be uttered), *cora, caura, pāṭaccara, granthi-bhedaka* or-*chedaka* (cut-purse), *aikāgārika* (house-breaker), *moṣaka, pratirodhī, parāskandī, malimluca, dasyu.* At some places, the following seven kinds of thieves are mentioned; that is probably due to the influence of *Caurya-śāstra :*

> Thief proper, one who betrays a thief, minister, one who is experienced in sowing seeds of dissension, buyer of stolen goods, one who maintains a thief, one who gives shelter to a thief.

It is interesting to note that theft is included in the list of sixty-four traditional arts to be acquired by cultured people[5]. (Princes had to be trained in it)[6]. In such an early work as the *Mahābhāṣya* (c. 2nd. cent. B.C.) there is mention[7] of the skill of thieves in stealing collyrium from a person's eyes and the deftness of cut throats in drinking blood from running people[8].

The notable stories of theft in the classical Sanskrit literature are recorded in the following works :

Daśakumāracarita (story of Apahāravarman; the very name *Apahāra*, meaning theft, is significant), *Mṛcchakaṭika* (Śarvilaka episode), Bhāsa's *Cārudatta, Kathāsaritsāgara*, Vidyāpati's *Puruṣa-parīkṣā, Vetāla pañcaviṃśati, Śuka-saptati,* Śivadāsa's *Kathārṇava, Pañactantra*. In the Buddhist *Divyāvadāna*, we find the description of garden-thieves (*udyāna-moṣakas*). Of the Jain works, containing the motif of theft, notable are the *Kathāratnākara, Prabandha-cintāmaṇi, Kathā-kośa, Pariśiṣṭa-parvan, Rauhiṇeya-caritra, Samyaktva-kaumudī, Samarāditya-saṃkṣepa, Malayasundarī-kathoddhāra.*

Bilhaṇa's *Caura-pañcāśikā* is a well-known poem utilising theft or stealthy means. References to theft are found in other works too (e.g. *Ka* p. 111)

A noteworthy feature of theft, depicted in the literary works, is that, in several cases, the person committing the evil act shows a golden heart. For example, Apahāravarman robbed the rich Peter to pay the poor Paul, and tried to help the union of two loving souls. Śarvilaka takes to the nefarious means only to secure the ransom of Madanikā, his beloved.

It is interesting to note that, in certain cases, thieves have been painted in noble colour. They do not belong to the type of thieves with whom the usual odium is associated. Their end appears to have justified the means adopted by them. We shall deal with such cases in due course.

In the *Daśakumāra-carita*, the name of Apahāravarman has been ingeniously conceived. The name literally means 'one whose armour is theft'. He is the Robin Hood of Indian literature. He used to rob the rich in order to pay the poor. He was no ordinary criminal. He performed also the noble service of bringing about the union of loving souls. In the same work, Pūrṇabhadra speaks of resorting to theft due to misfortune.

In the *Mṛcchakaṭika,* Śarvilaka, though a Brahmin, resorts to theft. But it is only for securing the ransom of the slave girl, Madanikā, whom he loves and wants to marry. He has other virtues too. He is the leader of a revolution against the unpopular king.

The *Caura (or, caurī)-surata-pañcāśikā,* briefly called *Caurapañcāśikā* consists of fifty verses purported to have been recited by Bilhaṇa who, accused of clandestine union with a princess, was being led to the place of execution. It is said that the king, pleased with the charming verses, set him free. The poem is so called, according to some, after its poet named *Caura*. Others think that the word 'cora' hints at the surreptitious union of the poet with his beloved. The legend is also the theme of the Sanskrit *Vidyāsundara*. In it, we find the lover coming to his beloved through a tunnel made under the palace. The idea of a tunnel for such a purpose appears to have been borrowed from old folk tale. It occurs in the *Mahā-nimagga-jātaka* (VI, No. 546).

In this connection, it should be noted that a regular science of theft appears to have been cultivated in India since very early times. From Lalla Dīkṣita's commentary on the *Mṛcchakaṭika* (III. 14) we learn of the existence of *Caurya-śāstra* (*Steya-śāstra, Cora-Śāstra, Steya-Sūtra*); seven methods of cutting holes in walls are stated. The seven kinds of tunnels or holes are called *padma-vyākośa, bhāskara, bālacandra, vāpī, vistīrṇa, svastika, pūrṇakumbha*. Tunnels are sometimes called *khātra, chidra, suraṅga, arsandhi*. In the *Cārudatta* of Bhāsa, these are named as follows : *jhaṣāsya, gajāsya, vyāghra-vāktra, pūrṇacandra, caṇdrārdha*. In some lexicons, tunnels of the types of *śrīvatsa* and *gomukha* are mentioned. The vogue of *Caurya-Śāstra* is attested also by the tradition of Mūladeva. The name of Mūladeva may have been derived from the word *mūla* or root used in duping or hypnotising people with a view to robbing them. The name may owe its origin to *mūla-karman*[9] or root-machination or employment of roots for magical purposes. Mūladeva is variously represented as a great magician, an adept in the use of cipher, a thief's instructor, a gambler, a prince of thieves, an author of *Steya-śāstra,* an accomplished hero (*nāyaka*). He is sometimes identified with Karṇīsūta or Goṇikāputra. The Jaina chronicler, Devendra, gives in Prākrit a biography of Mūladeva. It seems that originally Mūladeva was an *arbiter elegantiae* versed in *ars amatoria.* There are literary references to Mūladeva as a good conversationalist, brilliant narrator and great musician. In course of time, a mass of legendary matters gathered around him observing his real personality and raising him to the pedestal of a deity. The legend of Karṇīsūta, alluded to by Bāṇabhaṭṭa, probably goes back to the *Bṛhatkathā*, Karṇīsuta having been regarded traditionally as the author of a manual on the art of stealing. Mūladeva Karṇīsuta, as the initiator of *caurya-śāstra*, is mentioned in other works too, e.g. the lexicon *Hārāvalī. In the Daśakumāra-carita,* Apahāravarman is said to have followed the course shown by Karṇīsuta. Besides Karṇīsuta, the other epithets of Mūladeva appear to have been *Mūlabhadra Kalāṅkura,* etc.

In Devendra's commentary on the Jaina work *Uttarādhyayana,* there is a noteworthy story of Mūladeva. There is an autobiographical account of Mūladeva in the *Kathāsarit-sāgara.*

There is mention of Mūladeva and his activities in the *Vetāla-pañcaviṃśati*. *Dhūrtapati* Mūladeva is referred to in Kṣemendra's *Kalāvilāsa*.

The formulation of a regular code on theft seems likely in view of the fact that, in ancient India, communities or guilds of thieves and robbers existed; they appear to have rallied under the tutelage of goddess Durgā. It may seem strange that, while many works on various other branches exist, those on theft are well-nigh extinct. The reason of their paucity, if not lacking, lies probably in the fact that this *Śāstra* was cultivated in the narrow circle of thieves in the secret places like dense forests far away from human society. Literary evidences testify to the fact that the wild tribes, *Bhillas, Śabaras, Pulindas, Kīrātas*, etc., living in forests like those of the Vindhya, were organised robbers. The manuscripts, relating to this shady calling, preserved in their hide-outs, were gradually consigned to oblivion.

It is interesting to observe that even *Brāhmaṇas*, in some cases, could not get over the lure of theft. *Ṛgveda* I. 164, known as *Dīrghatamas hymn*, is regarded by some as essential for recitation by a *Brāhmaṇa* desiring to atone for the sin resulting from the theft of gold. Śarvilaka of the *Mṛcchakaṭika*, referred to above and Mātaṅga of the *Daśakumāra-carita* are *Brāhmaṇa* thieves.

In the *Daśakumāra-carita,* there is mention of an appliance, called *phaṇimukha* or *uragāsya* (resembling a serpent's face), for digging a tunnel. It was, perhaps, a sort of spade. In this and some other works, there is mention of underground tunnels.

In the aforesaid *Mṛcchakaṭika* (III. 12, 16 etc.) there are some references to certain interesting matters relating to theft. There is reference to the examination of a tunnel. There is provision for precaution against serpents in a tunnel. In this works, as well as in the *Cārudatta* of Bhāsa, there is mention of the practice of entering a dummy man (*pratipuruṣa*) through a tunnel in order to ascertain whether or not there is any danger at the other end of the tunnel in the room. In the *Cārudatta* and the *Daśakumāra-carita* there is reference to the musical instrument, called *kākalī,* which gives out a mild sound; it appears to have been played to test whether or not somebody within the house was awake. A thief appears to have carried a box containing moths or bees; these were let loose to put out the lights inside the house. It is stated that coughing by a thief is dangerous.

In the *Daśakumāra, Mṛcchakaṭika, Kathāsarit-sāgara* etc., the following appurtenances of a thief are referred to :

saṃdaṃśanikā (tongs), *karkaṭa-rajju* (rope resembling a crab or with a crab tied to it), *dīpa-bhājana* (blīnd lantern), *yoga-cūrṇa* (magic powder), *yoga-vartikā* (magic wick) etc.

The last one was, perhaps, used just as a lamp or for making others blind. *Yoga-cūrṇa* or *Yoga-rocanā* was used for making the thief himself invisible to others. A kind of collyrium appears to have been applied for making one look at a dark night like one dazzling with a crore of suns. The following *mantras* or charms are referred to : *Avasvapnikā* for inducing sleep; *Tālodghāṭinīvidyā* for breaking locks.

In the work, *Samarāditya-śaṃkṣepa*(VI. 114) the teacher, named Skandarudra, is described as teaching theft to his pupil, Caṇḍarudra. The teacher gives him a pill which, if applied over the eyes, can render a person invisible even to gods. In the same work (IV. 128 etc.), a teacher is found to instruct his pupil as to how to break locks.

The *Ṣanmukha-kalpa* is the only notable work on this *Śāstra* discovered so far. There is another work, called *Caura-caryā*, in manuscript (in Bhandarkar Oriental Res. Institute, Poona). Ṣanmukha or Kārtikeya is traditionally associated with the art of stealing[10]. *Sarabhū* (born in thickets), as an epithet of this deity is perhaps significant; it may hint at the genesis of this *Śāstra* among thieves whose haunts were the forests. According to mythology, Kārtikeya rent asunder the Krauñca mountain. Was this the reason why he was associated with thieves who used to make holes or tunnels into the hard walls or plinths ? This deity is supposed to be the custodian of the arms and ammunition of divine forces. This is also significant; thieves use various kinds of implements and weapons. This work contains details about how persons to be robbed can be made unaware of the mischief done to them, how thieves can make themselves invisible or walk over marshy lands. It contains also magic spells and formulae for *vaśīkaraṇa*(bringing others under control). Other topics, dealt with in it, are the opening of doors, rendering people incapable of seeing, release from confinement, cutting holes in walls, etc.

It is interesting to note that Sanskrit literature describes theft of not only material objects but also that of ideas and expressions from literary compositions. Plagiarists have been referred to at many places often with a spirit of condemnation. The *Sadukti-karṇāmṛta* quotes several verses on this subject. The poet Jalacandra, quoted in it, denounces those poetasters (*kavikhalas*) who indulge in the art of poetry, though devoid of the necessary equipment (*niḥsvavilāsins)* who, living by milching others' cows (*paragavī-dohena*)[11], have always a trembling heart[12]. Vaidya Gadādhara deprecates theft in the repository of the felicitous expressions of good poets as a sin difficult to expiate; it is indeed graver than the sin accruing from the following offences – theft of gold, adultery with the preceptor's wife, drinking of wine, turning to be a renegade, association of those who committed the above sins[13]. Poet Selhuka expresses concern having no means of protecting the cow (i.e. speech or poetical composition) from cow-stealers (i.e. plagiarists)[14]. Jitari gives vent to a sense of fear from wicked people in respect of poetical compositions[15].

Prison and Prisoner

Kauṭilya provides (II. 5) that prison should be located in the capital, separate places for men and women should be provided in it, and the entrance should be guarded carefully.

Manu is of the opinon that a prison should be near the highway (IX. 288). The idea is that people will see the hardship to which offenders are subjected; this will serve as a deterrent.

There are references[16] to the grant of amnesty of prisoners on certain happy or auspicious occasions, e.g. coronation, conquest of a new kingdom, birth of a son, king's birth anniversary, full moon day, etc. The *Bṛhatsaṃhita*, however, forbids the release of prisoners on any occasion if they are accused of an offence against the person of the king or the royal harem. According to Manu, forgiveness is forbidden in violent crimes like homicide. From the *Harṣacarita* we learn that a prisoner had long beard, and his body was covered with dust etc. .

Kauṭilya holds (II. 36) that the prisoners of the following types only should be released on special occasions : of tender or very old age, sick, helpless, one who has paid the prescribed fine or has furnished a written bond to do so.

All criminals, however, do not deserve forgiveness. Manu and Viṣṇu hold that, if the king forgives an offender, who is not repentant or commits crime repeatedly, the sin of the offender will taint him.

From some edicts[17] it appears that the king gave three days' time to a criminal sentenced to death. It is stated that, within twenty-six years, he granted amnesty twenty-five times.

Police System

From the *Manusmṛti* (VII. 114) we learn that a sort of police outpost (*gulma*) used to be vigilant against wrong-doers.

The term *Coragrāha* (e.g. *Nāradas-smṛti*, Supplementary verse 18) seems to denote an officer for catching thieves. *Corarajjuka* (e.g. *Arthaśāstra,* 4.13) was perhaps an officer whose duty it was to get a thief bound by a rope.

The word *Cauroddharaṇika*, meaning one who arrests a thief or eradicates him, occurs in some insriptions[18]. Perhaps synonymous with the above word is *coroddhartā* (*Yājñavalkya-smṛti*, II. 271).

Sthānapāla (Yājñavalkya, II. 173) appears to have been an officer engaged is guarding a specified place and finding out lost articles.

Dāṇḍika[19] was perhaps a high police official.

Daṇḍanāyaka(*Rājataraṅgiṇī*, VII. 951) is taken by some to denote the Police Chief.

According to Kane, *Dauhsādha-sādhanika*[20], *Dauḥsādhika*[21], *Mahā-dauḥsādha-sādhanika*[22] etc. refer to a man who used to arrest terrible robbers whose arrest was a difficult task.

Piśunavetrika[23] was perhaps a royal officer meant for chasing away undesirable elements with a cane.

Nāgarika (*Vikramorvaśīya* V, after verse 4; *Daśakumāra-carita*, II, pp., 58, 59-Bombay) denote Police Chief, according to some, the head of prisons according to others.

From the *Āpastamba-dharmasūtra* (II. 10.26, 6-8) we learn that an officer used to see that theft was not committed within a specified area.

The term *ārakṣaka*, occurring in the *Pañcatantra, Daśakumāra-carita* etc., probably refers to a guard or Police Magistrate.

In the *Mīakṣarā* commentary on the *Yājñavakya-smṛti* (II. 1.5) it is stated that complaints are of two kinds, *viz. śaṃkābhiyoga* (based on suspicion) and *tatlvābhiyoga* (based on fact).

According to the *Arthaśāstra* (4.6.2) arrests are of three kinds, *viz*.

Śaṃkābhigraha –	arrest on suspicion of theft, murder, adultery caused by extravagance, excessive addiction to wine and women, gambling, secret treatment of physical wounds, clandestine movement at night, etc.
Rūpābhigraha –	arrest of a person found in possession of stolen articles. If he can prove acquisition by purchase and the like, he is released.
Karmābhigraha –	arrest on *prima facie* evidence.

As in modern times, preventive detention prevailed. The following are some of the people who were kept confined without trial for prevention of crimes :

1. An unemployed person
2. Men and women gone astray
3. Drunkards
4. One engaged in clandestine sale or purchase of articles
5. One engaged in clandestine trade
6. A habitual offender.

Middle Indo-Aryan Literature

The *Cullavagga* of the *Khandhakas* state four kinds of legal matters requiring settlement. These are (1) dispute, (2) censure, (3) offence, (4) business. Thus, these four appear to have been common in the society.

Persons of eminent qualities were appointed on the jury. Disputes were settled by voting of which there appears to have been three systems—open, secret and whispering. If it was ascertained beforehand that those, whose opinion was in accordance with *dhamma*, were in the majority, voting was to be open. This was the first method. There were voting tickets of different colours, each colour representing a man of a particular opinion. If the polling officer found that those, whose opinion was against *dhamma*, were in the majority he would reject the votes. This was the second method. The polling officer was to whisper into the ear of each member of the jury as to which ticket represented what opinion. If it was found that those, whose opinion was against *dhamma*, were in the majority, the votes were to be rejected. This was the third method.

Adultery appears to have been very common in the society. The *pañcaśīla,* taught by the Buddha, includes it among the practices to be abjured. There is repreated mention of it in the scriptures as well as poetical works. From the *Bhikkhunīvibhaṅga Saṅghādisesa*, II, *Vinayapiṭaka*, IV, p. 225, we learn that women, accused of adultery, could escape punishment by entering the Order. But, when within the Order, they were strictly forbidden to associate with householders. For adultery a woman's nose and ears were cut off (*Cullapadma-jātaka* 193). The *Grāmaṇīcaṇda 57 and Kuṇāla (536) Jātakas* refer to the practice of getting such women devoured by dogs.

Section I of the *Bhikkhu Pātimokkha* mentions misconduct with women among the offences the punishment for which was expulsion from the Order. *Saṅghādhisesa,* section II, deals with thirteen offences the first five of which relate to sex matters. The prevention of adultery was obviously the object of the prohibition contained in the *Bhikkhunī Pātimokkha* (section II), that men should not intimately associate with householders.

Adultery is mentioned, in the *Mahādukkha khandhu Sutta* (*Majjhima Nikāya*, I, 83-90) among punishable offences.

In the *Dhammikasutta,* improper sexual intercourse is forbidden.

A glaring example of adultery was the birth of Vimala-kondañña, the illegitimate son of king Bimbisāra by the well-known courtesan, Ambapālī.

The *GS* testifies (IV. 60) to the fact that even a woman of a high caste had illicit connection with a vile person.

The *JC* (II.8) states that a queen was found dallying with a hump-backed man. Illicit sexual relation is referred to at some other places, e.g. *JC* II. 7,9 etc.

Some verses of the *GS* refer to illicit sexual relation between a man and his brother's wife. Verse I. 28 refers to a person striking certain limbs of his brother's wife with a creeper. Offensive conduct of a man towards his sister-in-law is hinted at in II. 59. In I. 35 the sister-in-law is exhorting her brother-in-law on pure conduct. Verse VII. 88 refers to the coaxing words of a person to his brother's wife. There is mention also of the unbecoming behaviour of a person relating to his sister-in-law.

The *GS* (III. 37) refers to *jāra-vaidya*, i.e. a physician having illicit connection with a female patient.

Abduction of women, particularly in forest regions, is referred to at certain places (e.g. *GS* II. 18).

Severe strictures appear to have been passed on a person if he was instrumental in the death of his wife (*GS* II. 78).

Robbery appears to have been a common crime. The *Dhammapada* mentions (IX. 8) highway robbery to which wealthy and ill-attended merchants fell victims.

The *Bhikkhu-pātimokkha,* section I, mentions robbery among offences for which the punishment was expulsion from the Order.

Theft appears to have prevailed widely. The *Bhikkhu Pātimokkha,* section I, includes it among offences for which the punishment was expulsion from the Order. Theft is prohibited in the *Sāriputtasutta.* In the story of Thera Revata in the *Theragāthā* commentary of Dhammapāla, we find that a receiver of stolen property was guilty of crime.

Among the punishable offences, mentioned in the *Mahādukkhakhandha Sutta (Majjhima,* I, pp. 83-90) are the following : burglary, robbery, adultery, etc. The modes of punishment are as follows : flogging, bastinado, bludgeoning, cutting off hands, feet, ears, nose, torture of the sauce-pan[24], chauk-shaver, the lanthorn,[25] wreath of fire,[26] fiery hand, hay-band,[27] bark-robe, black hart,[28] meat-hook,[29] pennies,[30] pickle,[31] bolting the door[32] or the palliasse,[32] spraying with boiling oil, throwing before starving dogs, impaling alive, chopping off the head.

Sedition was punishable (*GS* IV. 96). Quarrel appears to have been a common occurrence in the society. According to the *Cullavagga,* it is an offence calling for reprimand. Section II of the *Bhikkhunī-pātimokkha* (under Saṅghādisesa) deals with quarrelsome nuns. Disputes in an association appear to have been settled by votes (*Sunīla* 163, *Kasāya-Jātaka* 221).

Among the thirteen offences, dealt with in section II of the *bhikkhu-pātimokkha* (Saṅghādisesa), the eighth and ninth ones relate to false accusations.

Murder is referred to in the *Bhikkhu-pātimokkha,* Section I. From the *GS* (I. 29) it appears that if a person was sentenced to death, it was proclaimed by beat of drums.

Abortion appears to have been practised, sometimes with impunity. The *Brahamajāla-sutta* (*Dīgha*, I, pp. 1-46) mentions various charms one of which was meant for causing abortion. Sometimes it was caused by medicine (*Dhammapada Commentary,* I, pp. 45 f.f.). In the *Dhammapada Commentary* (Vol. I, pp. 45 f.f.) it is stated that a man beat his wife to death for causing the abortion of her co-wife and her eventual death. It is not clear whether such an action of the husband was culpable or not.

The following appear to have been some of the punishable offences committed by the people (*Sammāṭṭhi Sutta, Majjhima,* I, pp. 46-55) : killing, theft, sex indulgence.

The *Dhammika Sutta* of the *Sutta Nipāta* asks people to abjure the following offences : killing, abetment of murder, stealing, approval of theft, illicit sexual relation.

The *Kaṭāhaka Jātaka*, Vol. I, testifies to the practice of forgery.

The *Dhammapada Commentary* (Vol. I, pp. 208 ff.) refers to pilfering by maid servants.

The imposition of fines appears to have been a mode of punishment for comparatively light offences. King Bimbisāra is stated to have proclaimed the imposition of eight pieces of money on those who would, contrary to the royal order, refuse to see the dead body of Sirimā, a courtesan of exquisite beauty. The idea behind the proclamation was to impress upon the people, the transitoriness of human life, physical beauty etc.

Drinking appears to have been widespread. Perhaps it was why the Buddha included the prohibition of intoxicants among the *pañcaśīla*. Drinking was a part of merriment on festive occasions (*Jātaka* I, p. 489). The strong denunciation of this practice in the *Dhammapada* (XVIII. 13) seems to point to its wide prevalence. The *Dhammapada Commentary* (III, pp. 129 f.f.) refers to a rich man losing his wealth due to this vice. Even women used to drink wine. The *GS* VI. 44 refers to young girls drinking in spring festivals. Lovers sometimes used to appease the anger of their beloved by making them drink wine (III. 70). Verse II. 97 hints at the great fondness for old wine. Verse III. 27 mentions *pānakuṭī* or bar for providing wine.

Drinking is referred to in the *Karpūramañjarī* (e.g. I. p. 19, III. 14, IV. 6).

Gambling appears to have been a popular vice. The *Dhammapada Commentary* (III, pp. 129 f.f.) refers to a rich man losing his wealth due to addiction to it. The *Karpūramañjarī* refers to it (I. p. 20); it appears that evil women used to frequent gambling houses.

Besides drinking (IX. 21), the *KKC*. refers (I. 17) to theft and adultery. At one place (I. 5), there is reference to the son of an unmarried girl.

The *Bhk* (III. 21) refers to the existence of a large number of mischievous people like tale-bearers.

About prostitution in the society we have written under Economic life.

A good deal of information about vices, crimes and modes of punishment is available in the *Jātakas*. The *TANJ* refers to bribery. Theft is referred to at several places (e.g. *MAJ, LOJ, MVJ* etc.). Murder is mentioned in *MAJ, KLJ* etc. The *KLJ* mentions dacoity. Robbery and holding people as hostages are referred to at certain places (e.g. *VEJ, MUJ, ASJ, Śaṃkhadhara-jātaka, Vai J*). We are told that robbery was committed on highways and in forests. Sometimes the robbers confined people who were released on payment of ranson. Travellers are stated to have been tied up; sometimes one who was tied at the feet with ropes was kept hanging with head downwards. Adultery is referred to in *MVJ*. At one place (*PPJ*) there is reference to the practice of rendering a person unconscious by making him drink poisoned wine. The *Samudravāṇija-jātaka* states that carpenters, even after receiving advance payment, abstained from work. Repeated attempts to persuade them failed.

Certain criminals like dacoits were punished by getting them trampled by elephants (*KLJ*). Some offenders like hypocritical ascetics were whipped at the crossing of four roads (*SKJ*). Impaling appears to have been a mode of punishing thieves (*PRJ*). There was the practice of tying the hands of an offender at his back (*BMJ*). Fines are stated to have been a good source of income (*KLJ*). A fine of eight *Kāhaṇas* was prescribed for abusing people without any reason (*UBJ*).

REFERENCES

1. The following are *ātatāyins:* one who sets fire to another's house, administers poison, comes to attack with a deadly weapon, causes loss of money in such a manner as to starve another, misappropriates another's land, carries away another's wife.
2. See Manu, IX. 256 f.f.; Yājñavalkya, II. 18-20, 23, 24, 25.
3. For example, a clod of earth represented as a fragrant myrobalan by

infusing into it the fragrance of *Mallikā* flowers; a cat's hide is shown as tiger-skin after a finish with colour, a crystal represented as a ruby after changing its colour; cotton thread made by artificial means to look like silk thread; iron made to look like silver by changing its colour; a piece of *Bel* wood represented as sandal wood after imparting the fragrance of sandal to the former; cubebs sold as a sort of cloves; cotton cloth made to appear as silken.

4. See M. Bloomfield : Art of Stealing in Hindu Fiction, *American Journal of Philology,* XLIV, 1923.
   Character and Adventures of Muladeva, *Pro. of American Philosophical Soc.*, III, 1913.
   L.H. Gray : *WZKM,* XVIII, 1904
   J.J. Meyer : Trs. of *Daśakumāracarita* (Intro.)
   Ṣaṇmukhakalpa; ed. George, Marburg, 1966.
   S.C. Banerji : *Aspects of Ancient Indian Life*, Calcutta.
5. See *IHQ,* VIII, 857.
6. Vide *Daśakumāra-carita*, Kale's ed., p. 22.
7. Kielhorn's ed., II. 419.
8. Vide *Manu-smṛti*, ix, 290.
9. It may be noted that in, the *Atharvaveda* (*Pariśiṣṭa* XX), there is a ritual called *Skandayāga* or *Dhūrta-kalpa.* Thus, Skanda (or Kārtikeya) already figures as deceitful.
10. The word '*go*' means also a cow. We have a pun here.
11. V. 2166.
12. V. 2168 In *Smṛti-śāstra*, the following sins are classed as *Mahāpātaka* (grave sins): Killing a *Brahmaṇa*, drinking of *sura* (some kinds of wine) by the twice-born, theft of gold belonging to a *Brahmaṇa*, adultery with one's preceptor's wife, association with those who have committed any of the above sins.
13. V. 2169.
14. V. 2170.
15. e.g. *Mālavikāgnimitra* (IV. portion following V. 5), *Raghuvaṃśa* (XVII. 19), *Mṛcchakaṭika* (X), *Harṣacarita* (II, para 2; IV), *Kathaśāstra* (II. 36)
16. e.g. Delhi Topra Pillar Edict (*Corpus* I. 1, Vol. I, pp. 126-128 and E.I., Vol. II, pp. 258-59).
17. e.g. Gupta Inscription No. 46, p. 213, p., 216, Valabhi Grant of Dharasena II (Gupta era 252, 1. A., 15, p. 187 etc.
18. e.g. Gupta Inscriptions No. 46, p. 213 (p. 216).
    Bhāgalpur plate of Nārāyaṇapāta (1. A. 15, pp. 304, 306).
19. Bonskhera plate of of Harṣa (E.l., IV, p. 208, p. 271. Sevadi plates of Cāhamāna Ratnapāla, Saṃrat 1176 (E.l. XI, p. 310).
20. Lakṣmaṇasena's Grant (1122 A.D. E.l. XII., pp. 9, 306. Devapāla's Nālande plate, E.l., XI, p. 139, p., 141.
21. Nārāyaṇapāla's plate, 1.A. 15, pp. 304, 306.
22. Mahābhavagupta I's plate. E.l. pp. 93-94.
23. The skull is at first trepanned and a red hot iron ball dropped in so that the brains boil like porridge.
24. The mouth is fixed open and a lighted lamp thrust within.

25. The whole body, smeared with oil, is set ablaze.
26. From the neck downwards the skin is flayed into strips not severed at the ankles but there plaited like a hay-band to suspend the person till he falls down by his own weight.
27. The accused is fixed to the ground through elbows and knees with fire all around so as to char the flesh.
28. The accused is hung up with double hooks through flesh and tendons.
29. The flesh of body is shaved off with a razor.
30. Into gashes salt or alkali is rubbed with combs.
31. The head is nailed to the ground by a skewer passed through both the ear holes.
32. The skin is left intact and the bones are pounded till the whole body becomes soft like a straw mattress.

14

LEGAL SYSTEM

THE legal system reflects the outlook of the intelligentsia of the country concerned, and is an index to the degree of civilisation and culture attained by the people of the land. Law, in ancient India, was of two kinds, religious and secular. We are concerned here with the latter. It is not possible to deal here exhaustively with the legal system of ancient India. So, we shall give an outline for the general reader.

In ancient India, crime and sin were not clearly distinguished in the sense that the former is an offence against the state, and the latter is violation of certain ethical precepts and is an offence against God. Criminals also had to undergo expiation besides facing trial in a court of justice. For example, the murderer of a *Brāhmaṇa* was liable to both expiation and trial.

Titles of Law

The titles of law were generally eighteen, though some authorities added a few more. These were, according to *Manu*, (VIII. 4-7) non-repayment of debt, deposit, sale of an article by one other than its owner, partnership business, resumption of gift, non-payment of wages, breach of contract, repentance after sale or purchase, dispute between the master and the keeper (of cattle), boundary dispute, abuse, too severe punishment, theft, violence, adultery (including incest, rape), duties of wife and husband, partition of inheritance, gambling and animal betting.

Procedural Law

The procedural law was briefly as follows (*Yājñavalkya,* II.1, 2). A cause of action arises when a person, being harassed in a way contrary to the rules of *Smṛti* and usage, lodges a complaint. The judicial proceedings usually consist of four parts, *viz*. plaint, reply, evidence and judgement. Replies may be of four kinds, *viz*. admission, denial, demurrer or a special plea, relating to a former judgement (*res judicata*). Evidence is of three kinds, *viz*. document, possession and witness. In the absence of these human proofs, divine ones or ordeals are prescribed.

General Principles

Some general principles in connection with judicial proceedings are as follows : In case of conflict between two texts of *Smṛti*, equity according to usage is to be followed. In the event of conflict between a text of *Smṛti* relating to *dharma* and one relating to *artha,* the former prevails. The former prescribes rules regarding things unseen or otherworldly, while the latter is concerned with mundane matters.

An accused is ordinarily debarred from lodging a counter-complaint so long as the case against himself is not disposed of. In case of violent crimes, however, such a counter-complaint is allowed. Sureties are allowed.

Adverse Possession

Adverse possession confers right to the possessor if the owner who, even while seeing his property adversely possessed, does not raise any objection. An immovable property vests in the person adversely possessing it for twelve years without any objection from the owner. In the case of movables, the period is ten years. This rule does not apply to mortgage, boundary, deposit, and properties belonging to an idiot, minor, king, woman and a *Brahmin* possessed of *Vedic* learning.

Modes of Acquisition

The valid modes of acquisition of a property are purchase, gift etc.. Generally acquisition, by a valid mode, is a stronger evidence than possession. But, continuous possession for three generations is stronger than acquisition by lawful means. Acquisition, without even slight possession, is not valid.

In the matter of a legal transaction of royal officers, corporation of men belonging to different castes and different avocations, but living at the same place, an association of people of the same caste or different castes earning livelihood by the same kind of work and a group of relatives, cognates and people of the same caste, each preceding is stronger than the succeeding one.

Witness

Generally pious people are fit for being witnesses. Anybody, however, can be a witness if he is selected by both the parties. Perjury and suppression of evidence are punishable offences. But, when a true statement is likely to lead to the death of a member of a caste, a witness is allowed to give false evidence; for the expiation of the sin thus incurred he has to undergo slight expiation.

If there is conflicting evidence, given by witnesses, that of the majority is acceptable. In the case of two conflicting groups consisting of an equal number of witnesses, the evidence of the one containing more qualified persons is acceptable. If two groups of qualified witnesses differ, the evidence of those, who are most qualified, is to be accepted.

Mortgage

A mortgage vests in the mortgagee if it is not redeemed even after the principal amount is doubled. A mortgage, with a time-limit, lapses after the expiry of that time. A usufructuary mortgage is never lost. A mortgage is of two kinds, *gopya* (to be protected) and *bhogya* (to be enjoyed).

As regards partition and inheritance, there are two schools, *viz.* *Mitākṣarā* and *Dāyabhāga*. Their fundamental difference relates to a son's right to ancestral property. According to the former, a son acquires, at his very birth, rights equal to that of his father. According to the latter, the son acquires right either when the father gives him a share or after the death of the parents.

The mother's exclusive property, called *strī-dhana*, devolves upon the heirs in the following order: unmarried daughter, married but poor daughter, married and rich daughter.

One, earning something without using paternal property need not share it with others.

Among sons of different persons, the partition of ancestral property will be *per stirps*, and not per capita. For example, x, y, z have one, two and three sons respectively. In such a case, the property will be divided at first into three equal parts. The sons will share it as follows: 1/3, (1/6 + 1/6), (1/9 + 1/9 + 1/9).

Contracts, customary or written, had a sanctity. Their violation called for legal action.

Regarding partnership business, the general rule was that the profit and loss would be shared in proportion to the money invested by the partners, or in accordance with the contract, if any.

If any partner is crooked or fraudulent, others may expel him without giving him any profit (*YS*. II. 265).

In the case of artisans, working jointly, the directors of new methods are entitled to four shares, experts three shares, those who have studied the craft two shares and the apprentices one share (*Kātyāyana*, 632).

Heavy punishment was prescribed for distorting a balance, false weights and measures and for forging coins.

One, falsely posing as a physician, was heavily fined.

Crimes

Some other culpable offences were adulteration of medicine, oil, salt, rice, molasses, attempt to present jewels, metals, cloth etc. of small value as of high value, forcible sexual union with one's female slaves, refusal by prostitute to have sexual intercourse with a man who paid for it, sexual intercourse with animals, homosexuality, sexual enjoyment in parts of a woman's body like the mouth, sexual connection with a female mendicant.

Now we come to crimes. As regards murder, some authorities hold the following as murderers : one actually committing it, the instigator, one who approves it, helper and abettor, one who is chiefly instrumental. *Mens rea* or criminal motive plays a great part in the determination of the degree of punishment. Heavier punishment is prescribed for murder with intention than that without intention.

Punishable Suicide

Suicide is generally condemned. But, in certain cases, it is allowed by some authorities. For example, in the *Aparārka* commentary on the *Yājñavalkya-smṛti*, it is held, on the authority of Gārgya and others, that the following persons are allowed to put an end to their lives by entering into water or fire or falling from a precipice : One, attacked with a fatal malady, too old a person, one devoid of desires of the senses, one who has finished all the duties. For such an action the person incurs no sin; rather it is better than penance, because his life is useless. The *Parāśaramādhava* (I. pt. II. p. 228) also approves this practice on the authority of the *Agnipurāṇa*. According to Manu (VI. 31) and Yājñavalkya (III. 55), a *vānaprastha*, if a victim of an incurable disease or unable to perform his duties, is allowed to resort to this practice.

Permitted Suicide

The permission to court death under such circumstances reminds one of the mercy-killing advocated by some moderns in western countries.

In course of time, this practice came to be categorically prohibited. For example, the *Bṛhannāradīya-purāṇa* (*Pūrvārdha*, chap. 24.16) includes self-killing among *Kalivarjyas* or practices forbidden in the Kali Age. In the *Śuddhī tattva* (pp. 284.85, Jīvānanda's ed.), Raghunandana says that suicide by entering water etc. is prescribed only for *Śūdras*, and not for the three higher castes.

Post-mortem Examination

The *Arthaśāstra* (IV) provides for such examination in the case of *āśumṛtaka* or accidental death. Such a death aroused suspicion about suicide or murder.

In adultery, a forcible act takes place when there is enjoyment of a woman in a lonely spot against her will or when she is intoxicated, or when she shouts. Cheating a woman takes place when a passionate man brings a woman to his house by a ruse or overpowering her by *Dhattura*, etc.

Abuse consists in using filthy language to a person causing his sorrow or insult by loudly speaking ill of his country, caste, family etc. According to *Nārada* (18.2-3), abuse is of three kinds, *viz. niṣṭhura* (e.g. calling one a fool or rogue), *aślīla* (an utterance indicating bad taste or disgrace), *tīvra* (e.g. abusing a person as a murderer of a *Brāhmaṇa*).

Sedition, incitement to it, defalcation of government funds—these were the common offences to the state. Among other offences were obstruction to revenue-realisation, use of government property for self-interest, removal of things from mines or factories. Dishonesty of a judge or administrator, misconduct of the Chief of prisons, etc. are also mentioned. According to *Kauṭilya* (I. 14.25), the following classes of people are prone to sedition: *Kruddha* (angry), *Bhītā* (terrified), *Lubdha* (greedy) and *Mānī* (self-conceited).

Kauṭilya mentions a class of offenders called *Gūḍhājīva*. Their livelihood is clandestine. Among them are top-ranking officers and superintendents of departments. They can use their high position for selfish ends.

Witch-hunting was in vogue. According to *Kauṭilya* (4.4), women, who wanted to bring about clandestine love by magical charms, were guilty. It may be noted that, in England, up to the earlier half of the eighteenth century, some unfortunate old women were regarded as witches, and were punished and even hanged to death.[1]

According to *Manu* (IX. 290), use of charm or magic for causing harm to others is punishable.

Punishment

The main principle, underlying the award of punishment, was deterrent. The law-makers believed that punishment should cause horror not only to the offender, but also in the mind of the spectators so that they would not dare commit such an act. According to *Manu* (VII. 22), it is due to the fear of Daṇḍa (rod, punishment) that all the world becomes enjoyable. It was to create a sense of horror among the people that it was customary for the executioners to proclaim, by beat of drums, the fact that a criminal, sentenced to death, was being led to the place of execution.

Another purpose of punishment was to restrain the offender. The idea was that if an offender was kept confined, he would desist from anti-social activities at least for sometime. Banishment also serves this purpose.

Reformation of the offender was not ignored. The object of sublimating the instinct of an offender is clear in the modes of expiation prescribed for certain criminals besides physical punishment. The word *prāyascitta* means the performance of penance with the certain knowledge of washing off sin.

In the matter of punishment, the principle of *lex talionis* or retaliation is noticeable in the penal provisions of almost all ancient civilised countries. An eye for an eye, a tooth for a tooth

—this was the principle. This attitude is obvious in Hammurabi's *Code of Babylon* (c. 2200 B.C.), the *Twelve Tables* (table VIII) of Rome and in the ancient Hebrew Law, etc. *Manu* (VIII. 280), *Nārada* (*Pāruṣya*, V. 25), *Yājñavalkya* (II. 215) etc. provide that a low-caste offender, committing a physical offence to a *Brāhmaṇa,* shall have the very limb, with which the offence was committed, cut off.

Before inflicting punishment, the following factors were to be considered : the time and place of occurrence, the motive, capacity, learning, age, sex, caste, etc. of the offender. Also to be considered were the things involved, the extent of loss, the gravity of the injury, monetary value of the loss, etc.

In the present-day Criminology, there are generally two opinions about the reason behind the commission of crimes. According to one, the full responsibility of a criminal rests on himself. According to another, the reasons underlying crimes are many; e.g. physical, biological, social conditions, the mental state of the offender, his upbringing, environment, etc. The law-makers of ancient India do not appear to have paid much attention to these factors. Kauṭilya, however, lays stress on the circumstances under which a crime is committed, Medhātithi's commentary on *Manu*, and Vijñāneśvara's on *Yājñavalkya* hold that, in all cases, the same punishment should not be inflicted for a particular offence.

The modes of punishment can be divided into two classes, *viz.* physical and monetary. Physical punishments were as follows :

Caning, cutting of limbs, confinement, chaining, torture, capital punishment, killing by poison, trampling by an elephant, hitting with a sharp weapon, burning, drowning, impalement.

In the Buddhist literature, the following additional methods of physical punishment are stated :

flogging, bastinado, bludgeoning, chaukshave or the lanthorn, hay-band.

Death Penalty

As regards death penalty, there was difference of opinion. According to some, it should be inflicted whenever the law requires it. Others opine that it should not be ordained even in the case of the gravest offence excepting rebellion against the king (*Kāmandaka* 14.16, *Śukra* 4.1.93). Yet others think that death penalty should never be inflicted. According to *Manu* (IX. 236), death penalty should be inflicted only when the offender does not perform the prescribed expiation.

In a dialogue in the *Mahābhārata* (*Śānti*, chap. 268), a prince pleads for light punishment even for grave offences. He says that, if a criminal surrenders himself and swears that he will not repeat the crime, he should be let off after expiation. He further argues that if criminals like robbers are put to death, the innocent members of his family are subjected to great hardship. His father, however, is of the opinion that people, in the earlier age, were truthful and polite. The simple utterance of 'fie' would make an offender retrace his steps, but, in the Kali Age, offenders are not deterred even by the fear of death.

Torture is prescribed for extracting confession if there is a *prima facie* case.

The methods of torture were usually four, *viz*. beating with a stick for six times, seven lashes, hanging in two ways and pushing saline water into the nostrils with a pipe. Kauṭilya mentions the following :

> getting the offender stung by scorpions, burning his finger-joints. If necessary, torture to death is also prescribed (4.4.8).

Among various methods, the Pāli literature mentions the sauce-pan torture.[2]

It may be noted that torture has been in vogue in western countries from the time of ancient Rome down to the present day.

Fines of varying amounts were prescribed for different kinds of criminals. Depending on the degree of the offences fines ranged from a trifling amount to one's all the belongings.

According to *Manu* (IV. 129) and *Yājñavalkya* (1.367), mild reproof and harsh reprimand are also modes of punishment.

Other methods included disgrace of the offender by any of the following means :

Shaving the head, proclaiming the offender's crime by beat of drums, taking the criminal round on an ass, branding the criminal with marks indicating theft, adultery, etc.

A historical study of the penal provisions in ancient India reveals a gradual relaxation of the severity of punishments through ages.

Fa-hien (stay in India 401-410) testifies to the absence of

capital punishment. How far his testimony accords with fact we do not know.

Concession in Punishment

According to *Kātyāyana* (832-34) and *Bṛhaspati* (*SRE*, p. 364, verse 32), the following accused shall be punished in accordance with their capacity and the gravity of their offences :

> One who starts a violent act, abettor, one who determines the *modus operandi*, one who incites offenders to fight or beat, etc.

Mens rea or the criminal motive plays a great role. For example, one, committing murder with knowledge and criminal intent, will be liable to homicide. But, one unwittingly doing so will be liable to culpable homicide not amounting to murder. For example, a man throws a stone at another to scare him away. But, the stone strikes a vital organ of the other man causing his death. In such a case, it will be an offence of the latter kind.

Generally, half the extent of torture for men is prescribed for women.

According to *Kātyāyana* (487), in the case of an offence, for which death-penalty was prescribed, a woman had her limb concerned cut off.

Some *Smṛti* writers hold that, instead of corporal punishment, the following punishments may be inflicted on a *Brāhmaṇa* :

> Confinement in a secret place, giving food just enough for subsistence, rearing of cows and other kinds of work not befitting a *Brāhmaṇa*.

Discriminatory Punishment

According to *Kātyāyana* (786), there will be difference in punishment according to the difference of castes. The lower the caste of an offender, the lesser is the degree of punishment. According to *Manu* (VIII. 286), the degree of punishment will vary in accordance with the social status of the injured person and the nature of the injury.

In case of murder, the gravest offence is the murder of a *Brāhmaṇa*. *Brāhmaṇa*-murder is a grave sin. But, the murder of a person of a lower caste by a *Brāhmaṇa* is a minor offence.

Though adultery is generally punishable, yet, according to *Manu* (VIII. 365), a maiden has no fault for having sexual union with a man of a highter caste. But, union with a man of a lower caste is an offence.

Exemptions from Punishment

According to *Yājñavalkya* (II. 214), no offender should be punished for *daṇḍapāruṣya* if he acts through ignorance or under the influence of liquor. But, Kauṭilya provides for half the usual punishment in such cases.

The *Śāstras* exempt a person murdering an *ātatāyin* in self-defence. *Ātatāyins* are the following: one who sets fire to one's house, administers poison, comes to attack with a lethal weapon, steals money so as to cause starvation to the owner, misappropriates another's land, abducts another's wife.

There is difference of opinion about the murder of a *Brāhmaṇa ātatāyin*. According to some (e.g. *Manu* VIII. 350-1, *Matsyapurāṇa* 229. 115-17), an *ātatāyin*, even if versed in the *Veda*, may be killed with impunity. But, some (e.g. Sumantu quoted in the *Mitākṣarā* on *Yājñavalkya* II.21, Kātyāyana quoted in the *Smṛticandrikā*, Vyavahāra, p. 315) hold that a *Brāhmaṇa*, even though an *ātatāyin*, cannot be killed.

In the *Gītā*, Arjuna, perplexed at the sight of near and dear ones on the opposite side, is reluctant to fight as he does not want to incur sin by killing those *ātatāyins*. It is difficult to reconcile this with the above rule about the murder of an *ātatāyin*. Some hold that it is merely a literary statement, and is not in conformity with *Smṛtiśāstra*. In this connection, it may be pointed out that elsewhere in the epic itself (*Śānti* 22.5-6; 34. 17, 19; *Udyoga* 178.51-52), exemption is provided for the offender in the murder of an *ātatāyin* even if he is a *Brāhmaṇa*.

According to some authorities (e.g. *Yājñavalkya* II. 288), there is no fault of a man in enjoying a maiden of the same caste in accordance with her hint.

A liberal outlook is noticeable in the *Purāṇas* and *Smṛti*. *Nārada* states (XII. 61) that a chaste woman incurs no blame by willingly approaching a man if she is forsaken by her husband who is attacked with consumption.

Generally, the following kinds of offenders are exempted from torture: minor, old person, sick person, lunatic, an intoxicated person, one afflicted with hunger or thirst, one tired of journey or due to over-eating, one suffering from indigestion, a weak person, a woman in the family way, a woman within one month of delivery.

According to some authorities (e.g. *Viṣṇu-dharmasūtra* v. 1.), *Brāhmaṇas* are exempted from capital punishment.

Āpastamba (II. 10.27.16-17) holds that, for certain offences, for which a *Śūdra* offender has to die, e.g. homicide, theft, forcible misappropriation of others' land, etc. a *Brāhmaṇa* had only his eyes covered throughout life.

It should not be supposed that, in ancient India, a trial was conducted in blind conformity with the rules laid down in *Śāstras*. Some authorities clearly state that a judge should have a rational approach.

Bṛhaspati makes the position very clear. He declares: *Kevalaṃ śāstramāśritya na kartavyo* or, *vihi nirṇayaḥ/yuktihīne vicāre tu dharmahāniḥ prajāyate*[3]. No decision should be arrived at by depending merely on *Śāstra*. In a settlement, devoid of *yukti* (reasoning), *dharma* suffers.

These directions remind one of the principle of *acquitas* applied by the Roman proctors to the rigid law of earlier times. We are also reminded of the influence of equity in English law.

The travesty of justice in a trial without reasoning is illustrated by the story of *Māṇḍavya*[4]. A version of it is as follows. Some thieves, having kept stolen goods in the house of Māṇḍavya, concealed themselves. Asked by royal officers as to the way by which the thieves escaped, Māṇḍavya kept silent. The thieves were caught and, along with Māṇḍavya, were put to death. This story shows that the trial, without proper reasoning, led to the death of the innocent Māṇḍavya. A little exercise of the reasoning faculty would have convinced the judges that mere silence on the part of an accused does not lead to any definite conclusion.

REFERENCES

1. Vide Stephen, *History of Criminal Law of England,* Vol. II, p. 435; Lea, *Superstition and Force*, 1878, p. 425.
2. In it the skull is at first trepanned and a red-hot ball of iron dropped in so that the brain boils like porridge.
3. Quoted in *Vyavahāramātṛkā,* p. 7, *Parāśaramādhava,* III. p. 39, *Vyavahāramātṛkā*, p. 282.
4. Vide *Mahābhārata*, *Anuśāsana*, 18.46-50; Ādi. 107; *Arthśasāstra* IV. 8-12. Modified.

15

SOCIETY AS REFLECTED IN TANTRA

TANTRA is a vast literature. It is not possible to deal here exhaustively with the social conditions mirrored in it. We shall draw an outline of the society reflected in *Tantra*.

A study of the *Tantras* reveals a protest against the traditional religious rites, defiance of the age-old rules and regulations contained is *Smṛitiśāstra* about ascetic morality. The essence of *Tāntric* religion is the attainment of *mukti* (salvation) through *bhukti* (enjoyment). The highest goal can be attained not by denying all enjoyments of the senses, but by their gratification in the prescribed manner. In food, drink and sexual matters one should not be averse, but one should indulge in them with restraint.

Tantra does away with many of the caste-restrictions imposed by *Smṛtiśāstra*. It throws open the gates of religion to all including women and *Śūdras* who are debarred from many of the *Vedic* rites.

Instead of the mortification of the body, enjoined in many Brahmanical works, *Tantra* looks upon it as the microcosm, and, ways and means are prescribed for its preservation. *Tantra* believes that whatever is in the universe exists in the body. The body is believed to contain six *cakras* (circles like lotuses). It has three principal *nāḍis* (vein or artery). The dormant spiritual energy within the body is called *Kuṇḍalinī*. It is supposed to be like a serpent coiling round *mūlādhāra*; this *cakra* is in the middle of the body. *Tāntric Sādhana* aims at rousing this energy.

The *Guru* occupies a very important place in *Tantra*. While the priest (*purohita*) plays a prominent role in the Brahmanical religion, based on the *Veda*, he has no high place in *Tantra*. It is interesting to note that, according to some *Tantras* (e.g., *Prāṇatoṣiṇī, Kāṇḍa* II, *Pariccheda* II), one's mother is one's best *guru*.

The usual five accessories (*pañcatattva*) to *Tāntric sādhana* are *madya* (wine), *māṃsa* (meat), *matsya* (fish), *mudrā* (various hand-poses like *Kūrma-mudrā, Matsyamudrā,* etc. According to some *Tantras,* e.g. *Yoginītantra,* it appears to stand for corns like barley which can be chewed), *maithuna* (sexual intercourse).

Human nature has been divided into three main classes according to propensities and attitudes of mind. These are *Divya* (divine), *Vīra* (hero) and *Paśu* (animal).

In *Tāntric* worship, great stress is laid on *maṇḍalas, mudrās* and *yantras*. These mean respectively mystic circles, hand-poses and figures.

Tantra emphasises *yoga* in *Tāntric* devotion. The main types of *yoga* are the following:

Jñāna-yoga –	constant meditation on *Brahman.*
Mantra-yoga –	repeated recitation of *mantras*.
Rāja-yoga –	meditation on the six *Cakras.*
Laya-yoga –	meditation on the luminous Brahman in the thousand-petalled lotus in the head, after fixing the sight on the tip of the nose or between the eye-brows.

Kumārīpūjā (worship of a virgin girl of a certain age) forms an important part in *Tāntric* worship. For this purpose, a maiden of any caste, posssessing the requisite qualities, may be selected. The daughter of such a low-class man as a barber, washerman or even a *Caṇḍāla* is allowed.

As regards *pūjā* (worship), both internal (*mānasa*) and external (*bāhya*) *pūjās* are ordained, preference for the former is clear. In some works, great importance is attached to *antaryāga* or mental worship in which the five *Tattvas* are conceived as abstract, and not tangible things.

Tantra contains a lot of mysticism, occultism, magic and marvel. Worship on a corpse is held to be highly effective. The mystic syllables like *Hrīm, Krīm* etc. are believed to be of high potency.

Tantra contains many rites of the *abhicāra* type, calculated to cause mischief, even death to others. There are rites for *vaśīkaraṇa* (bringing others under control), and for acquiring wordly happiness. It is interesting to note that, contrary to the Brahmanical practice, *Tantra* includes the *Atharvaveda* among the subjects of study. Black magic or *abhicāra* appears to have originated with this *Veda*:

Haṭha-yoga – performance of the six acts called *Dhauti*, etc.

Among the deities, Kālī occupies a very prominent place. We find various conceptions of the goddess. These are *Dakṣiṇakālikā, Guhyakālī, Bhadrakālī, Rakṣākālī, Śmaśānakālī*, etc.

Tantra accords an exalted status to women. We have already seen that one's mother is regarded as one's best *guru*. The worship of *kumārīs* is a must in *Tāntric* worship. One's wife is one's *Śakti*. She is indispensable. A man without wife is not entitled to any rite. Of the *pañcatattvas*, essential for *Tāntric sādhana*, one is *maithuna* which is not possible without a woman. In certain rites, another man's wife can be worshipped. For this purpose, a *Śūdra* woman, a woman of the barber class, a washerwoman or even a prostitute is allowed.

It is curious that, while raising women to an elevated status, *Tantra* tabooes the following for women: *Sāvitrī* or *Gāyatrī*, *Praṇava* (*oṃkāra*), *Lakṣmī-bīja* (i.e. the syllable *Śrī*). They are debarred from worshipping even touching, *śālagrāma* stones.

While the corpses of men of certain kinds are recommended for *śava-sādhana*, the body of a woman is prohibited for this purpose.

Though making departure from the traditional caste-system, yet the *Mahānirvāṇa* holds that, for a *Brāhmaṇa*, only the wife of the *Brāhmaṇa* caste can be *dharmapatnī*. His wife of any other caste is *Kāmapatnī* (i.e. for enjoyment only). Thus, it is clear that this *Tantra* allows a *Brāhmaṇa* to marry women of other castes also. It should be added that, in later *Smṛti,* inter-caste marriage has been prohibited.

The *Mahānirvāṇa Tantra* (Chap. VI) vehemently condemns the enjoyment of others' wives, though this practice is allowed by some *Tantras*.

A person, taking to *Kulācāra* or a particular mode of *Tantric* life and worship, is urged to look upon women with great reverence. He should not beat them and speak ill of them. Crookedness towards them should be avoided.

Śūdras are equally entitled to *Tāntric dīkṣā* as members of the higher castes. A *Śūdra*, who has undergone *pūrṇābhiṣeka*, is allowed even to worship a *śālagrāma*. A *kumārī* of the *Śūdra* caste may be worshipped even by a *Brāhmaṇa* who can take her *prasāda* (remnant of food). A *Śūdra Avadhūta* is fit for salutation even by a *Brāhmaṇa*. In *Tantra*, *Śūdras* are subjected to the following disabilities : inability to worship a *śālagrāma* unless he is *pūrṇābhiṣikta*, recitation of the aforesaid *Sāvitrī*, *Praṇava* and *Lakṣmī-bīja*.

The *Mahānirvāṇa Tantra* recognises a caste in addition to the usual four castes. It is called *Sāmānya* (VIII. 5). A man of this caste is allowed (*Mahānirvāṇa*, VIII. 113) to take to the avocations of any caste, other than *Brāhmaṇa,* for livelihood. *Sāmānya* seems to have included all beyond the pale of the four conventional castes.

The *Tantras*, at least those of Bengal, do not recognise the usual four stages of life. For instance, the *Mahānirvāṇa*, followed by the *Prāṇatoṣiṇī*, recognise only two stages, *viz*. *Gārhasthya* (house-holdership) and *Bhaikṣya* (living on alms, mendicancy). All people are said to be entitled to do the duties of these two stages of life.

Though *Tantra* allows the devotee to enjoy the pleasures of life, yet it should not be supposed that it encourages levity. In some early *Tantras* (e.g. *Śrī-tattva-cintāmaṇi* XVIII. 574) a *Brāhmaṇa* is forbidden to drink wine. The drinking of wine appears to have been compulsory only for *Sannyāsins.* According to the *Mahānirvāṇa*, a householder should use *madhu-traya* (i.e. milk, sugar and honey) instead of wine.

As regards *māṃsa* and *matsya,* only specified beasts, birds and fish are allowed.

Though *maithuna* is a must for *Tāntric sādhana*, yet debauchery is not allowed. One *Sādhaka* is allowed to resort to one woman only. A man raping even a *Caṇḍala* woman deserves death-penalty.

16

FOLK ELEMENTS AND SOCIAL MISCELLANY

Sanskrit Works

IN dramas of the *prahasana* type, we find the wiles and quarrels of people of low character. Often does a courtesan figure among them. We shall take up only a few such farcical plays for the present.

The *Laṭaka-melaka* of Śaṃkhadhara (c. 12th century) brings together a number of roguish people in the house of the old bawd, Danturā, seeking the favour of her daughter, Madanamañjarī. The very names of the characters, assembled there, are an index to their nature. Sabhāsali, accompanied by his parasite, Kulavyādhi, is a profligate professor. He is tired of his fiercely quarrelsome wife, Kalahapriyā, and is in quest of diversion. Digambara Jaṭāsura and the Kāpālika Ajñānarāśi fall out. Then appears the cowardly village headman, Saṃgrāmavisara and his flatterer Viśvāsaghātaka. Among the other characters are the hypocritical *Brahmin* Mithyāśukla, the deceitful preceptor Phuṅkaṭamiśra, the loose-charactered Vyasanākara interested in a washer-woman etc. There is rivalry among the lovers, and the plot ends in the marriage between the old bawd and Jaṭāsura.

The *Dhūrta-samāgama* of Kaviśekhara (14th cent.) is another farce of this class. As the title suggests, in it there is an assemblage of knaves. The plot is the rivalry between the religious mendicant Viśvanagara and his pupil, Durācāra, over the charming courtesan, Anaṅgasenā. At the desire of the girl, the matter is referred to the *Brahmin*, Asajjāti, who keeps the girl himself, which his *Vidūṣaka*, too, covets her.

The *Hāsyārṇava* of Jugadīśvara throws some light on the life of the common people. It assembles rogues and rakes in the house of the bawd, Bandhurā the beauty of whose daughter, Mṛgāṅkalekhā, attracts them. Kalahāṅkura, a pupil of the court chaplain, Viśvabandhu, quarrels over the possession of a courtesan. We find also the quack Vyādhisindhu, the barber, Raktakallola, who operated upon a patient and let a profuse quantity of blood flow, the head of the police, Sādhuhiṃsaka (bearing malice against the good) according to whom the city is under the control of thieves. There appears *Raṇa-jambuka* (a fox in war) who can cut a leech into two and Mahāyāntrika who, though devoid of all knowledge of astrology, passes as an astrologer. We find the teacher and his pupil trying to get a damsel whom another religious preceptor, Madāndhamiśra, and his pupil succeed in winning. The play is full of vulgarities and obscenities of the life of low-class people.

Dispute over a courtesan occurs also in the *Kautuka-sarvasva* of Gopīnātha.

A *Brāhmaṇa*, named Kapaṭa-veśa-dhārin, appears in the *Kautuka-ratnākara* of Kavitārkika (16th cent.) as the abductor of the queen of the country. A good deal of vulgar pleasure is indulged in by the odd characters of the play.

In the *Dhūrta-nartaka* of Sāmarāja Dīkṣita (17th cent.), we meet with an ascetic in love with a dancing girl.

In the above works, we find rogues and rascals moving in a vulgar atmosphere and indulging in carnal pleasures. Thus, they mirror true folk-life in its natural setting.

The *Mālatī-mādhava* of Bhavabhūti has the love of the student, Mādhava, for Mālatī, daughter of a minister, as its principal theme. The curious incidents, through which the plot is carried to the denouement, makes one feel as though moving in the fantastic world of folk-tale. The tigers running wild on the roads, ghosts screaming in cemeteries, *Kāpālikas* performing grim rites, maidens carried away for murder, people, versed in occult sciences, flying through the air—all this conjures up an atmoshpere of folk-tale.

The *Mṛcchakaṭika* portrays several aspects of folk life. We have already noticed in it the thief, the gambler, the courtesan, etc. Besides, we find Śakāra, the villain. Though brother-in-law of the king, yet he has the frolics and foibles of an ordinary man with his carnal propensities and designs on women. There are also Viṭas, a friend of Śakāra and another, an attendant of Vasantasenā, Ceṭa Sthāvaraka, his servant, Saṃvāhaka, the shampooer addicted to gambling, Māthura, keeper of the gambling den, Dardura, the gambler, Dyūtakara, a gambler, Karṇapūraka, servant of Vasantasenā, Ceṭa Vardhamānaka servant of Cārudatta, Ceṭa Kumbhīlaka, attendant of Vasantasenā, Bandhula, a bastard-parasite of Vasantasenā and the executioners. We meet with Rebhila, a merchant. Among the females of the common class are Radanikā, maidservant of Cārudatta, Madanikā, maidservant of Vasantasenā, Chatradhāriṇī, an attendant of Vasantasenā.

Other similar works are the four one-act plays, commonly known as *Caturbhāṇī*. These are the *Ubhayābhisārikā, Padma-prābhṛtaka, Dhūrta-viṭa-saṃvāda* and the *Pādatāḍitaka* attributed respectively to Vararuci, Śūdraka, Īśvaradatta and Śyāmalika. In these we find a curious assemblage of motley characters drawn from actual common life. These contain pictures of rogues, rakes, harlots, etc. The scene in each of the works is laid in the city. But, the works contain the pictures of loves, scandals, adventures and gossips of such classes of people as move about in every city.

The *Mattavilāsa* of Mahendra-Vikrama-Varman affords a glimpse of folk-life. It describes the activities of a drunken mendicant, his wanderings with his wench, his tussle with a monk etc.

Of the Bhāsa-plays, at least one, *viz*. the *Avimāraka,* appears to be based on folk-tale. The main theme is the love of a prince, disguised as an outcaste sheep-killer, for a princess. The important elements of the plot are the motifs of recognition and of the magic ring effecting invisibility. These appear to have been taken from folk-tale.

In the *Vikramorvaśīya*, the transformation of the ruthless, passionate and selfish Urvaśī into a loving wife may have been influenced by the ideal of a good spouse current among the people in general.

Recognition through a memento, as a motif in the drama, e.g. in the *Avimāraka* and in the *Abhijñāna-śakuntalā*, appears to be derived from folklore.

We have dwelt on clandestine love elsewhere. Love as a theme dominates the Prākrit poetical literature which appears to preserve the tradition of folk-literature to a great extent. The best example of such Prākrit works is the *sattasaī* of Hāla. The predominance of love, as a sentiment, is found in several Sanskrit poems of which the most noteworthy are the *Amaruśataka*, *Śṛṅgāra-śataka* of Bhartṛhari and the *Āryā-saptaśatī* of Govardhana. Verses with erotic themes, abound in the anthologies. Some of these verses reflect the highly sensuous erotic experience that leaves scars of nails and teeth on the bodies of both the partners. For example, Rājśekhara says (*Subhāṣita-ratnakoṣa*, 612) :

> The nail-marks of the lover appear on the sides of the breasts of a woman (from whose face) liquid lac-dye is trickling down. Methinks, the sparks of the fire of Cupid, increased within, have pierced through the heart. Elsewhere the friend of a woman, who enjoyed sexual sports overnight, tells her that her lower lip, having the colour of a ruby, is extremely beautiful even with the scar (caused by the teeth of her lover). So, she need not unnecessarily hide it with her hand.
>
> (*Ibid*. 629)

These reflect the practices of the unsophisticated common people who did not learn the art of glossing over the visible marks of erotic enjoyments.

The husband, enjoying a woman other than his wife, is a common sight. The following verse of Vākkūṭa contains the clever reproach of an indignant woman to her infidel husband who seeks to appease her wrath :

> Why do you fall at my feet ? Husbands, indeed, are independent. You have enjoyed yourself somewhere for sometime. What is your fault ? I am at fault, because I survived during separation from you. Women have husbands as their lives: so, rather I should appease you.
>
> (*Subhāṣita-ratnakoṣa*, 643).

There are many pictures of women, not content with their husbands, stealthily going out in the stillness of night to meet their paramours with whom trysts have been arranged. A young woman, in separation from her husband, cleverly hints at her desire to enjoy herself with a traveller to whom she says :

> The aged mother lies down here, here sleeps the very elderly father, there rests the female slave utterly exhausted by the chores of the household. Here remain I alone, the wretched one, with my husband gone abroad for a few days.
>
> (*Ibid,* 812)

The treacherous go-between (*dūtī*), sent by a woman in separation to her husband, bears marks of herself having been enjoyed by the man. So, the wife, with wounded self-respect, skilfully chides the *dūtī* in the following words :

> Why do you cover your breasts and face with the hands ? Heroes, lower lips and breasts look beautiful with scars alone.
>
> (*Ibid*, 838)

The picture of the villain appears to reflect folk life or attitudes of common people. A few examples are given below :

> Who does not fear an evil man whose cruel malice arises without any reason ?
>
> *SRK* 1258
>
> With a pleasant exterior but an evil heart, a bad man befools others like a *Kimpāka* fruit (looking beautiful, but ugly within) ?
>
> *SRK* 1260
>
> The snake, trampled or struck with a stick, kills the man whom it bites, but a slanderer, surpassing a serpent, touches one man's ear, but slays another.
>
> *SRK* 1268
>
> The bad man extends his arms from afar, has tearful eyes, offers half of his own seat, embraces closely, talks pleasantly; skilled in stratagem, he is pleasant outwardly but has poison within—this is indeed a peculiar dramatic performance learnt by a wicked fellow.
>
> *SKM* 2178

Some common sights, usually associated with rural life, have been very artistically depicted, particularly in the anthologies. We note a few of them below. These are :

> a dog chasing a cat (*SRK* 1163), a quail picking up seeds at the edge of a loamy field (*SRK* 1181), sparrows scratching in the furrows (*SRK* 1162), a woman of the cultivator class scared by a bull (*SRK* 1176), rushing in the rain into a hut, an old dog wagging its tail into a hut, an old dog showing white teeth, a cock fight (*SRK* 1171), a person boasting of quite a number of tank-fish (*SRK* 1148), heavily spiced and fried in oil, swallowed even without washing the same, a village desolated by oppression (*SRK* 1175), human sacrifice in a dense forest (*SRK* 1190), rural life in which mustard oil is prepared (*SRK* 318), the peasant woman singing (*SRK* 1178, 1182, 314), keeping time with the crushing of grain[1], the farm workers laying down their implements to chase hares during harvest (*SRK* 300), the shepherd resting on a cool spot on the river bank (*SRK* 282), urchins with sticks in hand and smeared with mud running after the fish coming to the surface of water in the paddy field flooded with water where frogs croak (*SRK* 226), walking barefooted in hot summar dust eroding the toe-nails (*SRK* 204), walking through snow and frost in a chilly winter morning (*SRK* 307-9), a person seeking shelter in the rain but denied by the irate housewife (*SRK* 1316), a man expressing grief at the uselessness of his bull which every day kicks or gores people, tramples down the crops, refuses to bear the yoke and move (*SRK* 1683).

In some works, particularly the anthologies, we find charming descriptions of the flora and fauna in a rural setting. In fact, these descriptions conjure up idylls before our inward eye. A few word-pictures are given below. The stately banyan tree is thus described :

> This banyan tree does not cause any direct delight nor does it remove danger out of affection, nor does it please the ears of the high-minded persons with good works of solace. Owing merely to the residence in it of the lord of the daughter of the

ocean, it takes away bad dreams told before it.

SKM 1899

(It refers to the popular belief that one gets rid of evil dreams by telling a tree the subjects of such dreams.)

The *śālmali* tree is looked down upon in the following words :

The root is overgrown with thorns, the inside is devoid of substance, the flowers are not fragrant, the fruit is useless in one's hunger, the leaves are never charming, the growth is for the resort of vultures. O brother *śālmali* what else is there to be said—you have nothing befitting a noble one.

The tree on a road is thus praised :

You spread out extensive shade, please people with sweet fruits, you are bent low but high, you are on the way and often praised by other travellers. You alone are thought of by travellers for rest.

SKM 1916

The bull, victorious in fight, is described thus :

With the throat and face bent low due to the moving of the curved and sharp horns, with eyes slightly contracted, striking the ground with hoofs, scattering the chaff with very frequent breath, the victorious bull is jumping upon the cows in the pasture.

SKM 2013

Here we have a realistic picture of a kingfisher—

He rushes high up, shakes his wings; looking below he quickly aims at the target. Then he plunges into the water, and rises with a fish.

SRK 1155

A typical picture in cultivated land :

The village sparrows hop about near the furrow striking at the clods with the tips of their claws. They quickly blink their eyes for fear of being hit by the wind-borne particles of dust raised by themselves by beating their wings.

SRK 1162.

A common sight near a river with water :

The fish-hunting crane moves cautiously in the clear water of the stream looking this way and that. With one foot raised at times, it cocks its neck, and casts a longing glance at a trembling leaf.

SRK 1164

The movements of bees are described thus :

The swarm of bees, having left the mango-blossoms, has gone to the *Navamālikā* flowers. Thence they have resorted to red *Aśoka* flowers and then have gone to the *Kadamba* tree. Thence having remained for long in the *Kunda* flowers they proceed to the lotus. People, disliking familiar qualities, seek over new things.

SKM 1778.

A tank in the rainy season is described as follows :

The birds in it are singing sweetly, the bathing place is pleasant, beneath the trees on the bank there is beatiful moss; all this is good of the tank, but the water has been rendered turbid by fresh water.

SKM 1741.

A realistic description of the fish that falls a prey to birds :

'O *Pāṭhīna* fish, leave this bad river because here the beating of the sharp beaks of ospreys will fall heavily upon your soft body when you will rise after drinking the water mixed with the mud of the ever falling earth of the bank.'

SKM 1756

Some aspects of country life have been delineated with great vividness and attention to details.

A deserted village is thus depicted :

Due to the oppression of an unkind district lord, all but a few families, clinging to their mother land, have deserted the villages which are devoid of grass and where walls are crumbling down and mongooses move about freely. These show their deepest sadness in a garden resonant with the cooing of gray doves.

SRK 1175.

Not only the manifold colour of the village life has attracted the poet's eye, but its sound also has caught his ears :

> The songs of women, husking the winter rice, are charming as these are mixed with the sound of their bracelets, striking against one another on their arms swinging with the bright and smoothly rising pounder and accompanied by the drone of *hüm hüm* breaking from their sharply heaving breasts.
>
> *SRK* 1178.

Here we find not only a graphic scene of a tribal festival, but also a crude belief and a queer custom of the tribesmen :

> The tribesman worship with many animals the forest goddesss Durgā, living in rocks and caves, pouring the blood to the deity (or spirit) living near the tree. Then, at the end of the day, accompanied by young women, they enjoy merriment with the gourd-lute alternating with draught of old wine from cups of *bel* fruits.
>
> *SRK* 1191.

Of great charm and intense literary flavour are the word-pictures of the different seasons as they appear in the country side. A few specimens are given below.

A vernal picture :

> Black bees hold a drinking bout in calyxes of delicious *jambū* flowers. Parrots peck at them mistaking them for ripe berries. The bees again mistake the parrots for green leaves of the *Kiṃśuka* tree, and fall upon their beaks taking them to be (*Kiṃśuka*) flowers.
>
> *SRK* 157

A sight in sweltering summer :

> The water of the pond is hot on the surface, but pretty cold beneath. The wells on the way go dry. The travellers, coming at noon, stir with their arms and drink the tank-water covered with floating moss and muddy due to the wallowing of buffaloes not yet yoked to the plough.
>
> *SRK* 206.

Some common sights in the rainy season :

> The walking doe looks at the locusts mistaking them for sprouts of grass. The hen broods for long on mushroom tops thinking them to be her eggs. In the forest the peacock, longing for a feast of snakes, shakes his head from afar and chases the swarming line of ants.
>
> *SRK* 219.

The advent of autumn :

> Gone are the swans. The turbidity of water has disappeared quickly. The moon is clear. The rays of the sun are spread widely. The directions have been enlarged. The blue colour of the sky is wide.
>
> *SKM* 1310

A typical scene in early winter :

> The houses of peasants are attractive, being happy in the first harvest of the winter rice and sweet with the fragrance of fresh grain stored in jars. The young women take the pounder, lift and shake and smoothly let it fall, their bracelets tinkling, as they raise their arms.
>
> *SKM* 1337

An appropriate sight in late winter –

> The mustard moves to and fro with small branches weighed down by spike-shaped pods, children standing under the tree pick the jujubes from the branch bent low, the sugar-canes, crushed by the manually operated press, emit juice.
>
> *SRK* 316

In the *Uttararāmacarita* (II. 29) we have a realistic picture of nature. It is as follows : Here is the mountain Krauñcavata, where the tribes of crows are silent in the vast expanse of bamboo clumps whistling in the wind, among which the flocks of owls hoot in the bowers which are their homes; upon this the serpents, scared by the notes of the peacocks running hither and thither, climb up on the branches of the old sandal trees.

From the *Śiśupālavadha* we gather the following information :

Shops run in tents (V. 24), signs of a *Pañacabhadra* horse

regarded as auspicious (125), camels used as beasts of burden (XII. 18), small bells were put on a camel's neck (*Ibid*) and on the neck of a horse (V. 518), some ornaments were used to decorate an elephant on its neck (XVIII. 10).

The *Harṣacarita* contains the following information: elephants were decorated with chowries (I. 32) and *paṭṭabandhas* (II. 132) on their heads. The use of a *nālikā* or *nāḍikā* (water-clock) for ascertaining time is mentioned (VIII. 247). This work mentions the use of red arsenic as medicine for eyes (VIII. 230), use of the blood of hyenas in preparing medicines (VIII. 215), the practice of inhaling smoke as an austerity (VI. 136), *Caṇḍālas* taking the shrouds of corpses (VI. 125). There is reference (1. 25) to *śāsanapaṭṭa* which means a grant (generally on copper plate or silk cloth) of land or a proclamation announcing a royal order. The work testifies to the use of glass (III. 201).

From the *Kirātārjunīya* we learn as follows :
The Himālayas were held in veneration (V. 22), Badarikāśrana was regarded as a holy place (XII. 33), there was a tribe called *Kirāta* (XII. 42).

From the *Naiṣadhacarita* (II. 83) we learn that artificial lions were placed on mansions, and that dolls were kept before them. The eating of areca nuts and *acacia cstechu* is attested by the same work (VII. 46). XI. 15 refers to the use of palanquins.

The *Kādambarī* gives us the following information:
Public recitation of *Purāṇa* and *Itihāsa*, the practice of *dhūmavārtipāna*[2] (*Ka* p. 49, 55), presence of tribes called *Kirāta* and *Śabara* (*Ka* pp. 99, 100), the use of *ghaṭikā-yantra*[3] for determining time (*Ka* p. 244), signs for ascertaining the quality of a horse (*Ka* p. 269), use of *ghaṭī-yantras* (*Ka* p. 706) which were probably jars attached to pullies for drawing water from the wells . The *H* (II. 29) mentions *dhārāgṛha* which appears to denote shower bath. The *Ka* testifies to the use of *dhārāgṛha* and *jalayantra i.e.* a bath-room containing showers (*Ka* pp. 663, 705), prevalence of dental treatment (*Ka* p. 743), use of boar tusks for breaking stones (*Ka* p. 743).

In the *Kādambarī* (*Ka* p. 262) the following weapons are mentioned : bow, disc, swords, *Śakti* (spear, lance, dart, pike), *Tomara* (iron club, javelin), axe, mace. The shield is also mentioned.

From the *Kirātārjunīya* (I. 6) and *Naiṣadha* (III. 35, VII. 63), *Kādambarī* (*Ka* p. 263) we learn that the following were the subjects of study.

Sixty-four arts, *Nāṭyaśāstra, Gāndharva-veda* (music), elephant-lore, horse-lore, palmistry, painting, determination of the positions of planets and stars etc., art of writing books, dicing, preparation of fragrant substances, knowledge of the significance of the cries of birds, astrology, lapidary science, making various articles with wood and ivory, house-building, medical science, cure of effects of poison, making subterranean tunnels, swimming, jumping, climbing, erotic science, magic, art of knowledge of narratives, dramas, poems, epics, *Purāṇas*, history, linguistics, metrics, etc. Bāṇabhaṭṭa mentions the branches of knowledge in connection with a prince. At some places, four branches of knowledge are mentioned. These are, perhaps, *Ānvīkṣikī, Trayī, Vārtā, Daṇḍanīti.* At some places, fourteen branches of knowledge are referred to.

About houses we learn that these contained posts with large space at the top for supporting beams. There are references to multi-chambered houses and houses covered with canopies. As a decorative design there were pigeon-holes having wooden pigeons inside.

According to some *Tantras* (e.g. *Prāṇatoṣiṇī* on authority) the subjects of study are as follows :

Four *Vedas,* four *Upavedas*, six *Vedāṅgas, Purāṇa, Nyāya, Mīmāṃṣā, Dharmaśāstra.*

Among the *Upavedas* are included *Āyurveda, Gāndharva, Daṇḍanīti* and *Dhanurveda.*

The following philosphical systems are mentioned: *Bauddha, Śaiva, Brāhma, Saura, Vaiṣṇava, Śākta.* The atheistic and hedonistic *Cārvāka-darśana* has been condemned as *atigarhita* (extremely reprehensible).

Sthāpatya (architecture) has been recognised on the authority of Śaṃarkācārya. Works on various arts like *Kāmaśāstra, Nāṭyaśāstra* etc. are also included in the approved subjects of study.

Wooden and earthen dolls are mentioned in the *Kādambarī* (Siddhāntavāgīśa, pp. 312, 319). This shows that doll-making was the occupation of some people.

We learn (*Ka* p. 56) that dolls were inscribed on pillars in halls. From the *H* (VI. 53) we learn that there were clay-workers who made clay-figures of fish, tortoises, crocodiles, coconuts, banana trees and betel plants.

Arts and Crafts

These have been dealt with in a general way under economic life. Here we state some of the callings found in some prominent works in classical Sanskrit. A study of these reveals that various arts and crafts were resorted to by the common people for livelihood. In the *Śakuntalā* (Act VI) we find the fisherman hauled up for the alleged theft of a ring with the king's name inscribed on it. Policemen are also mentioned in this connection. The *Mṛcchakaṭika* acquaints us with the *Saṃvāhaka* (shampooer), whose occupation was to shampoo the limbs. The *Śakāra*, corresponding to the *miles glorissus* of the Greek drama, is prominent in the *Mṛcchakaṭika*. He is represented as a king's brother-in-law through one of his inferior wives. He speaks the low Prākrit dialect, called *Śākārī,* in which '*S*' is the only sibilant. He is depicted as a foolish, frivolous, proud, vile and a cruel man. As Keith aptly observes, he is skilled only "in perfidy and deceit". From *Pāṇini* (IV. 1.130) the term *Śakāra* appears to have been derived from *Śaka* (Scythian) with the affix-*ārak* added to it. Thus, it seems that such a person had a Scythian origin. His possession of a chariot and a park in the *Mṛcchakaṭika* need not lead one to suppose that he belonged to the upper class in society. His possession is a perquisite a royal relative was privileged to enjoy. Keith suggests that the *Śakāra* may have belonged to the class of mercenary soldiers common in the society of those days.

We meet with the snake-charmer (*viṣa-vaidya*, *jāṅgulika*) at several places. For example, in the *Kirātārjunīya,* I. 24, we have a reference to serpents lowering their heads at the recitation of incantations. The *H* refers (I. 90) to *Jāṅgulika* which means *viṣavaidya*. In the *Mudrārākṣasa* (act II), Virādhaka, an agent of Rākṣasa (minister of the Nandas) is in the guise of a snake-charmer.

The magician *(aindrajālika)* is found to be demonstrating his art at some places. In the *Daśakumāracarita* we find the magician, Vidyeśvara, performing the difficult task of bringing about the marriage of prince Rājavāhana with princess Avantisundarī, by creating an illusion before the royal court. References to magic are found also in the works : *Prabodha-candrodaya, Kathāsarit-sāgara, Ratnāvalī.*

A class of people appears to have taken to the profession of showing pictures to people at various places. A reference to this profession is found in the *Mudrārākṣasa* (i) where a man goes about displaying a piece of cloth or canvas on which Yama, with his attendants and punishments of hell, are depicted, such a man being designated as *Yamapaṭika* in the *Harṣacarita*.

Gate-keepers and watchman are frequently found. A class of such people was called *Āhiṇḍika* (e.g. *Manu-smṛti,* X. 37). Descended from a *Niṣāda* father and a *Vaidehī* mother, such a person appears to have been employed as a watchman outside a jail.

Gambling

Gambling, though condemned as a vice, appears to have been not merely a pastime, but also a profession serving a means of livelihood to many people. We meet with the Sabhika who used to own a house where gamblers stayed, and resorted to gambling. It was a source of income for him. The professional gamblers used to keep stakes. The term *glaha* means wager agreed upon by gamblers. Gambling was of two kinds, *Dyūta* and *Saṃāhvaya*. In the former, the participants used to play with dice (*akṣa*), a flat piece of leather for playing upon with dice (*carma-paṭṭika*), an oblong piece of ivory or bone used in gambling (*śalākā*), chess-men, etc. In the latter, the participants used to play with birds like cocks, pigeons etc., wrestlers, animals like rams, buffaloes etc. In short, gambling with inanimate objects was called *Dyūta*, while that with living beings was known as *Samāhvaya.*

Rural Life and Landscapes

The majority of Indian population, ever since the dawn of civilisation, used to live in villages. No wonder, therefore, that pictures of rural life are found in many works. We shall note a few well-known references.

In the *Raghuvaṃśa* (I. 45) we find people of the cowherd class presenting fresh ghee to King Dilīpa proceeding towards the hermitage. In *Raghu*, I. 43, the poet speaks of the fragrance of lotuses in tanks. In *Raghu*, II. 12, Kālidāsa describes the sound produced from the holes of bamboos filled with wind.

In the *Bhaṭṭikāvya* (Canto II), there is a charming pen-picture of the cowherd-women appearing to dance as they were churning milk. In the same work, we read of the glossy paddy plants, the hunter, enraptured by the cacklings of swans, forgetting his target, the deer, which stood motionless on hearing the humming of bees. We find descriptions of tanks full of lotuses, clouds resting on the slopes of mountains, water shimmering under the rising sun, cowherds without any dress, modest women with straightforward nature, and graceful glances, the dancing deer, white swans lost in white lotuses, and in sandy banks whitened with foams. The panoramic view of autumnal scenes all around has been delineated with delicate touches; the poet's pen seems to be like the painter's brush. We also read of grazing fields in which there are rustic people devoid of guile and artificial beauty like that of dresses. There is a fine description of rural women with unobtrusive movements, artless glances and upright nature inspiring confidence. Here are fine pictures of village women :

> On the forehead is a spot of collyrium, in the hands is lotus-sprout bright like moonrays, the head-dress of fruits, covered with the foam, is reaching the ears, the hair is naturally glossy as if rubbed with the juice of sesamum leaves. The dress of the village women renders the pace of travellers slow.
>
> (*Sadukti-karṇāmṛta*, Calcutta, No. 577)

Adverse Possession

Adverse possession of movable and immovable properties appears to have been common. The main law, according to the *Yājñavalkya-smṛti* (II. 2.24, 25) was that the adverse possession of a movable property continuously for ten years, within the knowledge of the owner but without any protest by him, would confer the title on the possessor. With regard to immovable properties, the law was the same with twenty years instead of ten. In such a case, the law, however, gave protection to minors, women, learned *Brāhmaṇas*, the mentally retarded persons and royal properties. The legality of adverse possession was not applicable in the following cases too : mortgage, boundary and deposit.

Slavery

Slave-system has been a blot on the Indian society from hoary antiquity; in the *Ṛgveda*, there are many references to *dāsas*. They appear to have been pre-Aryan aborigines with whom the Aryans were at feud. Those *dāsas*, who were subjugated by the Aryans, were perhaps employed by the victors as their servants or even slaves. At one place, Sāyaṇa explains *dāsa* as *garbhadāsa,* i.e. a slave by birth. *Dāsas* are referred to very frequently, e.g. I. 92.8, II. 12.4, III. 12.6, IV. 30.14, 21; V. 30.5, 7, 9; VI. 60.6; VIII. 40.6, X. 38.3 etc. I. 92.8 contains a prayer for possession of *dāsas*. VIII. 56.3 is a prayer for one hundred *dāsas*. There are references to *dāsīs* also; they were wives of *dāsas,* and were probably employed as female slaves. Both male and female slaves are mentioned in *AV* XII. 3,13; their duty, among other things, was to make foodgrains fit for consumption.

We have already seen under Economic Life that the *Mitākṣarā* enumerates fifteen classes of slaves.

Infanticide

Some people think that infanticide[4] or exposure of children was in vogue in ancient India. *RV* II. 29.1. is cited as an evidence. This *Vedic* passage refers to the practice of a woman's casting off an illegitimate child. It does not imply that legitimate children also were thrown away. Another evidence, furnished by some scholars, is the *Taittirīya Saṃhitā* (VI. 5.10.3). It means that people keep aside a female child when born, and greet the son. This passage appears to indicate that a female child was not greeted with enthusiasm with which a male child used to be. This feeling, prevailing in the society, is clearly indicated by the *Aitareya Brāhmaṇa* (33.1) which holds that a daughter is distress or humiliation whereas a son is light in the highest heaven. A similar opinion about a daughter is voiced by the *Mahābhārata* (*Ādi* 159.11). All the above references confirm the fact that a daughter was generally looked upon with a sense of sorrow. But nowhere is there any reference to exposing female children to death. There are many evidences to show that a daughter enjoyed certain legal rights. For example, Nārada argues (*Dāyabhāge*, V. 50) that both the son and the daughter continue the line of the father so that, in the absence of the former, the latter succeeds as heir. Bṛhaṣpati says that the daughter is born from the limbs of the parents as much as the son. So, when she is alive nobody else can take her father's property.

We know of the prevalence of infanticide at one time in some parts of India, e.g. Rājputana (Rajasthan). This appears to have been resorted to for certain reasons; e.g. the difficulty of protecting a girl and preserving her honour, the crushing burden of her marital expense. But the practice had no *Śāstric* sanction behind it.

Architecture

The subject has been elaborately dealt with in the works on *Vāstuvidyā, e.g. Mānasāra, Mayamata, Samarāgana-sūtradhāra, Aparājitapṛcchā*, etc. Some information in this regard is available also in the epics, some *Purāṇas* (e.g. *Matsya, Viṣṇudharmottara, Mārkāṇḍeya, Vāyu, Agni*), *Arthaśāstra, Bṛhat-saṃhitā, Atri-saṃhitā, Kālikāgama*, etc.

There appear to have been two main schools of architecture, *viz.* northern called *Nāgara,* and the southern called *Drāvida.* These two apply chiefly to temple architecture. The term, *Vesara,* found in southern works, applies, according to some, to Orissa architecture alone. Others hold that it had two sub-divisions, *Āndhra* (southern) and *Kāliṅga* (Orissa). In some works, the types called *Lāṭa, Vairāṭa* and *Bhūmija* etc. are mentioned. In certain works, as many as twenty types of temple-architecture are mentioned. The *Atrisaṃhitā* of the south mentions four types of temple architecture, *viz. Brahmacchanda, Viṣṇucchanda, Indracchanda* and *Rudracchanda.*

The terms like *Chandi, harmya, dhruva*, etc., occurring in the *Ṛgveda,* indicate various types of buildings in the remote *Vedic* age. The terms *vaṃśa, sthūṇa, upamit, pramit,* relating to architecture, occur in the *Atharvaveda*.

The examination of the soil for house-building was in vogue in ancient times. The *Āśvalāyan Gṛhyasūtra* (II. 7-9) gives the following method. After digging a hole in a part of the proposed land, it should be closed with the earth dug up. If the quantity of earth fails to fill the hole, the soil is bad. Otherwise it is good.

The *Purāṇas* show familiarity with *harmya, prāsāda, devāyatana, nagara,* etc. Some *Purāṇas* contain description of pillars, measurement of brick-built houses, plan, classification, etc.

In the *Arthaśāstra* there is mention of houses made of bamboo or wood plastered with clay. The use of stones is also attested. There are references to fencing, arrangement for the disposal of rubbish, waste water etc., outlet for rain-water, lanes between neighbouring houses and windows in side-walls.

It is stated that a man, making doors and windows even in his house, causing inconvenience to neighbours, will be liable to punishment. The water of one's house should not pass into another's. In between two houses a specified space must be left vacant.

The *Kālikāgama* mentions as many as twenty types of houses made of brick.

In certain works, we find particular attention to the position and dimension of the doors and arrangements for ventilation. In various parts of the house, particularly on doors, there should be paintings and images of gods. The subjects of painting are natural objects, birds, beasts, gods, goddesses and legendary incidents.

The sizes of the biggest and smallest bricks mentioned in the different works, are 18"x18"x6" and 8"x4"x2" respectively.

The *Mānasāra* mentions a twelve-storied palace as the tallest.

In certain literary works, some incidental references to house-building are available. The *Harṣacarita* gives the picture of a royal palace. It appears to have had three compounds besides the harem.

The *Rājataraṅgiṇī* mentions *vānaśālā* (huge mansion surrounded by walls and moats), *caitya, vihāra*, etc. The *Meghadūta, Śiśupālavadha, Mṛcchakaṭika* and *Uttararāmacarita*, reveal familiarity with cities and buildings. The *Śiśupālavadha* mentions (III. 50) a house with posts having large space at the top for supporting beams. There is also reference to a multi-chambered house.

The *Kādambarī* refers (*Ka* p. 56) to dolls inscribed on pillars in halls.

From the *Śiśupālavadha* (III. 51) it appears that, in some houses, certain portions had many holes with wooden pigeons inside. These might be meant for ventilation or decoration only.

Middle Indo Aryan Literature

Aspects of folk-life flash from certain similes. In connection with comparisons of various sorts, the *DP* refers to the following :

> A thatched house (I. 14), a cowherd counting cows (I. 19), race-horse (II. 29), a fletcher straightening his arrow (III. 1), a cowherd driving cows to a pasture-ground (X. 7), cranes sitting near a lake (XI. 10.11), *Khattaka* reed bearing fruit for its own destruction (XII. 8), birds escaping from a net (XIII. 8), winnowing chaff (XVIII. 18), a sucking calf clinging to a cow (XX. 12), flood washing away a sleeping village (XX. 15), invisible arrows shot out at night (XXX. 15), a blade of grass cutting the hand (XXII. 6), a driver controlling an elephant (XXIII. 7), taming of elephants, horses and mules (XXIII. 3), an elephant sunk in the mud (XXIII. 8), an elephant freely roaming in a forest (XXIIII. 10), a monkey jumping here and there (XXIV. 1), spreading *bīraṇa* grass (XXIV. 2), drops of water falling from a lotus leaf (XXIV. 3), digging up *bīraṇa* grass to get *uśīra* roots (XXIV. 4), one running like a hunted hare (XXIV. 9), a spider following its web (XXIV. 14), weeds growing in fields (XXIV. 23), an empty boat moving lightly (XXV. 10).

Some information is available about the furniture and appurtenances in a house. The *Cullavagga* states (VII. 7) that monks were allowed to have, as seats or beds, benches against the walls, bedsteads with short removable legs, arm-chairs, sofas, cushioned chairs, carpets, pillows, bolsters stuffed with wool, cotton, etc. Bedsteads, made of split bamboo, are mentioned. Chairs were of various kinds, e.g. arm-chair, state-chair, chair on a pedestal, chair with many legs, cane-bottomed chair, straw-bottomed chair, etc. Mats of grass are also mentioned;

section IV of the *Bhikkhu Pātimokkha* mentions woollen mats. The above work refers to jars, brooms, fans, mosquito-fans, flower-stand etc.

From the *Mahāvagga* (V. 13.3) we learn that the skin of the following animals was used as covers of beds and seats : *elaka* (ram), *aja* (goat), *miga* (deer).

The *SV* mentions (Pt. I, pp. 84-87) the following kinds of seats:

Āsandī –	Big seat.
Gonaka –	Carpet with long hairs.
Koseyya –	Silken seat bedecked with gems.
Kuttaka –	Woollen seat on which sixteen girls can dance together.
Pallaṅka –	Seat having legs with figures of deer, etc.
Patālika –	Woollen seat.
Vekatika –	Having the figure of a lion or tiger.

From the *Cullavagga* we learn that a bathroom can be enclosed in three ways – with brick, stone or wood. The use of stools is allowed in it. The bathroom may have an ante-chamber. Water-vessels of three kinds are mentioned – made of brass, wood or skin. The use of towels is referred to.

According to this work, the basement of a house may have a brick, stone or wooden facing. The use of a balustrade is known. The monks are allowed to put up a railing for the cloister. There is reference to chimney. The floor may be made of brick, stone or wood. There is evidence of the system of drainage. Whitewash and colourwash are known. Chambers of the following shapes are mentioned : palanquin, quart-measure verandah, covered terrace, inner verandah and overhanging caves are mentioned.

Abodes of the following descriptions are allowed for monks : *vihāra, addhayoga* (shaped like a *Garuḍa* bird), storied dwelling, attic, cave.

The above work refers to the use of needles and needle-cases of bamboo. It mentions an instrument to remove ear-wax. The use of tooth-picks is referred to.

The *Dhammapada* commentary (III. pp. 183 ff.) refers to the practice of making a canopy with parts of *śāla* wood, under which people can sit on some occasions.

The *Mahāvagga* (VI. 1.5, 15.10 etc.) mentions the use of the following as medicine : urine, butter, cream, oil, honey, molasses, animal fat, roots, herbs, leaves, fruits, gum, salt, raw meat, blood, gruel, broth. The following astringent decoctions appear to have been used as medicine : *nimba, pakkava* (a creeper), *nattamāla, kutaja*. There is reference to the practice of inhaling some medicines. Medicine and surgery are referred to also in the *Brahmajāla-sutta* (*Dīgha,* I, pp. 1-46). The *Papañcasūdanī* (p. 90) mentions five kinds of medicines, *viz*. ghee, butter, oil, honey and molasses. The *Dhammapada* commentary (Vol. III, pp. 295 ff.) mentions white leprosy (leucoderma) as an infectious disease. Hot bath, purgative, ointment, dressing of wounds are also mentioned.

The *GS* mentions (I. 50) ordinary fever, fever caused by dysentery or indigestion (I. 51). Verse V. 58 refers to the practice of putting a sort of plaster (*dhavalapaṭṭa*) on scars and wounds. There are references to bitter medicine (IV. 17) and *sañjīvanauṣadhi* (IV. 36) i.e. a medicine for curing a patient about to die. There are references to deafness and blindness (VII. 95) as well as dumbness (VII. 96).

The *GS* gives us a glimpse of rural life. The following features of village life are available :

> Cultivation and cultivators (e.g. II. 34, VI. 67, VII. 89), cultivators gleefully singing after a rich harvest (VII. 89), food for cultivators brought by their women to the field at noon (VII. 92), fence around a cultivator's house (III. 20, 21, 57), holes in the fence for seeing distant objects (V. 40), houses made of grass (IV. 15), *alinda* before a house (V. 40), a big banyan tree near or in the middle of the village (I. 94, III. 94-95), tanks (II. 10, VII. 26), lotus-tanks (I. 8), flowers like *Kāśa* (V. 34), *Kunda* (V. 26), *Kuvalaya* (II 8), *Kamala* (I. 78, II. 10, V. 95, VII. 41), *Kuravaka* (I. 6), *Kadamba* (II. 77, IV. 14, VI. 65, VII. 36), *Kandoṭa* or blue lotus (VII. 22), *Mālatī* (I. 92), *Bakula* (I. 63), *Navamalikā* (III. 81), *Palāśa* (IV. 8), *Kusumbha* (II. 45), *Madhuka* (II. 4), *Śephālikā* (V. 12), *Pāṭala* (V. 68) *Marubaka* (VII. 77).

Among the trees are *Aśoka* (I. 7), *Kaṅkella* (V. 4-5), *Āmra* (IV. 31), *Eraṇḍa* (II. 57), *Kārpāsa* (IV 59-60); the *Mādhavī* creeper is also mentioned (IV. 22).

The fruits mentioned are *Nimba* (I. 30), *Āmra* (I. 62), *Badara*

(II. 100), *Tāla* (IV. 98), *Jambu* (II. 40).

The pulse, *Tuvari* or *Aḍahara* is mentioned (IV. 58).

Villagers appear to have had pet birds (III. 20). The householders are stated to have felt ashamed when a caged parrot divulged details about their sex-sports before the superiors (VI. 52, 89).

Among domestic birds, besides parrots, are mentioned the peacock (I. 52), pigeon (I. 64), swan (II. 10), cock (VII. 98). The crow (II. 5) and crane (I. 4) are also mentioned.

Among aquatic creatures are mentioned the crab (I. 19) and conch-shell (I. 4).

The insects, mentioned in the *GS*, are the spider (I. 63), bee (I. 37).

The following beasts are mentioned : deer of various kinds (e.g. III. 851, VII. 29), cow (III. 71), bull (III. 38), elephant (II. 73), buffalo (II. 72), monkey (II. 71), cat (III. 83), dog (vii. 62), lion (II. 75).

Rathyā (road) has often been mentioned (e.g. II. 19, V. 19, VII. 82). There is reference to village roads being water-logged and filled with slush (IV. 92).

Verse III. 94 mentions a well of cold drinking water. V. 90 refers to pots for raising water with a mechanical device called *Rahatta* or *Arahatta.* A sort of artificial fountain, located in a tank, appears to be referred to (V. 91).

Verse VI. 54 refers to a machine for producing molasses.

Housewives were preoccupied mainly with cooking (I. 13, 14).

A householder, maintaining distressed relatives, is described as wearing poor cloths (I. 18).

The exchange of jesting remarks between the husband and the wife is referred to in I. 11, 13.

Some verses (e.g. III. 44, VII. 71) refer to letter-writing. Letters are stated to be sent by wives to their husbands gone abroad.

There are observations (e.g. I. 17, 49, 77, 94, 98; I. 36, 39, 70, 98) containing various sentiments relating to the householders gone abroad, and the wives in separation. In some cases, a wife, unable to bear long separation, is found to be attracted to other men (I. 66), particularly to another woman's husband staying abroad (VII. 67).

A wife is stated (VII. 11) to be emaciated in summer at the

thought of the husband going abroad. In the rainy season, the wife in separation is drenched in tears (VII. 21). The absent husband, in this season, wants to hasten back home (VII. 94, 98). He feels distressed at the sight of a tank in autumn (VII. 22). He is pained at the touch of southern breeze in spring (V. 46).

There is reference to *ekagrāma-pravāsa* (I. 43). It means that a lover and the beloved, though living in the same village, cannot be united and, therefore, suffer.

There is reference (e.g. VIII. 28) to the *grāmaṇī* or village headman; the post appears to have been hereditary (VII. 32). The *tittillas* or gate-keepers appear to have played an important rôle in the defence of a village (VI. 56).

From the *Jātakas* we learn that when crops grew, the cattle were not allowed to graze in the fields. The animals used to be placed in charge of one herdsman, hired by villagers collectively, and sent to the common pasture (I. 194). The herdsman was required to leave milk in the udders.

No individual proprietor was to fence off his portion of the field. There was a common fence (*Vinaya* I. 287).

Villagers appear to have worked together to build rest-houses, reservoirs etc., roads and lay out parks. Even women participated (I. 199).

Some biographical works in Apabhraṃśa throw a little light on folk elements. For example, in the *Jasahara-cariu* of Pupphadanta, king Yasodhara is stated to have prayed to Kaulācārya Bhavananda for capacity to fly in the air.

Vinayacandra Sūri's *Neminātha-caupai* (12th century A.D. end) contains, among other things, *Vāramāsyā* or the description of the activities in twelve months of the year. It reflects popular life.

Some works glorify *vratas* which appear to have had wide popular appeal. For example, the *Bhavisayatta-kahā* of Dhanapāla glorifies the five-year-long *pañcamī-vrata.*

A picture of folk-life emerges from certain *Jātakas* in which robbers, vagabonds, gamblers and courtesans play important parts. We also hear of people's insolence, women's infidelity men's weakness, etc. For considerations of space we do not recount the relevant stories here. Some *Jātakas* (e.g. *Nanda* 39, *Khadiraṅgāra* 40, *Sataṃkila* 73, *Rabhree* 137 etc.) refer to the practice of burying money underground for fear of thieves, enemies, king, water and fire.

The *Karpūramañjarī* contains some information about the life of common men. For example, a popular practice was to sprinkle water on a knot in a hempen rope to make it tighter (I. p. 23). A hen-pecked husband appears to have been an object of contempt (III. p. 70).

People are stated to have used palm-leaf fans in summer (III. 20). There is reference to people being besprinkled with drops of water coming from the fans which were obviously soaked (IV. 8).

Shower-baths appear to have been used to reduce summer heat (III. 20, IV. 10). A showering machine is mentioned (IV. 10). Bathing pools are referred to (IV. 4).

In summer, sandal is stated to have been made more fragrant with powdered camphor (IV. 5).

The *KKC* (II. 9) refers to the following weapons: sword, disc, spear, dagger, bow, javelin.

The above work mentions the tribe called Bhillas. They are described as dark-complexioned and having eyes red like *Guñjā*. It appears that they were bird-catchers (VIII. 7, 8). A class of people, known as *Takku* (hailing from the Punjab) appears to have dealt in horses (VIII. 16). A tribe called *Pulinda*, is mentioned in IV.

REFERENCES

1. In the *Bhaṭṭikāvya* (II. 16), we find the following graphic description of cowherd women engaged in churning curd :-
   their sides are moving, limbs are making graceful movements, their dance is delightful on account of their buttocks moving high and low.
2. It was, perhaps, like smoking a cigarette or tobacco in the Indian style.
3. It appears to have been a mechanical device filled with water. The trickling of water, drop by drop, indicated the time.
4. On this practice among some barbarous and civilised communities of ancient countries, see Westermark, *Origin and Development of Moral Ideas*, Vol. I. 1906.

Appendix I

Chronology of the Principal Works Consulted

THE works, consulted in preparing this work, belong to different periods. With a view to enabling the reader to form an idea about the time of the works, in which various aspects of social life are recorded, we give below the chronology of these works. Though chronology is a weak point in the history of Indian literature, yet we shall note the dates, some of which are tentative, as fixed by modern scholars. As regards the works, the dates of which have not yet been determined, no guess has been made.

B.C.

2500 (or 2000) – 750 – Origin and evolution of *Ṛgveda* (acc. to Winternitz). According to D. Frawley, 12,500 B.C. (Vide *Glory of India a quarterly journal* published by Motilal Banarsidas, Delhi) Vol. V, Nos. 3-5, 1981.

Later than *Ṛgveda* – *Atharvaveda* (Extant text).

Between the conclusion of hymn-composition and *Ṛgveda-saṃhitā* and the rise of Buddhism (acc. to Winternitz) – *Brāhmaṇas*.

486 – Buddha's Enlightenment (acc. to Cantonese tradition). *Kalpasūtras* approximately synchronous with the rise and first spread of Buddhism.

4th century – Pāṇini, Kauṭilya, *Arthaśāstra*. *Telakaṭāhagāthā* (origin). According to a recent view, the extant text dates back to the 2nd cent. A.D.

2nd cent. – Patañjali, author of the *Mahābhāṣya*.

2nd or 1st cent. – *Caraka-saṃhitā*

Between 2nd cent. B.C. and 2nd cent. A.D. – *Manu-smṛti*. in its present form (acc. to P. V. Kane).

A.D.

Beginning of the Christian era according to some—*Caturbhāṇī*

c. 1st cent.—*Divyādāna*

c. 1st—2nd cent. or earlier—extant *Yājñavalkya-smṛti* (according to P.V. Kane)

c. 1st cent. (acc. to some)—*Gāthāsaptaśatī* ,*Paümacariya* (4 A.D. according to some, 2nd or 3rd cent. according to others).

c. 2nd cent.—Final form of the extant *Rāmāyaṇa* (according to Winternitz), *Avadānaśataka*.

c. 3rd cent.—*Kāmasūtra*. Upper terminus of the date of the *Gāthāsaptaśatī* (acc. to some) and of the *Vāyupurāṇa*.

c. 4th cent.—Bhāsa. Amarasiṃha, author of the *Nāmaliṅgānuśāsana*.

c. 400—Lower limit of Kālidāsa's date.

c. 4th cent.—Final form of the extant *Mahābhārata* (according to Winternitz).

5th cent.—Bhaṭṭi, author of the *Bhaṭṭikāvya, Sumaṅgalavilāsinī*.

Between 4th and 5th cent.—*Dīpavaṃsa*. 5th-6th cent.—Rise of original *Tantras*. Time of Varāhamihira, author of the *Bṛhat-saṃhitā*.

6th cent.—Śūdraka, author of the *Mṛcchakaṭika*. Lower terminus of the date of *Pañcatantra*. Conjectural date of the *Mahāvaṃsa*. Supposed lower terminus of the date of the *Caṇḍī*, a portion of the *Mārkaṇḍeya-purāṇa*.

634—Lower limit of Bhāravi's date.

500-650—Lower terminus of the date of the *Bhāgavata-purāṇa*.

7th cent.—Lower terminus of the period of composition of the old extant *Purāṇas*.

Bāṇabhaṭṭa, author of the *Kādambarī* and *Harṣacarita*.

Subandhu, author of the *Vāsavadattā*.

Bhavabhūti, author of the *Uttararāmacarita, Mahāvīracarita, Mālatimādhava*.

Between 5th and 7th cent. supposed time-limit of the *Viṣṇudharmottara*. Mahendra Vikramavarman, author of *Mattavilāsa*. Bhartṛhari, author of the three *Śatakas*. Harṣa, author of *Ratnāvalī* , etc.

7th-8th cent.—according to some, date of the *Kāśikā* comm. on the *Aṣṭādhyāyī*.

8th cent.—Daṇḍin, author of *Daśakumāracarita*. *Amaruśataka*. *Gaüḍavaho*. *Harivaṃśa-purāṇa* (783 A.D.)

8th-9th cent.—Dāmodargupta, author of *Kuttanīmata*. Jaina *Rāmāyaṇa* of Svayambhū.

9th cent.—Viśākhadatta, author of *Mudrārākṣasa*. According to some, *Agnipurāṇa* was compiled. Līlāśuka variously assigned between 9th cent. and the 15th.

9th-10th cent.—Rājaśekhara's works.

10th cent.— Lower terminus of the date of the *Caturbhāṇī* which are believed to be later than Bharata's *Nāṭyaśāstra*.

Bhavisayatta-kahā appears to have been composed in this century. *Kālakācārya-kathānaka, Nāyakumāra-cariu*. Supposed date of the *Mayamata*.

1063-82—*Kathāsaritsāgara*.

11th cent.—Bilhaṇa's *Caurapañcāśikā*. Works of Kṣemendra. Kṛṣṇamiśra, author of *Prabodha-candrodaya*. *Karakaṇḍa-cariu*. *Samarāṅgaṇa-sūtradhāra* of Bhoja.

12th cent.—Jayadeva, author of *Gītagovinda*. Govardhana, author of *Āryā-sapaśatī*. Śrīdhara-dāsa, compiler of *Sadukti-karṇāmṛta*. Kalhaṇa, author of the *Rājataraṅgiṇī*. Cintāmaṇi Bhaṭṭa's enlarged version of *Śuka-saptati*. Śaṃkhadhara, author of *Laṭakamelaka*. Vidyākara, compiler of *Subhāṣita-ratnakośa*. *Kathākośa*. *Neminātha-caüpai*.

13th cent.—*Saṃgīta-ratnākara* of Śārṅgadeva. *Siṃhāsana-dvātrimśikā*. *Pāṇḍava-carita* (c. 1200).

14th cent.—Viśvanātha, author of *Sāhitya-darpaṇa*. Vidyāpati, author of *Puruṣaparīkṣā*. Kaviśekhara, author of *Dhūrta-samāgama*. *Rasavāhinī* (probably earlier part of this cent.)

1400—Lower terminus of the period of composition of later *Purāṇas*.

Between 11th and 15th cent.—supposed time-limit of the composition of the *Mānasāra*.

15th cent.— *Kathāmahodadhi*.

1486-1533—Lifetime of Caitanya. Rūpa Gosvāmin, a contemporary. Jīva Gosvāmin, son of a brother of Rūpa. Kavikarṇapūra, a later contemporary of Caitanya.

16th cent.—Kavitārikika, author of *Kautuka-ratnākara*. *Pāṇḍava-purāṇa* (1551 A.D.).

17th cent.—Sāmarāja, author of *Dhūrta-nartaka*. 16th-17th

cent.—*Kathā-ratnākara*.

18th-19th cent.—according to some, the date of the *Mahānirvāṇa-tantra*.

19th cent.—Compilation of the *Prāṇatoṣiṇī*.

Appendix II

Popular Elements in Similes

SANSKRIT literature is rich in the use of figures of speech, particularly simile. The traditional eulogy, conveyed by the two words *Upamā Kālidāsasya*, represents Kālidāsa as an adept in the use of simile. It is a remarkable feature that, in many of the similes, the poets refer to common things of life. There are cases in which recondite similes, invovling philosophical matters or things fancied by the poet, are employed. But, in a large number of comparisons, the poet seeks to bring home an idea intimately to the reader by using such sights or objects as are familiar to the people in general. For the present purpose, we shall confine ourselves to the following works only : *Ṛgveda,* and Kālidāsa's works. As illustrations of popular elements in similes, we shall refer to only a few cases; it requires a separate volume to collect all such similes.

In the similes of the *Ṛgveda*, the cow, horse, goat, dog, birds, flowers, fish, boat, fowlers, dice-players, instruments commonly met with in life, etc. figure prominently. We breathe a rustic air in them – sometimes bordering on vulgarity, according to modern taste. A few specimens are given below:

Cow

vāśreva vidyunmīmāti vatsaṃ na mātā siṣakti	I. 38.8	Lightning rumbling like a cow from whose udders milk is trickling.
pra sugopā yavasaṃ dhenavo yathā	III. 45.3	As a good cowherd nourishes cows (so Indra nourishes the sacrificer).
dhenumivāyatīmuṣāsam	V. 1.1.	To *Uṣas* coming like a cow.

śiśāno vṛṣabho yathāgniḥ śṛṅge davidhvat	VIII. 60.13	Agni shaking its head as a bull does after sharpening its horns.
Boat		
pra te nāvaṃ na samane vacasyuvam	II. 16.7	Indra, like a boat, rescuer from danger.
vācamariteva nāvam	IX. 95.2	As a sailor starts a boat....
Horse		
agnir-hotā no adhvare vājī san pariṇīyate	IV. 15.1	Agni brought to sacrifice like a horse.
atyo no vājī raghurajyamāno babhru	V. 30.14	Babhru moved like a swift horse.
Goat		
ajeva yamā varamā	II. 39.2	*Aśvins* fancied like two powerful goats.
Dog		
śvāneva no ariṣaṇyā tanūnām	II. 39.4	(They are requested to protect the bodies of sacrificers against violence) as a dog gives such protection.
Bird		
udgāteva śakune	II. 43.2	Vulture crying like a breeding horse neighing near a mare.
Miscellaneous		
emīdeṣāṃ niṣkṛtaṃjariṇīva	X. 34.5	As a concubine goes to her paramour, so the gambler goes to the house of playmates.
. . .Vidhaveva devaraṃ maryaṃ na yoṣā kṛṇute Sadastha	X. 40.2	As a widow fondles her brother-in-law at bedtime.

ubhe dhurau vahnirā-pibdamāno'ntar-yoneva carati dvijātiḥ	X. 101.11	As one husband of two wives performs sexual intercourse.
apa tye tāyavo yathā nakṣatrā, yantyaktubhiḥ	I. 50.2	Stars disapper like a thief.
śvaghnī va kṛtnur-vija āmimānā	I. 92.10	As the wife of a fowler kills a bird.
Flowers		
simbalaṃ cid vivṛścati	III. 53.22	As *Simul* flowers are easily severed.
Instrument		
tāmasya rītiṃ paraśoriva	V. 48.4	Action of Agni like that of an axe.

In Kālidāsa's works, the common things, figuring in *Upamā,* are aquatic creatures like *Śapharī*, birds like pigeon, osprey, cuckoo, parrot, swan, domestic animals like the bull, calf, ass, dog, insects like the fire-fly, bee, other creatures like the serpent, rat, monkey, jackal, etc. Of the other common things, mention may be made of parts of the body, like the face, hair, lip, breasts, etc. The patient and medicine, so common in society, appear in some cases. Fire, lamp etc., so very familiar to all, are also used. Among the common flowers are the *Kunda, Ketaka, Japā* and *Śirīṣa*. Honey and sweetmeat, which are in common use, appear in some similes. The familiar fruit, *Bimba*, occurs in some cases. The commonest food grains, *Yava* and *Śāli* are found in some similes. Various articles in the common man's house are mentioned on some occasions; these are *argala* (bolt), *kavāṭa* (door-leaf), *dvāra* (door). Articles in common use, like the umbrella, raft and measuring rod are seen at some places. Of ordinary instruments and appliances, there are the *aṅkuśa* (hook), *parigha* (iron club) and *śmaśānaśūla* (stake for impaling criminals in a burning ground). Among metals, the most widely used one, *viz.* iron, occurs at several places. Of the miscellaneous popular elements, mention may be made of laughter, traveller, lover, thief, oil, dwarf. The common ornament is the *niṣka,* and the popular cosmetics are *añjana* (collyrium) and *kuṅkuma* (saffron). Of the plant-kingdom, *Kāśa* grass and the reed called

Śara are mentioned. The commonest fruit, *Kadalī* or banana, occurs at places. *Cūta, Kadamba, Bakula,* which are frequently met with, have been mentioned in some similes. Some other things, which are part and parcel of folk-life, are *kulya* (channel), *kūpa* (well), *jalāśaya* (tank), *palvala* (puddle). While rivers in general are mentioned, the Gaṅgā and the Yamunā are stated on several occasions. Among women of various kinds, we find *Kāminī* (a loving woman) and *navavadhū,* the most popular aspects of the female species, are used. Below we shall set forth some of the passages from Kālidāsa's works containing the similes concerned.

Abbreviations

RS – Ṛtusaṃhāra.	*AS – Abhijñānaśakuntala.*
KS – Kumārasambhava.	*RV – Raghuvaṃśa.*
VU – Vikramorvaśīya	*MD – Meghadūta.*

Aquatic Creatures

Śapharīṃ hrada-śoṣa-vikalāvāṃ *KS* IV. 39
prathamā vṛṣṭiriva
As the first rain-fall does to the small glittering fish (*Cyprinus saphore)* distressed due to the drying up of a lake.

Birds

Kapoṭa-karburam *KS* IV. 27
Variegated like a pigeon.
Vignā kurarīva *RV* XIV. 68
Like an alarmed osprey.
Kokilā-mañju-vādinīm *RV* XII. 39
Sweet-spoken like a female cuckoo.
Śukodara-śyāmam *VU* IV. 17
Green like the belly of a parrot.
Haṃsa-mālā śaradīva gaṅgām *KS* I. 30
As rows of swans go to the Ganges in autumn.

Domestic Animals

Vṛṣa-skandha *RV* 1.13, XII. 35
Having shoulders like those of a bull.
Śubhra-trinayana-vṛṣotkhāta-paṅkopameyām *MD* I. 54
Like mud raised by the white bull of the three-eyed (Siva).
Rāsabha-kaṇṭha-dhūsaram *KS* XV. 21
Grey like the throat of an ass.

Śvānaḥ pramattā iva kārtike-niśi KS XV. 41
Like dogs mad in a night of the month of *Kārtika*.

Insects

Khadyotālī-vilasita-nibhām MD 2.24
Like the sparkling of rows of fire-flies.
Bhramara iva vibhāte kundam antastuṣāram AS V. 19
As a bee (can neither reject nor take to) a jasmine flower, with frost within, in the morning.

Serpent

Na tu sarpa iva tvacam RV VIII. 13
Not as a serpent does to its slough.

Other Animals

Biḍāla-gṛhīta mūṣika iva AS VI. 27
Like a mouse caught by a cat.
Śivā-ghora-svanām RV XII. 39
Fiercely crying like a jackal.

Parts of the Body

Vāra-yuvati-mukhābham RS III. 23
Having complexion like that of a beautiful young woman.
Aṅgulībhirtva keśa-saṃcayaṃ saṃnigṛhya KS VIII. 63
As if pressing the lock of hair with fingers.
Nitambam iva medinyāḥ srastāṃśukam RV IV. 52
Like the earth's hip stripped of cloth.
Madhye śyāmaḥ stana iva bhūvaḥ
śesa-vistāra-pāṇḍu MD II. 18
Like the earth's breast dark in the middle and pale (or white) in the rest of its expanse.
Sagarbha-pramadā-stana-prabhaiḥ RS II. 2
By those which were of the colour of the breast of a woman in the family way.

Disease and Medicine

Asādhya iti paricchidya ātura iva vaidyena VU III. 14
As a patient by a physician having determined that his disease is incurable.
Ārtasya yathauṣadham RV I. 28
Like medicine to an ailing person.

Fire

Hemnaḥ saṃlakṣyate hyagnau viśuddhiḥ śyāmikāpi vā *RV* I. 10
In fire is tested the purity of alloy or gold.
Dīpa ivānilāhataḥ *RV* U.37
Like a lamp struck by wind.

Flowers

Hima-kliṣṭa-kiñjalkam iva paṅkajam *RV* XV. 52
Like a lotus with its filaments battered by frost.
Bhramara ivavibhāte kundam antastuṣāram *KS VIII. 58*
See above under insects.
Pūrva-diṅmukhaṃ ketakairiva rajobhir-āvṛtam
Like the eastern horizon covered with the pollens of *Ketaka* flowers.
Pratinava-japā-puṣpa-raktam *MD* I. 38
Red like a fresh *japa*-flower.
Śirīṣa-puṣpādhīka-saukumāryaḥ *RV* XVIII. 45
More delicate than a *Śirīṣa* flower

Food

Madhu navam anāsvādita-rasam *AS* II. 10
Fresh honey not yet tasted.
Khaṇḍa-modaka-sadṛśaḥ *VU* III. 6
Like a sweetmeat made of candied sugar.

Fruit

Pakva-bimbā-dharoṣṭhī *MD* II. 18
Having lips like a ripe *Bimba* fruit.

Grain

Yavāṅkurā-pāṇdu-kapola-śobhī *RV* XIII. 49
Looking beautiful with cheeks slightly pale like the sprouts of barley.
Apragalbha-yava-sūcī komalāḥ *KS* VIII. 62
Soft like the tips of immature barley.
Phalītā iva śātayaḥ *RV* XV. 78
Fructified like Śāli grains.

House

Purārgalā-dīrgha-bhujaḥ *RV* XVIII. 4
With arms long like the bolt to the city-gate.

Kavāṭa-vakṣāḥ *RV* III. 34
With chest wide like a door-leaf.
Śṛṅgāntaraṃ dvāram ivārtha-siddheḥ *RV* II. 21
The intervening space between the horns, like the door to the fulfilment of an object.

Various Articles
Sva-hasta-dhṛta-daṇḍam ivātapatram *AS* V.6
Like an umbrella of which the handle has been grasped by one's own hand.
Titīrṣur-dustaraṃ mohād uḍupenāsmi sāgaram *RV* I. 2
Out of delusion I am desirous of crossing an ocean, difficult to cross, with a raft.

Instruments
Aṅkuśaṃ dviradasyeva *RV* IV. 39
Like the goad of an elephant.
Śmaśāna-śūlasya na yūpa-satkriyā *KS* V. 73
There is no worship of the sacrificial post of a stake in the cremation ground like that of a sacrificial post.

Metals and Minerals
Ayoghanenāya ivābhibaptam *RV* XIV. 33
Like hot iron (struck) by a hammer.

Miscellaneous
Savibhrama-vadhū-hasitā-vadātāḥ *RV* VI. 23
By those which were white like the laughter of a sportive woman.
Chāyā-vṛkṣam ivā-dhvagāḥ *RV* X. 5
As a shady tree (is resorted to) by travellers.
Ataskaras-taskara-saṃgato yathā *KS* XV. 42
Like one, not being a thief, united with a thief.
Apāṃ taraṅgeṣviva taila-bindum *RV* XIV. 38
Like a drop of oil in the waves of water.
Prāṃśu-labhye phale lobhād udvāhur-iva vāmanaḥ *RV* 1.3
Like a dwarf with his hands raised out of greed for a fruit capable of being obtained by a tall person.

Ornaments and Cosmetics
Prabhinnāñjana-rāśi-sannibhaiḥ *RS* II. 2
By those which were like a heap of mixed collyrium.

Kaṇṭhe niṣkam ivārspitam *KS* II. 49
Like a necklace put round the neck.

Grass
Vikasat-kāśa-cāmaraḥ *RV* IV. 17
The chowrie of *Kāśa* grass that is blooming.
Śara-pāndureṇa *RV* XIV. 26
By that which was white like *Śara* grass.

Plants and Trees
Sarasa-kadalī-garbha-gauraḥ *MD* II. 36
White like the interior of a juicy *Kadalī* fruit.
Anantarāśoka-latā prabālaṃ prāpyeva cūtaḥ pratipallavena *RV* VII. 21
Like a mango tree which has held with a leaf the leaf of an *Aśoka* creeper which is close to it.
Kadamba-mukula-sthūlaiḥ *RV* XV. 99
By those which were big like the buds of *Kadamba* flowers.
Sphurad-bāla-kadambakalpaiḥ *KS* III. 68
By those which were like the shining buds of *Kadamba* flowers.

Water
Kulyevodyāna-pādapān *RV* XII. 3
As a channel waters garden trees.
Tṛṇa-cchanna-Kūpopamasya *AS* V. 22
Of (you) who are like a well covered with grass.

River
Nadyo nabhaseva vivardhitāḥ *RV* XVII. 41
Like rivers enlarged by the rainy season or the (cloud-pouring) Sky.
Gaṅgā-rodhaḥ-patana-kaluṣā gṛhṇatīva prasādam *VU* I. 9
As if becoming clear like the Ganges rendered muddy by the fall of its banks.

Women
Jahāra catureva kāminī *RV* IX. 69
Stole like a clever loving woman.
Raktāṃśukā nava-vadhūriva *RS* VI. 19
Like a newly married woman dressed in red cloth.

Appendix III

Folk-Elements in Grammatical Illustrations

WE have seen that the *Aṣṭādhyāyī* and the *Mahābhāṣya* contain a lot of information on the folk-life of ancient India. It is interesting to note that the commentators have drawn many illustrations of grammatical rules from common life. The intention seems to have been that such instances, within the ambit of common experience of the pupils, would leave a vivid impression on their minds. We shall collect some such illustrations confining ourselves only to the *Siddhānta-kaumudī*. We shall note the illustrations, and give references to Bhaṭṭoji's numbering of the *Sūtra* concerned. Below the words or expressions we shall give their English rendering. It is interesting to add that the cow figures prominently in the popular illustrations. This is, of course, natural in a country in which economy was largely agricultural, and cows played an important role in agricultural operations.

1001 *Aja-kṣīram*
Milk of a she-goat.
2688 *Apaskirate Vṛṣo hṛṣṭaḥ*
The delighted bull scratches (the earth).
713 *Ardha-pippali*
Exact half of the peepul tree.
698 *Aśva-ghāsa*
Grass for horse.
504 *Aśva-patikā*
Female keeper of horses.
916 *Aśva-vadavau*
A horse and a mare.
913 *Kākolūkam*
A crow and an owl.
536 *Kukkuṭāṇḍam*
Egg of a hen.
484 *Kuṇḍodhnī gauḥ*
A cow with udders resembling a bowl shaped vessel.
916 *Kuśakāśam*
Grasses called *Kuśa* and *Kāśa*.
1040 *Kṛṣīvala*
Cultivator.
846 *Keśākeśi*
A fight between persons dragging

913 *Ahi-nakulam*
A snake and a mongoose.
637 *Āyukto gauḥ śakaṭe*
The cow is yoked to the cart.
624 *Āścaryo gavāṃ doho' gopena*
The milking of cows by one who is not a cowherd is surprising.
825 *Ikṣu-cchāyam*
Shade of sugarcanes.
544 *Ubhayataḥ Kṛṣṇaṃ gopāḥ*
The cowherds are on both sides of Kṛṣṇa.
Ulūka-pucchī Senā
An army having the rear like *that of an owl.*
746 *Go-vehat*
The cow that causes its abortion.
916 *Go-mahiṣāḥ*
Cows and buffaloes.
709 *Ghaṭānāṃ nirmātuḥ*
Of a maker of pitchers (i.e. Potters).
617 *Caurasya niprahaṇanam*
Severe beating of a thief.
914 *Takṣāyaskāram*
The carpenter and the blacksmith.
846 *Daṇḍādaṇḍi*
A fight between persons beating each other with sticks.
568 *Daṇḍena ghaṭah*
A pitcher made with a stick.
915 *Dāsī-dāsam*
A female servant and a male servant.
980 *Dāsī-putra*
Son of a female servant or, slave.
568 *Dāsyā saṃyacchate kāmukaḥ*
The passionate man.
852 *Dīrgha-sakthi śakaṭam*
A cart with long shafts.
1051 *Dūrvā-vanam*
Jungle of *Dūrvā* grass.
906 *Mārdaṅgika-pāṇavikam*
A company of instrumentalists playing *Mṛdaṅga* and *Paṇava.*

each other by the hair.
633 *Keśeṣu camarīṃ hanti*
He kills a *Chamari* deer for the sake of hairs.
915 *Gavāśvam*
The cow and the horse.
638 *Gavāṃ kṛṣṇā bahukṣīrā*
Of the cows, the black one yields plenty of milk.
539 *Gāṃ dogdhi payaḥ*
He milches milk from the cow.
746 *Go-gṛṣṭiḥ*
The cow that has borne a calf once.
504 *Go-pātikā*
Female keeper of cows.
572 Gopī marāt Kṛṣṇāya tiṣṭhate
The female cowherdess waits for Kṛṣṇa out of passion.
539 *Devadattaṃ śataṃ muṣṇāti*
He robs Devadatta of one hundred.
1051 *Devadāru-vanam*
Forest of *Devadaru* trees.
617 *Dhānā-peṣaṇam*
Crushing of corn.
1044 *Niṣāda*
A low-class man called *Niṣāda.*
463 *Naukā*
Boat.
853 *Pañcāṅgulaṃ dāru*
A piece of wood with five finger-like *parts for exposing paddy, etc.*
838 *Pācikā-bhāryaḥ*
One whose wife is a cook.
916 *Plakṣa-nyagrodhau*
The trees *Plakṣa* (Indian fig *tree) and Nyagrodha* (a species of the same).
916 *Badarāmalakam*
Jujube fruits and myrobalans.
847 *Bāhūbāhavi*
A fight in which the fighters drag each other by the hand.
540 Bhakṣayati batīvardān śasyam
He makes the bull eat corn.
541 *Bhṛtyaṃ kaṭaṃ kārayati*
He causes the servant to make a straw-mat.

846 *Muṣṭīmuṣṭi*
A fight in which the rivals strike each other with fists.
505 *Yavānī*
Bad barley.
590 *Yavebhyo gāṃ vārayati*
He prevents the cow from (eating) barley.
617 *Vṛṣalasya peṣaṇam*
Thrashing of a *Śūdra.*
916 *Vrīhi-yavam*
Paddy and barley.
2686 *Vyādadate pipīlikāḥ patangasya mukham*
Ants stretch the mouth of the insect.
852 *Sthūlakṣā Veṇu-yaśṭi*
A bamboo staff with big joints.
1051 *Śrīṣa-vanam*
Forest of Sirisa flowers.
916 *Śuka-bakam*
Parrots and cranes.
454 *Śūdrī*
A female *Śūdra.*
509 *Surāpītī*
A woman drinking wine.

The names of the four kinds of head-rules or *Adhikāra-sūtras* are taken from objects found in common life. They are *go-yūtha* (herd of cows), *siṃha-drsti* (look of a lion), *maṇḍūka-pluti* (frog-leap) and *gaṅgā-srotaḥ pravāha* (flow of the current of the Ganges).

Appendix IV

Folk-Elements in the Upaniṣads

THE *Upaniṣads* deal with esoteric and abstruse philosophical and metaphysical matters. So, naturally we cannot expect popular beliefs and practices in these works. It is, however, not correct to think that these treaties are totally devoid of folk-elements. Sometimes the preceptors of *Upaniṣads* mention popular sights and objects in order to bring an idea home to the mind of the disciples. Here we shall note just a few things of common life in the principal *Upaniṣads*.

In the *Chāndogya* we find the following folk-elements. There is this comparison. As a (fisherman) finds fish in shallow water, so Death saw the gods in the rites performed with the *mantras* of *Ṛg, Yajus* and *Sāma-vedas*. (I. 4-3). We get, in the following, an idea of the food and habits of common men. In the *Kuru* land, crops having been destroyed, one, named Uṣasti, took shelter in *ibhya-grāma* (village of elephant-drivers). There he found that a man had been eating loathsome *māṣa* (i.e. a kind of pulse). Uṣasti having begged food of him, the latter offered him the remnant of his food and drink (I. 10. 1 ff). From this we learn that, in those days, people having a particular occupation used to live in a village which was meant solely for them. It is also found that they did not hesitate to offer food-leavings even to a guest. From II. 17.2 it appears that slander was a popular practice which people of the upper strata did not like to indulge in. From IV. 2.1 we come to learn that people were accustomed to using *aśvatarī-rathas* (chariots drawn by mules) as vehicles. In the story of *Satyakāma Jāvāla* (IV. 4. ff) there is a clear indication of the prevalence of adultery in public life. IV. 17.7 refers to the practice of melting or mending articles of gold with a particular salt, silverware with gold, *raṅga* (borax) with silver, lead with *raṅga*, iron with lead, wood work with iron or leather. V. 13.2 testifies to the use, *inter alia*, of necklaces not only by women but also by men. V. 24.4 refers to the practice of the remnants of food given by a man of an upper class to a *Caṇḍāla*. In VI. 9.2 we find the following comparison. Bees gather honey from flowers, various trees and plants. Honey is an amalgam of different kinds of juice which lose their individual character. So also the individual souls become one with the supreme Soul. VI. 16.1 refers to the practice of administering the ordeal of heated axe to a thief. In VII. 6.1 we find that common men used to indulge in quarrels, discovery of faults in others and the spread of scandal.

In the *Umā-Haimavatī*, story of the *Kenopaniṣad* (III) we find an element of folk-belief. In the story we find that the lesser gods could not burn or lift even a blade of grass overpowered as they were by the will of the Supreme Being.

In the *Muṇḍaka* (III. 1.1) we find a reference to birds sitting on trees—some eating fruits with others looking on.

The *Śvetāśvatara* (II. 8) refers to the use of rafts to cross waterways. In the same *Upaniṣad* (VI. 10) we find this simile. As a spider covers itself with web, so the Supreme Being covers itself under *Māyā* (illusion).

The *Bṛhadāraṇyaka* says (I. 4.7) that one has to know all the mysteries by knowing the *Ātman*. It is like finding out lost cattle tracking them down by means of their footprints. In II. 2.2 there is mention of a calf with its rope and the post to which it is tied. The idea is that as a rope keeps a calf united with a post, so *anna* (food) is the cause of unification of the *Liṅgaśarīra* and *Sthūlaśarīra*. II. 5.16 refers to *Madhu-vidyā*, a magical charm capable of working miracles. II. 3.18 likens the movement of *pūrṇātmā* in both the states of sleep and wakefulness to the movement of a great fish on both the eastern and western coasts. In IV. 3.20, it is stated that, as a big bird, tired of flying, flies towards its nest with outstretched wings, so the *puruṣa* speeds towards such a state in which, being asleep, he covets no object nor does he dream of anything. In IV. 3.36, it is stated that when *jīvātman*, within the body, goes upward being in possession of *paramātman*, it makes a sound like a cart which is heavily burdened. As a leech goes to the end of a blade of grass, and then jumps to another, so also *jīvātman* leaves one body to resort to another (IV. 4.3). As a goldsmith takes some gold to fashion it in a beautiful way, so also *jīvātman,* leaving one body goes to a new one which it builds nicely (IV. 4.4). As a slough, cast on an ant-hill, lies there similarly the body of one who knows *Brahman,* lies (IV. 4.7). In V. 8.1, *Vāk* is conceived as a cow with *Svāhā, Vaṣaṭ, Hanta* and *Svadhā,* as the four udders. *Prāṇa* is like the bull to the *Vāk*-cow and *Menas* is her calf (V. 8.1). When *Prāṇa* was about to go up, it dislocated the senses as a horse from Sindhu-deśa uproots the pegs used for tying its legs. (VI. 1.13). VI. 4.13 mentions the following ten kinds of corns which seem to have been produced in those times :

> *dhānya, yava, tila, māṣa, aṇu, priyaṅgu, godhūma, masūra, khalva and khalakula.*

This *Upaniṣad* records the following beliefs and practices (VI. 4.13 ff.). A man, desiring issues, should get paddy husked by his wife who has bathed after three days of monthly impurity. A person, desiring to have a son of fair complexion and long life and versed in one *Veda*, should cook rice, obtained in the above manner, in milk and, mixing it with ghee, eat it along with his wife. One wishing to have a long-lived son of tawny complexion, versed in two *Vedas*, should cook rice with curd, and eat it mixed with ghee. One intending to be the father of a dark-complexioned, red-eyed and long-lived son, versed in three *Vedas*, should cook rice in water, and eat it mixed with ghee. A man, desiring to have a learned and long-lived daughter, should cook rice with sesame and eat it mixed with ghee. One, wishing to get a famous, long-lived, sweet-tongued son, capable of participating in learned assemblies and versed in all *Vedas*, should prepare *palānna* with the meat of a young or aged bull. It is interesting to note that it attests the vogue of beef-eating in that age. Towards early morning, oblation should be offered in fire, and the remnant of *caru* rice should be eaten by the husband who should give what remains to his wife. The husband will also sprinkle the wife thrice with consecrated water.

Appendix V

Supplementary List of Folk Cults[1] and Festivals

In addition to the folk-cults, mentioned in the body of this work, there are a few others. We note some of the additional cults below with a short description of each.

Name of cult	Source	Description
Dhanurmaha	*Harivaṃśa* II. 22. 91, 26.4, 27.32, 101.64	A festival in which archers used to give a demonstration of their skill. The practice appears to have been in vogue since early times when people took to archery in war and hunting. When Kaṃsa desired Kṛṣṇa to come to his court at Mathurā he arranged for *Dhanurmaha* festival. The *Harivaṃśa* testifies to its holding in connection with Śiva-worship. A sort of *Dhanurmaha* is connected with the Rāma legend too. Rāma's breaking the bow at Janaka's court appears to have taken place in such a festival.
Girimaha	*Harivaṃśa* II. 16.1 *Mahābhārata Āśvamedhika 59.4-Raivataka Maha.*	Cowherds are stated to have taken to this festival. Kṛṣṇa's lifting the Govardhana hill was, perhaps, connected with such a cult. The festival consisted in merriment,

Name of cult	Source	Description
		distribution of sweets etc. The food was at first offered to the mountain deity.
Indramaha (also Śakramaha)	*Harivaṃśa* II. 15.4, 19.59 A text of the *Atharva-Pariśiṣṭa* is called *Indra-mahotsava.* *Nāṭyaśāstra* I. 58-59, 64-70 *Rāmāyaṇa, Kiṣkindhā* 16.37	Indra appears to have been worshipped by cultivators. From the *Mahābhārata* (*Ādi,* 57) and some other works we learn of of *Indradhvaja* festival in which a flag-staff in honour of Indra used to be worshipped.
Nadīmaha	*Kāśikā* Comm. on Pāṇini V. 1. 109 (Gaṅgāmaha)	The tradition of looking upon rivers as goddesses or mothers is very old. The rivers Gaṅgā, Yamunā, etc. are invoked to render water holy.
Samudramaha	*Harivaṃśa* II. 88.4, 27-28, (Samudra-yātrā) 57-60	

REFERENCES

1. This list is based on V.S. Agrawala's book entitled *Ancient Indian Folk Cults,* Varanasi, 1970, which may be consulted for details.

GLOSSARY

Technical Terms and Unfamiliar Words Used in the Work

[In English Alphabetical Order]

Abhicāra or *Ābhicārika* : Rite or incantation supposed to cause harm to others.

Abhivartamaṇi : Name of an amulet.

Abhūti : A malevolent deity.

Adhivastra : Outer cover or veil.

Ādikauśika : According to some, a mendicant showing images of gods; according to others, snake-charmer. *Kauśika,* according to some, denotes a class of people practising music, dance, etc.

Āgrayaṇa : A religious ceremony in which the first fruits of the season are offered to god.

Āji-dhāvana : Horse-race.

Alinda : Terrace before the house-door; Square-shaped place at the door.

Ambuvācī : 10th to 13th day of the dark half of the month of *Āsādha,* when the earth is supposed to be unclean.

Ānandapaṭa : The cloth put on by a woman during her first menstruation.

Āpaṇa : Liquor-shop; a drinking party.

Arcā : Image of a deity.

Arhat : A Buddha, the highest rank in Buddhist hierarchy.

Ārhata : A Jaina, a follower of the Jaina doctrine.

Aṣṭakā : The eight days of three months, on which the manes are to be propitiated.

Aśvamedha : Horse-sacrifice.

Āśvina : The distance traversed by a horse in course of one day.

Ātatāyin : Dangerous enemies of the following kinds: an incendiary, a poisoner, one armed with a weapon, a robber, one who wrests a field or carries away one's wife.

Aumaka : Cloth made of yarn of flax (*umā*).

Avadātikā : A kind of wine.

Āvarilla : Upper garment.

Avidyā : Nescience.

Ayaḥśūlika : A class of ascetics who used to pierce their tongues, arms or some other limb with iron spikes.

Āyogava : Craft of weaving nets; name of a mixed caste sprung from the union of a *Śūdra* male and *Vaiśya* female.

Bhāṇḍāgārika : A particular minister.

Bhāṭaka : Paid servant.

Bhuśiṇḍī : A mechanical device used for throwing stones in war.

Bodhi : Enlightenment.

Brahmacarya : Nīlakaṇṭha, a commentator of the *Mahābhārata*, defines it as *brahmaṇyeva cāre vāk-kāya-manasāṃ pravṛttiḥ*, i.e., to contemplete *Brahman* alone with speech, body and mind.

Brahmarihāra : Attitudes of mind, called *Maitrī* (friendliness), *Karunā* (compassion), *Muditā* (delight at others' joy), *Upekṣā* (equanimity).

Bṛhatikā : Perhaps an upper garment thrown over the shoulders, and hanging down to the knees.

Catuḥsama : An unguent of four ingredients – sandal, agallochum, saffron and musk.

Caṭuka : A vessel out of which alms are given.

Caturaṅgabala : Game of chess in which the chessmen are

represented as hastin (elephant), *aśva* (horse or cavalry), ratha (chariot) and *padāti* (infantry) – the four wings of an army.

Cetiya : Sanskrit *Caitya*, Memorial mound, monument, tomb-stone, a place of worship, temple, a religious tree or any tree growing by the side of a street.

Challi : A kind of dance.

Cīvara : Robe of a Buddhist monk.

Cūḍākaraṇa : Sacrament of tonsure.

Daiṣṭika : Follower of the famous Makkhali Gosāla, well-known in Pāli literature.

Daṇḍājinaka : A class of people masquerading as ascetics merely by the outward signs of staff and deer-skin.

Dhammacakka : The wheel of *dharma*. A particular discourse is called *Dhammacakka-pavattana-sutta.*

Dhānā : Fried barley or rice.

Dhāraṇī : Protective spell.

Dhavalapaṭṭa : A sort of plaster for wounds.

Dhigvana : A low-caste person living by leather-work and sale of leather.

Dhopana : Name of a ceremony in which the bones of a dead relative are dug up, washed and besmeared with scent. Then the people eat various kinds of food, drink wine while crying for the departed relative.

Diśākāka : A crow for ascertaining directions in the sea.

Gaṇa : Same as *Saṃgha.*

Gāndharva : A singer; the art of music; a form of marriage by mutual consent of a man and a woman.

Gāṇikya : A group of harlots.

Goṇi or *Goṇītarī* : Small sack.

Goṣṭhī : An assembly, association, a sort of club for meeting and discussion.

Grāmaṇī : Village headman.

Guṭikāpāta : A process for ascertaining the culprit by using wooden pieces.

Haiyaṃgavīna : Clarified butter prepared from the previous day's milk; fresh ghee.

Harimāṇa : Name of a disease, Jaundice.

Jāmbunade : Gold.

Jana : A political body.

Janapada : A self-governed political unit comprising a sizeable area.

Jaṅgiḍa : Name of an amulet.

Jekkāra : Loud utterance of glory.

Jeṭṭhaka : Leader of a union.

Kālakarṇī : Designation of a person through whose fault shipwreck is supposed to occur.

Kalama : A kind of paddy.

Kālikā : A kind of wine.

Kaṇapa : A kind of weapon.

Kañcuka : A sort of bodice.

Kāpālika : A class of *Tāntric* devotees.

Kapiśāyana : A drink.

Karambha : Flour or meal mixed with curds.

Karaṅka : Begging bowl.

Kārtāntika : Fortune-teller.

Kaṭhina : Name of a Buddhist ceremony for making robes.

Kaula : A class of *Tāntric* devotees.

Kauśika : See *Ādikauśika.*

Kāyastha : Scribe.

Kedāra : A field under water, a meadow, a basin for water around the root of a tree.

Khala : Threshing floor.

Khaśa : Name of a people and of its country (in North India)

Kimīdin A class of demons who, according to Sāyana move about shouting *Kim idam Kim idam.*

Kīnāśa : Cultivator.

Kṛsara : Rice boiled with sesamum.

Kṛtyā : An evil spirit or a demigoddess supposed to cause injury or mischief.

Kṣapaṇaka : A Buddhist or Jaina mendicant.

Kṣattā : Charioteer.

Kṣviṅkā : According to Sāyaṇa, *Śabdakāriṇī*— shouting; a kind of bird.

Kulāla : Potter.

Kulmāṣa : Gruel.

Kumba : A kind of head-dress.

Kumba-kurīra : According to some, golden ornaments attached to the head-dress of the sacrificer's wife, according to others, hair-net.

Kuppāsa : A sort of bodice.

Kurīra : A head-dress or head-ornament.

Kuśī : Ploughshare.

Kutū or *Kutupa* : Leather jar.

Lāja : A kind of fried paddy.

Lāsya : Tender dance.

Loḍhaa : A machine for separating seeds from cotton.

Lokāyata : Materialism, atheism.

Madhuparka : A mixture of certain delicious substances offered to deities in religious rites or to distinguished guests. Opinions of some authorities, who differ on the ingredients, are : mixture of curd and honey; mixture of water (or milk), honey and meat .

Madhuvidyā : A mystical doctrine supposed to transform poison into nectar.

Mahāpaśu : A human being intended to be sacrificed before a deity.

Maireya (ka) : Distillation of wine.

Mānatta : Suspension of a person from the Order for some ecclesiastical offence.

Māṇava : A gang of dacoits.

Māsara : A mixture of several articles of food, e.g. barley, fried grain.

Maskarin : A class of wandering medicants.

Masūsya : A variety of paddy.

Medhi : A pillar, post, especially a pillar in the

	middle of a threshing floor, to which oxen are tied up.
Mūlakarman :	Use of roots for magical purposes.
Nagnahu :	Generic name of certain roots, herbs, spices, etc. serving as yeast.
Nagnikā :	A girl before mensturation.
Naigama :	A sort of trade-union.
Navānna :	A ceremony held with new rice or grain.
Nigantha or *Nirgrantha* :	A naked Jaina mendicant of the *Digambara* class.
Nimitta :	Omens and signs.
Nirbāna or *Nibbāna* :	Complete extinction of individual of worldly existence; perfection, perpetual calm.
Niriṅgī :	A veil for a woman.
Nirṛti :	An evil spirit or a demigoddess supposed to cause injury or mischief.
Niṣka :	Gold coin; necklace in which such coins are stringed together.
Pakṣiṇī heti :	Same as *sasarparī* (q.v.).
Pakṣyā :	Same as *sasarparī* (q.v.).
Pānakuṭī :	Bar for providing wine.
Pañcakṛṣṭi :	Differently expalined : Rotation of five crops in the same field; Growing of five kinds of crops in different fields.
Pañcarātra :	A form of ritualistic Vaiṣṇavism so called because in it a sacrifice had to be performed on five successive nights. Some take it to mean a mysterious area of knowledge said to have been taught by Viṣṇu to Brahmā who learned it in five nights.
Pañcasīla :	Five rules of conduct, *viz.*, abstinence from intoxication, abstinence from violence, abstinence from adultery, not to take what is not given.
Pāṇdusopāka :	A low-caste person born to a *Caṇḍala* by a *Vaidehī* woman.
Pāṇḍva :	A garment.
Pāramitā :	Perfection.

Parivāsa :	Parched rice fried in butter.
Pārśvaka :	A lier, pilferer, thief.
Pāṣaṇḍa :	Heresy, heretic.
Paṭavāsa :	Perfumed powder.
Pattana :	Port on a river or sea.
Paṭṭiśa :	A kind of sword.
Pavāranā :	Post-rains ceremony of the Buddha.
Pāyasa :	A preparation of milk mixed with ghee, honey and sugar.
Pāyasya :	A mixture of curd and milk.
Phāṇṭha :	Perhaps a hot drink or butter made from the cream of the day's milk.
Plava :	Catamaran.
Pośakārī :	Female embroiderer.
Prahelikā :	Riddle.
Praheṇaka :	Sweets etc. distributed among people on festive occasions.
Praśnadūtī :	Riddle.
Pratidhi :	Probably part of a woman's dress.
Pratiloma :	In reverse order e.g., a husband of an inferior caste, and the wife of a superior one.
Pṛthukā :	Flattened rice (*cipīṭaka*).
Pukvasa or *Pulkasa* :	A mixed caste.
Puruṣamedha :	Human sacrifice.
Putrikāpurta :	A sonless man's daughter's son appointed to be his own son; A sonless man's daughter appointed to be his own son.
Rājasūya :	A great sacrifice performed by a universal monarch. In it, the tributary princes also participated. It was performed at the time of coronation as a mark of his undisputed sovereignty.
Rājika :	Black mustard.
Rāṅkava :	Probably a costly wrapper.
Rāsa (ka) :	A kind of dance said to have been performed by Kṛṣṇa and the cowherds, but particularly by *gopīs* or cowherdesses of Vṛndāvana in the

	Pūrṁimā tithi (full moon) of the month of *Kārtika*.
Riktā :	Name of the 4th, 9th and 14th days of a lunar fortnight.
Rukma :	Gold or golden ornament.
Sadampuṣpā :	Name of an amulet.
Sahaja :	A mode of *sādhana* which enables one to attain the goal by easy means.
Sāhasa :	Violent crime.
Śailūṣa :	Actor.
Sairāvatī :	Sea-going vessel.
Sairika :	Bull.
Sairindhra :	Arrangement of the dress of rich people.
Śakuna-vidyā :	Knowledge of the indications of the behaviour of animals and birds.
Salākābhatta :	Distribution of food by tickets, a sort of rationing system.
Sālākiya :	Occultism.
Śāli :	A kind of paddy.
Samaja :	A multitude of beasts or birds; a number of fools.
Samana or *Śramaṇa :*	A Buddhist ascetic.
Samāvartana :	Return, especially of pupil's return home after finishing his holy studies.
Saṃgha :	A group of people holding similar views and owing allegiance to a particular person; Buddhist Monastic Order.
Saṃghāti :	Double waist-cloth.
Samudaya :	Origin.
Saṃyāva :	A sort of cake of wheaten flour fried with ghee and milk, and made up into an oblong form with sugar and spices.
Sānnāyya :	Mixture of curd and milk.
Saptasvasāraḥ :	Seven rivers, according to Sāyaṇa.
Sasarparī :	An evil spirit capable of bestowing great power.
Saṣpānī :	Malted rice.
Śataghnī :	A kind of cannon; According to some, a huge slab of stone so called because it

	could kill one hundred people at a time.
Śatavāra :	Name of an amulet.
Sauvīra :	Soar gruel.
Setu :	Dam.
Śikhā :	A kind of interest payable daily.
Simbidhānya :	Rain crop.
Sīmantonnayana :	Parting of the hair; one of the sacraments (*saṃskāra*) or purificatory rites observed by a woman in the fourth, sixth or eighth month of her pregnancy.
Sinīvalī :	First day of New Moon.
Śīpada :	A disease.
Śiśnadeva :	A phallus-worshipper or one who plays with his genital organ.
Sītya :	Ploughed land.
Śobhanaka :	A kind of actor.
Sphya :	Oar.
Śrāṇā :	Cooked vegetables.
Śreṇī :	Guild, union of traders.
Sruti :	Royal thoroughfare.
Stūpa :	Relic mound.
Śukadhānya :	Autumn crop.
Śukaramaddava :	Meat of a grown-up hog, neither too young nor too old.
Śūlagava :	An ox fit for a spit offered to Rudra.
Suṇḍāpaṇa :	A shop where liquor is sold; a bar.
Śvagaṇika :	Hunter, dog-feeder.
Śvetapata :	A *Śvetambara* Jain.
Śvetasurā :	Perhaps same as *Avadātikā* (q.v.).
Śyāmūla :	According to some, a woollen garment according to others, a kind of blanket
Tādaṅka :	Ear-ring.
Takṣā :	Carpenter.
Tāṇḍava :	Violent dance.
Tārpya :	Various meanings suggested : cloth soaked in ghee; cloth made of a material obtained from the *Tṛpā* tree; a silk garment or under-garment;

cloth made of yarn thrice dipped in water before weaving.

Tilaka : Name of an amulet.
Tiṇṭa : Gambling house.
Tirīṭa : A kind of head-dress.
Titthiya or *Tīrthika* : A pilgrim, an ascetic *Brāhmaṇa* visiting holy places.
Tittila : Gate-keeper.
Tokmāni : Malted barley.
Triśaraṇa : The Trio, *viz. Buddha, Dhamma, Saṃgha.*
Trivṛt : Name of an amulet.
Tulāoḍi : Anklet for a woman.
Tunnavāya : Tailor.
Tvaksāra : Bamboo and similar other plants.
Udaṃcana : A bucket, a pail for drawing water from a well.
Ukhā : A boiling vessel, a boiler or cooking pot like a saucepan.
Upabarhaṇa : A pillow.
Upadaṃsa : Probably thing like radish, ginger, etc.
Upanayana : A sacrament (*saṃskāra*). Literally, it means taking of a boy near his preceptor investiture with the sacred thread.
Upasampadā : Ordination.
Upasaṃvyāna : A lower garment.
Upavasana : Veil.
Uposatha : Periodical meeting of the Buddhists; a sort of sabbath.
Ūrṇa : Wool.
Uttarāsaṃgha : Single upper robe.
Vādinī : A female musician.
Vaidhṛti : A conjunction of sun and moon when they are in the same *Ayana* and of equal declination, the sun of the longitudes amount to 360 degrees.
Vaila : Hair of a rat.
Vaisāriṇa : An aquatic creature.
Vandanamālikā : Welcome-garland.
Vāpa : Barber.

Vāramasyā :	An account of joy and sorrow, caused by the infulence of nature, in the twelve months of a year
Varatrā :	Long rope.
Vardhakin :	Carpenter.
Varṇaka :	A kind of woollen blanket.
Vārṣadaṃsa :	Furs of cats.
Vāruṇī :	Any spirituous liquor.
Vassāvāsa :	Residence in the rainy season.
Vavri :	Upper garment.
Vicchitti :	Paints and unguents for colouring the body.
Vihāra :	Buddhist monastery.
Vikṛnta :	A kind of gangster.
Vipāṭha :	A kind of arrow.
Vīrudh :	Name of an amulet.
Viś :	A political body.
Viṣṭi :	Labourer working on wages in kind.
Vīṭā :	A piece of wood or an iron ball.
Vrātya :	Anti-Aryan people or Aryans who were non-conformist in outlook and practice.
Vyāma :	Span from the tip of the middle finger of one hand up to the tip of the middle finger of another when a person stands with arms outstretched.
Vyatipāta :	An astronomical *yoga* when sun and moon are in opposite *Ayanas* and have the same declination, the sum of their longitudes being 180 degree.
Yamapaṭṭaka :	A piece of cloth or canvas on which Yama, with his attendants, and the punishments of hell were depicted.
Yantraka :	One expert in the construction of canals etc.
Yātudhāna :	An evil spirit, demon.
Yātumāvat :	One working with something magical and consisting of witchcraft; one engaged in magic and deception; according to Sāyaṇa; *Yātudhāna* (q.v.); *Rākṣasa* causing torments.

BIBLIOGRAPHY

TEXTS AND TRANSLATIONS

Abhijñānaśakuntala of Kālidāsa, ed. M.R. Kale.

Advaita-brahma-siddhi of Sadānanda, ed. *Bib. Indica*, Calcutta, 1890.

Advaita-siddhi of Madhusūdana, NSP. ed., 1917.

Alaṃkāra-sarvasva of Ruyyaka, NSP. ed., 1893.

Āpastamba-gṛhyasūtra, ed. Winternitz, Vienna, 1893.

Arthasaṃgraha of Laugākṣibhāskara.

Atharvaveda—Śaunaka recension, ed., with Sāyaṇa's comm., Hoshiarpur, 1960-64. Trs. into Eng. by R.T. Griffith, Benares, 1895-96.

Ātmabodha of Śaṃkara, ed. F. Hall, Mirzapore, 1852.

Ātmapurāṇa of Śaṃkarānanda, Bombay.

Ātma-tattva-viveka of Udayana, ed. J. Vidyasagara, Calcutta, 1873.

Bālamīmāṃsā-praśasti of Śaṃkarabhaṭṭa.

Bhāmatī of Vācaspatimiśra, *Bib. Indica*, Calcutta, 1880.

Bhāṣāpariccheda of Viśvanatha, ed. L.N. Vasak, Calcutta 1871.

Bhāṭṭarahasya of Khaṇḍadeva.

Bhāṭṭikāvya Bhavisayattakahā of Dhanayāla, ed. Dalal Gune, Baroda, 1923.

Bhedadhikkāra of Nṛsiṃha, Benares, 1904.

Bhuvaneśa-laukika-nyāya-sāhasrī.

Brahmasūtra-bhāṣya of Śaṃkara, Anandasarma ed., Poona, 1890-1.

Brahmasūtra-tātparya-vivaraṇa, pub. in the *Paṇḍīt*, 1882.

Bṛhadāraṇyakopaniṣad-bhāṣya-vārtika of Sureśvera, Anandasarma ed., 2 Vols., 1892-94.

Bṛhatī—comm. on *Śabara-bhāṣya.*

Cārudatta of Bhāsa, in *Bhāsa-nāṭaka-cakra,* ed. C.R. Devadhar

Poona, 1937.
Caura-pañcāśikā of Bilhaṇa, ed. in *Kāvyamālā*, xiii , Bombay, 1903 (*Bilhaṇa – kāvya*).
Citsukhī, *Paṇdit*, 1882-83.
Dakṣiṇāmūrti-stotra of Śaṃkara.
Daśakumāracarita, ed. L. Pansikar, NSP, 10th ed., Bombay, 1925.
Deśopadeśa of Kṣemendra, ed. M. Kaul, Poona, 1923.
Dhammapada, ed. S. Radhakrishnan.
Dhvanyāloka of Ānandavardhana, NSP, 1891.
Dīgha Nikāya, PTS eds. Vols. I, II by T.W.R. Davids, J.E. Carpenter, 1889.
Dīpavaṃsa – trs. into Eng. by E.M. Coomaraswamy, Colombo, 1901.
Divyāvadāna
Gaṇaratna-mehodadhi of Vardhamāna, ed. Eggeling, 1879-81.
Gāthāsaptaśatī, ed. trs. into Bengali by R.G. Basak, Calcutta.
Gaüḍavaho of Vākpatirāja, ed. S.P. Pandit, Bombay, 1887/2nd ed. 1927.
Harivaṃśa-purāṇa of Jinasena.
Harṣacarita of Bāṇabhaṭṭa, ed. P.V. Kane, Bombay, 1918.
Haṭhayoga-pradīpikā of Svātmārāma.
Hitopadeśa, ed. Peterson, Bombay, 1887.
Jīvanmukti-viveka of Vidyāraṇya, Ānandāśrama, Śaka 1811.
Jaiminīya-nyāyamālā-vistara, Ānandāśrama, 1892.
Jaina Rāmāyaṇa of Svayambhū. *Jātaka*, ed. Fausböli. Trs. by various scholars, ed. Cowell and Rouse, Camondee, 1895. Trs. into Bengali by I. Ghosh, Calcutta.
Kādambarī of Bāṇabhaṭṭa, ed. M.R. Kale, Bombay, 1928.
Kālakācārya-Kathānaka
Kalāvilāsa of Kṣemendra, ed. *Kāvyamālā*, I.
Kalpataru – Same as *Vedānta-kalpataru* (q.v.).
Kāmasūtra of Vātsyāyana, ed. with Skt. and Hindī comms., by D. Sastri, Benares, 1964.
Karakaṇḍa-cariu, ed. H. Jain, 1964.
Karpūramañjarī of Rājasekhara, NSP. ed., 1887. Also ed. S. Konow. Trs. Lanman.
Kathākośa of Śrīcandra.
Kathāmahodadhi of Somacandra, Jamnagar, 1916.
Kathāratnākara of Hemavijaya, Jamnagar, 1911.
Kathārṇava

Kathāsaritsāgara—ed. Durgaprasad and Parab, NSP, Bombay, 1889 (Reprinted 1915). *Ocean of Story*, Eng. trs. by Tawney, ed. Penzer, Vols. 1-10.
Kāvyādarśa of Daṇḍin, *Bib. Indica*, Calcutta, 1863.
Kāvyālaṃkāra of Rudraṭa, NSP ed., 1886.
Kāvyapradīpa of Govinda, NSP. ed., 1891.
Kāvyaprakāśa of Mammaṭa, ed. M. Nyātaratna, Calcutta, 1866.
Khaṇḍanakhaṇḍa-khādya of Śrīharṣa, Reprint from *Paṇḍit*, 1888.
Kirātārjunīya of Bhāravi, ed. Godbole and Parab, with Mallinātha's comm., NSP, Bombay, 6th ed., 1907.
Kṛṣi-parāśara, ed. G.P. Majumdar and S.C. Banerji. Asiatic Society, Calcutta.
Kumārasambhava of Kālidāsa, ed. Parvanikar Parab and Pansikar, with comm. of Mallinātha (i-viii) and Sītārāma (ix-xvii), NSP, Bombay, 10th ed., 1927.
Kusumāñjali of Udayana, *Bib. Indica*, Calcutta, 1880-85.
Kuṭṭanīmata of Dāmodaragupta, ed. T.M. Tripathi, with Skt. comm., Bombay, 1924.
Kuvalayānanda of Appayadīkṣita, ed. J. Vidyasagara, Calcutta, Śaka, 1796.
Laukika-nyāya-saṃgraha.
Mahābhārata, Bombay, Śaka 1799.
Mahābhāṣya, ed. Kielhorn, Bombay, 1880-85.
Mahānirvāṇa-tantra.
Mahāvaṃsa, ed. Geiger, PTS, 1908.
Majjhima Nikāya, PTS. ed., Vols. I-III. Trs. PTS. in 3 Vols.
Mālatīmādhava of Bhavabhūti, ed. Telang, with comm. of Jagaddhara Tripurāri (i-vii) and Nānyadeva (viii-x), NSP, Bombay, 1926.
Malayasundarī-kathoddhāra.
Manu-smṛti—Ed. J.L. Shaśtri, Delhi, 1983.
Meghadūta of Kālidāsa, ed. S.K. De, New Delhi (Sāhitya Akademi).
Mīmāṃsā-nyāya-prakāśa of Āpadeva.
Mīmāṃsā-sūtra of Jaimini, *Bib. Indica*, Calcutta, 1873-89.
Mṛcchakaṭika, ed. K.P. Parab, with comm., NSP, Bombay, 5th ed., 1922.
Mudrārākṣasa, ed. Telang, Bombay, 1884.
Naiṣkarmya-siddhi of Sureśvara, Bombay, 1891.
Nāyakumāra-cariu of Pupphadanta.

Nemināthа-caüpai.
Nītisāra of Kāmandaka, *Bib. Indica*, Calcutta, 1884.
Nyāyabindu-ṭīkā of Dharmottara, *Bib. Indica*, Calcutta, 1889.
Nyāyakandalī of Śrīdhara, *Vizianagram. Skt. Series*, 1895.
Nyāyakaṇikā of Vācaspati Miśra, *Paṇdit.*
Nyāyamakaranda of Ānandabodha, Benares.
Nyāyamañjarī of Jayanta, *Vizianagram Skt. Series.*
Nyāyaratnākara — comm. on *Ślokavārtika.*
Nyāya-siddhānta-dīpa of Śeṣadhara *Paṇḍit.*
Nyāyasudhā of Someśvara, Benares.
Nyāyavārtika, Bib. Indica, Calcutta, 1887-97.
Nyāyavārtika-tātparya-ṭīkā of Vācaspatimiśra, *Vizianagram Skt. Series*, 1898.
Padamañjarī of Haradatta (Comm. on *Kāsikā-vṛtti*).
Pañcadaśī of Vidyāraṇya, ed. J. Vidyasagara, Calcutta, 1882.
Pañcapādikā of Padmapāda, *Vizianagram Skt. Series*, 1891.
Pañcatantra, the Pañcatantra Reconstructed, New Haven, Conn. 1924.
Pāṇdavacarita of Devaprabha Sūri, ed. *Kāvyamālā,* 93 Bombay, 1911.
Pāṇḍava-purāṇa of Śubhacandra.
Paramārthasāra of Śeṣu, Lucknow, 1876.
Paribhāṣenduśekhara of Nāgojī, ed. & trs. Kielhorn, Bombay, 1868-74.
Parimala — Same as *Vedānta-kalpataru-parimala* (q.v.).
Pariśiṣṭaparvan of Hemacandra, *Bib. Indica*, Calcutta, 1891.
Pātimokkha, ed. Minayeff, St. Petersburg, Akad., 1869 with trs. and notes. trs. R. Davids and Oldenberg, *SBE*, Vol. 13.
Paümacariya of Vīmalasūri, Ed. Jacobi, Bhavnagar, 1914.
Prabandha-cintāmaṇi.
Prasanna-rāghava of Jayadeva, NSP, 1893.
Raghuvaṃśa, ed. Durgaprasad, Bombay, 1892-96.
Rāmāyaṇa, NSP, 1888.
Rasagaṅgādhara of Jagannātha, ed. Durgaprasad, 1888.
Rasavāhinī of Vedeha, ed. B. Devarakkhita, Colombo, 1917.
Rauhiṇeya-carita.
Ṛgveda, ed. with Sāyaṇa's comm., Vaidika Saṃśodhana Maṇḍala, Poona, Vols. I-V. Eng. Trs. by H.H. Wilson, 6 vols., Poona, 1925-26.
Ṛjuvimalā of Śālikanātha, Benares, 1929.

Śabarabhāṣya, Anandasrama ed.
Ṣaḍ-darśana-cintanikā of M.M. Kunte, Poona, 1877-82.
Ṣaḍ-darśana-samuccaya of Haribhadra, Benares, 1905.
Saduktikarṇāmṛta, ed. S.C. Banerji, Calcutta.
Sāhityadarpaṇa, *Bib. Indica*, Calcutta, 1851.
Sāhityakaumudī of Vidyābhūṣaṇa, NSP, 1897.
Samayamātṛkā of Kṣemendra, ed. Durga Prasad and Parab, Bombay, 1925.
Samyaktva-kaumudī.
Śaṅkaravijaya of Ānandagiri, *Bib. Indica*, Calcutta, 1868.
Sāṃkhya-sūtra-vṛtti of Aniruddha, *Bib. Indica*, Calcutta, 1888.
Sāṃkhya-tattva-kaumudī of Vācaspati Miṣra, ed. T. Tarkavacaspati, Calcutta, 1871.
Sāṃkṣepa-śārīraka of Sarvajñātmamuni, *Paṇḍit*, Vols. IV-X.
Sanatsujātīyam Adhyātmaśastram of the *Mahābhārata,* ed. G.P. Haldar, Calcutta, Śaka 1851-53.
Śāṇḍilyasūtras, ed. Ballantyne, Calcutta, 1861.
Saptapadārthī of Śivāditya, *Vizianagram Skt. Series*, 1893.
Sarasvatī-kaṇṭhābharaṇa of Bhoja, ed. A Barooa, Calcutta, 1883.
Sarva-darśana-saṃgraha of Mādhava, *Bib. Indica*, Calcutta, 1858.
Śāstradīpikā of Pārthasārathi, Benares, 1891.
Siddhāntaleśa of Appaya Dīkṣita, *Vizianagram Skt. Series,* 1890.
Śiśupālavadha, ed. T. Tarkavacaspati, Calcutta, Śaka 1769.
Subhāṣitāvalī of Vallabhadeva, ed. Peterson & Durgaprasad, Bombay, 1886.
Subodhinī—Comm. on *Mīmāṃsā-sūtra.*
Somanāthī—*Mayūkhamālikā*, comm. on *Śāstradīpikā,* NSP, 1915.
Syādvāda—mañjarī, comm. on Hemacandra's *Vītarāga-stuti*, Benares, 1900.
Śukasaptati—Textus Simplicior, ed. R. Schmidt, Leipzig, 1893. Textus Ornatior, ed. R. Schmidt, München, 1898-99.
Sumaṅgalavilāsinī of Buddhaghosa, ed. PTS. in 3 Vols., 1886, 1931, 1932.
Svapnavāsavadatta of Bhāsa, ed. Kale, 1945.
Taittirīya Prātiśākhya, ed., trs. Whitney, New Haven, 1871.
Taittirīyopaniṣad-bhāṣya-vārtika of Sureśvara, Anandasrama ed., Śaka 1811.
Telakaṭāhagāthā, Ed. Goonaratne, JPTS, 1884.
Tantraratna of Pārthasārathi.
Tantravārtika of Kumārila, Benares, 1890.

Tārkikarakṣā of Varadarāja, Benares, 1890.

Tattvabindu of Vācaspati Miśra, *Paṇḍit*, 1892.

Tattva-muktā-kalāpa of Veṅkaṭanātha, Benares, 1900. Cited as *tattva-muktāvalī* in *Sarva-darśana saṃgraha.*

Theragāthā, ed. Oldenberg and Pischel, PTS, 1883. Eng. trs by R. Davids, PTS, 1937.

Therīgāthā, ed. Oldenberg and Pischel, PTS, 1883. Eng. trs by R. Davids, PTS, 1909.

Ṭuptīkā of Kumārila, ed. K.Sarasvati; also rarely Anandasrama ed.

Udāna, PTS, 1885.

Udbhaṭa-sāgara – Collection of verses by P.C.De, Calcutta.

Upakrama-parākrama of Appaya Dīkṣita.

Upamiti-bhava-prapañca-kathā of Siddharṣi.

Uttararāmacarita of Bhavabhūti, ed. P.V. Kane, with comm., Bombay, 1921.

Vākyasudhā or Śaṃkara, pub. with *Vivaraṇopanyāsa* (q.v.).

Vedāntakalpataru of Amalānanda, *Vizianagram Skt. Series,* 1895-97.

Vedāntakalpataru – Parimala of Appaya Dīkṣita, *Vizianagram Skt. Series*, 1895-98.

(References to the above ed. of *Kalpataru* are given by mentioning the full title of the work and the page numbers. References to NSP, ed. 1917, are indicated by simply *Kalpataru* and the no. of the *Sūtra* concerned). References to *Parimala* are indicated by page nos. References to NSP. ed. are by the no. of *Brahmasūtra* concerned.)

Vedāntasāra of Sadānanda, ed. Jacobi, NSP, 1894.

Vedānta-siddhānta-muktāvalī of Prakāśānanda, ed. & trs. A. Venis. Reprint from *Paṇḍit.*

Vetālapañcaviṃśati – Śivadāsa's version ed. H. Uhle, Leipzig, 1884. Jambhaldatta's version ed. M.B. Emaneau, with Eng. trs., New Haven, Conn., 1934.

Vidhi-rasāyana of Appaya Dīkṣita, Benares, 1901.

Vinayapiṭaka, ed. PTS, 1879-83. Eng. trs. by R. Davids and Oldenberg. Also see *Vinaya texts, SBE*, Vols. XIII, XVII, XX.

Vivāraṇa-prameya-saṃgraha of Vidyāraṇya, *Vizianagram Skt. Series*, 1893.

Vivaraṇopanyāsa of R. Sarasvati, Benares, 1901.
Yājñavalkya-smṛti, NSP. ed., 1926.
Yaśastilaka of Somadeva, NSP, 1901-3.
Yogasūtra of Patañjali, ed. Bodas, Bombay, 1892.
Yogavārtika of Vijñāna Bhikṣu. Reprint from *Paṇḍit, 1884.*
Yogavāśiṣṭha, Bombay.

MISCELLANEOUS WORKS

Agrawala, V.S. : *India as known to Pāṇini,* Varanasi, 1963 (2nd ed.).
Agrawala, V.S. : *Ancient Indian Folk Cults*, Varanasi, 1970.
Aiyar : *Agricultural and allied arts in Vedic India.*
Ambedkar, B.R. : *Who were the Shudras* ? Bombay, 1946.
Anand, M. (ed.) : *Satī.*
Apte, V.M. : *Social and Religious life in Gṛhyasūtras*, Bombay. 1953 (2nd ed.).
Apte, V.S. : *Sanskrit-English Dectionary*, Delhi.
Asko Parpola et. al. : *Decipherment of the Proto-Dravidian Inscription of the Indus Civilisation*, Copenhagen, 1969.
Asko Parpola et. al. : *Progress in the Development of Proto-Dravidian Indus Script*, 1969.
Asko Parpola et. al : *Futher Progress in the Decipherment of the Proto-Indus Script*, 1969.
(Sri) Aurobindo : *Foundations of Indian Culture*, Pondicherry, 1975 (6th ed.).
Bader, G. : *Women in Ancient India* (Moral and Literary Study).
Banerji, G. : *Marriage and Strīdhana*, Calcutta.
Banerji, N.N. : *Vedic Socialism*, New Delhi, 1980.
Banerji, S.C. : *Dharmasūtra—A study etc.*, Calcutta, 1962.
Banerji, S.C. : *A Companion to Middle Indo-Aryan Literature*, Calcutta, 1977.
Banerji, S.C. : *The Castaway of Indian Society*, Calcutta, 1989.
Banerji, S.C. : *Crime and Sex in Ancient India*, Calcutta, 1980.
Banerji, S.C. : *Aspects of Ancient Indian Life*, Calcutta, 1972.
Banerji, S.C. : *A Brief History of Tantra Literature*, Calcutta, 1988.
Banerji, S.C. : *Tantra in Bengal*, Calcutta, 1977.
Banerji, S.C. : *Indian Society in the Mahābhārata*, Varanasi, 1976.
Basham, A.L. : *The Wonder that was India*, Fontana, 1971.
Basham, A.L.: *Cultural History of India* (ed.), O.U.P., 1975.
Basu, J. : *India of the Age of Brāhmaṇas,* Calcutta, 1969.

Bhattacharya, A. : *Modern Commercial Concepts in the Mahābhārata*, Calcutta.
Bhattacharya, A. : *Modern Accounting Conception in Kauṭilya's Arthaśāstra*, Calcutta.
Bhattacharya, S.C. : *Some aspects of Indian Society* (from c. 2nd cent. B.C. to 4th cent. A.D.), Calcutta, 1978.
Bloomfield : *Kauśikasūtra of Atharvaveda,* Delhi.
Brough, J. : *Early Brahmanical system of gotra and pravara*, Cambridge, 1953.
Buch, M.A. : *Economic Life in Ancient India,* Allahabad, 1979.
Bülcke, C. : *Rāmakathā* (Hindi), Prayag (Allahabad), 1950.
Burrow, T. : *Sanskrit Language.*
Chakladar, E. : *Studies in Kāmasūtra of Vātsyāyana : Social Life in Ancient India*, Calcutta, 1929.
Chanana, D.R. : *Slavery in Ancient India*, New Delhi, 1960.
Chandra, R.C. : *Ornaments and Jewellery of Vedic Indians*, Varanasi.
Chatterji, H. : *Studies in some aspects of Hindu saṃskāras in Ancient India*, Calcutta, 1967.
Chatterji, H. : *The Law of Debt in Ancient India*, Calcutta, 1971.
Chatterji, H. : *Studies in the social background of the forms of marriage in Ancient India*, vols. 1,2.
Chattopadhyay, D.R. : *Science and Society in Ancient India*, 1979.
Crawford, S.C. : *Evolution of Hindu Ethical Ideals*, Calcutta, 1974.
Dange, S.A. : *Pastoral Symbolism from the Ṛgveda*, Poona, 1970.
Dange, S.A. : *Vedic Concept of Field and Divine Fructification*, Bombay, 1971.
Datta, N. : *Early Monastic Buddhism*, Vol. I, Calcutta, 1941, Vol. II, Calcutta, 1945.
De, S.K. and Das Gupta, S.N. : *History of Sanskrit Literature*, Calcutta.
De, S.K. : *Ancient Indian Erotics and Erotic Literature*, Calcutta, 1959.
Deb, R.K. : *Śabda-kalpadruma*, Calcutta.
Derrett, J.D.M. : *Hindu Law, Past and Present,* Calcutta, 1957.
Dubois, M.L. Abbe : *Hindu Manners, Customs etc.*, trs. H.K. Beauchamp, Oxford, 1906.
Fergusson, J. : *Tree and Serpent-worship,* 1872.
Ganguly, A.B. : *Sixty-four Arts in Ancient India.*

Hazra, R.C. : *Studies in the Puranic Records on Hindu Rites and Customs*. Dacca, 1940.
Jairajbhoy, R.A. : *Foreign influence in Ancient India*, Bombay, 1969.
Jolly, J. : *Recht Und Sitte* (Eng. trs. by B.K. Ghosh-*Hindu Law and Custom)*.
Kane, P.V. : *History of Dharmaśāstra*, Poona, vols. I-V, particularly Vol. V., pt. II, 1962, pp. (1339-51).
Kantawala, S.G. : *Antharvavedic Civilisation.*
Keith, A.B. : *Sanskrit Drama.*
Keith, A.B. : *Religion and Philosophy of the Veda and the Uapaniṣad, HOS*, 1925.
Law, B.C. : *A History of Pāli Literature*, Vols. I, II, London, 1933.
Maity, S.K. : *Economic Life etc.*
Majumdar, G.P. and Banerji, S.C. : *Kṛṣiparāśara*, Asiatic Society, Calcutta.
Meyer, J.J. : *Sexual Life in Ancient India*, 2 vols., London, 1930.
Mitra, Subal : *Saral Vāṅglā Abhidhān*, Calcutta.
Mookerji, R.K. : *Ancient Indian Education* (Brahmanical and Buddhist), 2nd ed., London, 1951.
Mukherjee, P.; *Beyond the four Varṇas* (untouchables in India), Delhi.
Pakrashi, K. : *Female Infanticide in India*, 1970.
Patil, D.R. : *Cultural History of the Vāyapurāṇa*; Poona, 1946.
Patil, D.R. : *Proceedings of Indian History Congress*, (Indoor and outdoor games in Ancient India by T.N. Roy).
Puri, B.N. : *India in the times of Patañjali*, Bombay, 1957.
Radhakrishnan, S. : *Hindu View of Life*, Great Britain, 1927.
Ram Gopal : *India of Vedic Kalpasūtras*, Delhi, 1959.
Renou, L. : *Hinduism*, London, 1961.
Rhys Davids, T.W. : *Buddhist India*, Calcutta, 1950.
Rhys Davids, T.W. : *Early Buddhism*, 1908.
Roy, B. : *India from 6000 B.C.*
Roy, J. : *Ancient Indian Life*, Calcutta, 1948.
Roy Chaudhuri, S.P. : *Agricultural Practices in Ancient India*, New Delhi.
Sarasvati, K. : *Mīmāṃsā-kośa*, Wai, Satara, ph. I, 1952; ph. II, 1953.
Sarda, H.B. : *History of Ancient Hindu Society.*
Sastri, Sukhamay : *Mahābhārater Samāj* (In Bengali), Calcutta.
Satyavrat : *The Rāmāyaṇa*, Delhi, 1964.
Sen, S.N. : *India through Chinese Eyes,* Calcutta, 1979.

Sengupta, N.C. : *Law and Society in Ancient India.*
Sharma, K.L. : *Vaidik Sāhitya men Śakun evaṃ abdhut ghaṭanāem,* Saharanpur, (U.P.), 1970.
Sharma, R.S. : *Shudras in Ancient India,* Delhi, 1958.
Sharma, T. : *Woman in Ancient India* (from 320-1200 A.D.).
Shende : *Religion and Philosophy of the Atharvaveda*, Poona 1952.
Singh, S.D. : *Polyandry in Ancient India*, Delhi.
Sternbach, L. : *Gaṇikā-vṛttasaṃgreha*, Hosiarpur, 1953.
Sternbach, L. : *Mahā-subhāṣita-saṃgraha,* Vol. I.
Sttutley, M. : *Ancient Indian Magic and Folklore.*
Tarkavācaspati, T. : *Vācaspatya*, Calcutta.
Thakur, U. : *History of suicide in India*, 1963.
Thapar, R. : *Ancient Indian Social History.*
Thapliyan, U.P. : *Foreign elements in Ancient Indian Society*, 1979.
Upreti and Upreti : *The Myth of Satī*, Bombay, 1991.
Van, P. : *Gods on earth*, Delhi.
Verma, N. : *Society and economy in Ancient India.*
Vyas, S.N. : *India in the Rāmāyaṇa Age*, Delhi, 1967.
Winternitz, M. : *History of Indian Literature*, Vols. I-III.

PAPERS

American Journal of Philosophy, XLIV, 1923 (Bloomfield on art of thiving).
Journal of American Oriental Society, XL, 1920 (Bloomfield on *dohada* as fiction-motif); XLIV. 1924 (Do on false ascetics and nuns in Hindu fiction). XLVIII. 1927 (W.N. Brown on Change of sex as a Hindu story motif).
Journal of Royal Asiatic Society, 1917 (E.W. Burlingame on the Act of Truth : A Hindu spell and its employment as a psychic motif in Hindu fiction).
Journal of Asiatic Society of Bengal, XIV, 1876 (R.L. Mitra on Human sacrifices in Ancient India).
Proceedings of American Philosophical Society, LII (Do), LVI, 1917 (Bloomfield on the art of entering another's body as a fiction-motif).
WZKM, XVIII, 1904 (L.H. Gray on burglary, role of the parrot, etc.).
Summaries of Papers, A.I.O.C., 1974 (S.C. Adhikari, Position of Love-lorn disappointed maidens in ancient Indian society (upto c. 600 A.D.).

INDEX

B

C

D

N

O

T